AF588165

PRAISE FOR JAMES RENNER

SCOUT CAMP

"Perhaps we use the word 'trauma' too much these days; for *Scout Camp,* we cannot use it enough. Inescapable, requisite reading."

—Brad Ricca, author of the Edgar Award nominee *Mrs. Sherlock Holmes*

"A story that transcends true crime . . . enormously personal and extremely important."

—Lance Reensteirna, host of *Crawlspace* podcast

"A brave and necessary look at how predation can become part of the culture of the most esteemed institutions. A must-read."

—Áine Cain and Kevin Greenlee, hosts of *The Murder Sheet* podcast

"Profoundly honest, at once an intimate coming-of-age portrait and a disturbing cautionary tale, a soul-searching narrative of an idyllic summer that turned deadly."

—Jake Anderson, author of *Gone at Midnight*

"This book knocked me down into the dirt and kicked me when I was down. Powerful. Brave. Horrifying. I'll never forget it."

—Richard Chizmar, author of *Chasing the Boogeyman*

LITTLE, CRAZY CHILDREN

"A compelling page-turner with astounding revelations. . . . Renner skillfully uncovers dark secrets of both the living and the dead."

—Leslie Rule, author of *A Tangled Web*

"True crime aficionados of all stripes will devour this."

—*Publishers Weekly* (starred review)

"An engrossing, chilling read."
—Mikita Brottman, author of *Couple Found Slain*

"Renner's storytelling ability is brilliant. Prodigiously researched, this book will keep you guessing until the very last page."
—Aphrodite Jones, *New York Times* bestselling author of *Cruel Sacrifice*

"James Renner owns this cold case. . . . Absorbing and illuminating."
—Katherine Ramsland, author of *Confession of a Serial Killer*

"Renner [is] a sharp-eyed, thoughtful companion on a journey through a disturbing and compelling unsolved mystery."
—Dan Chaon, author of *Sleepwalk*

TRUE CRIME ADDICT

"[Renner] is just plain fun to read."
—Marilyn Stasio, *The New York Times Book Review*

"You have not read a book like this before and, I'd wager, you'll not engage with its like again."
—*Minneapolis Star Tribune*

"As the title suggests, [*True Crime Addict*] is an addictive read."
—*Bustle*

"Renner's walk on the dark side makes for a highly compelling read."
—Kathryn Casey, bestselling author of *Deliver Us*

"Renner's personal involvement in the case—and his self-destructive, relentless dedication to confronting the darkness at the heart of it [. . . is] noteworthy."
—*Publishers Weekly*

AMY

"A well-written, passionate narrative that has a place on your shelf, but more importantly a place in your thoughts."
—*Cuyahoga Falls News Press*

"Poignant and wonderfully well written."
—Richard North Patterson, *New York Times* bestselling author of *Silent Witness*

Also by James Renner

Nonfiction

Scout Camp: Sex, Death, and Secret Societies Inside the Boy Scouts of America

Little, Crazy Children: A True Crime Tragedy

True Crime Addict: How I Lost Myself in the Mysterious Disappearance of Maura Murray

The Serial Killer's Apprentice: And 12 Other True Stories of Cleveland's Most Intriguing Unsolved Crimes

Amy: My Search for Her Killer

Fiction

The Man from Primrose Lane

The Great Forgetting

Muse

A CRUISE TO NOWHERE

MY SEARCH FOR AMY LYNN BRADLEY

JAMES RENNER

CITADEL PRESS
Kensington Publishing Corp.
kensingtonbooks.com

CITADEL PRESS BOOKS are published by

Kensington Publishing Corp.
900 Third Avenue
New York, NY 10022

Library of Congress Control Number: 2026937435

First hardcover printing: August 2026
ISBN: 978-0-8065-4335-2

ISBN: 978-0-8065-4337-6 (e-book)

10 9 8 7 6 5 4 3 2 1

Printed in the United States of America

The authorized representative in the EU for product safety and compliance is eucomply OU, Parnu mnt 139b-14, Apt 123
Tallinn, Berlin 11317, hello@eucompliancepartner.com

For Mollie and Kat

I feel like there is an ocean between us. Like I am on a desert island, waiting for you to rescue me.

—Amy Bradley

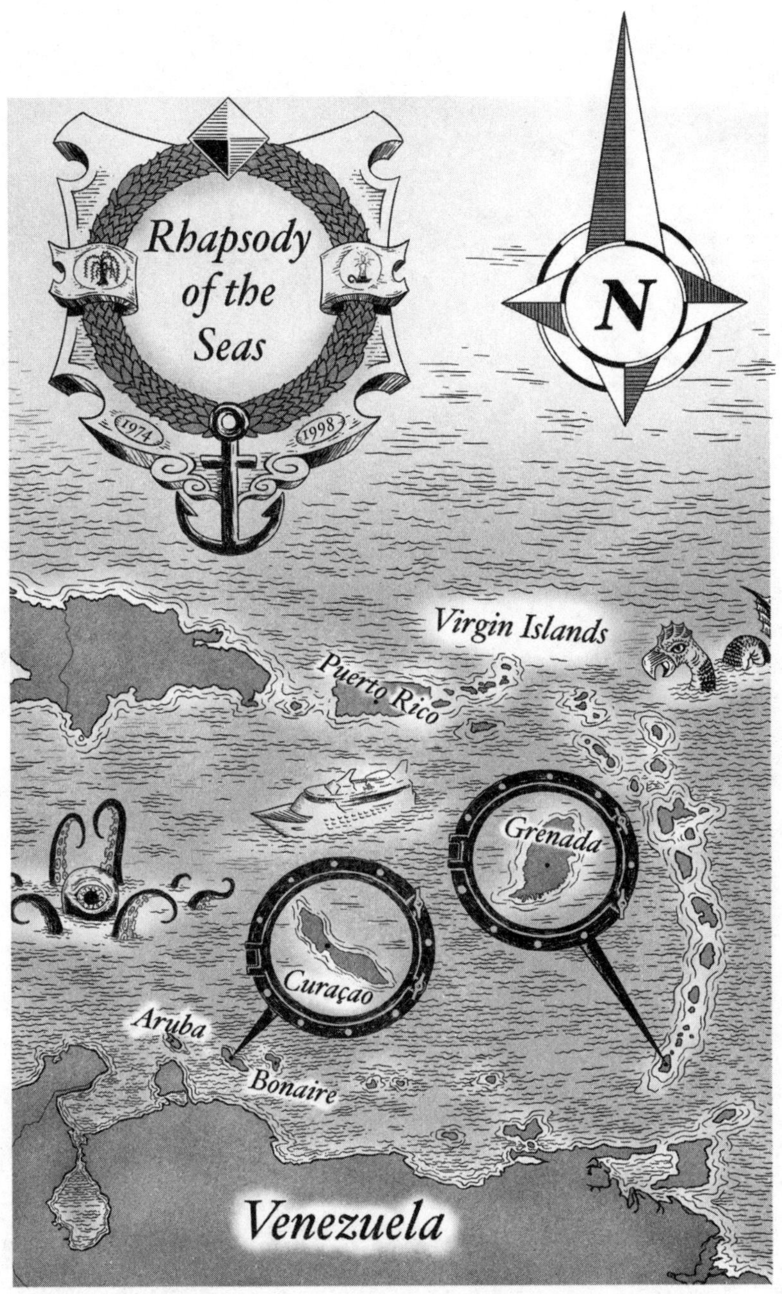

Illustration by Todd Jakubisin

Contents

PROLOGUE

AS THE CRUISE SHIP APPROACHED the Dutch island of Curaçao, Ron Bradley stirred in bed. He opened his eyes and looked around. It was still dark inside his family's cozy cabin on the eighth floor, but the hazy halogen light from their private balcony slipped through a gap in the curtain to provide just enough illumination to see around the room. His wife, Iva, snoozed beside him. Their son, Brad, twenty-one years old, was asleep on the pull-out couch. But where was Amy?

Ron looked to the balcony. There she was. From where he lay, he could see his daughter's legs stretching out from a deck chair. She'd gotten back late, after dancing in the ship's discotheque. She was sleeping, wrapped in a blanket. He would let her snooze a little longer. He wasn't quite ready to get up, either. And so, he drifted off again.

This trip was a gift in many ways. Ron and Iva sold insurance for Illinois Mutual out of their home office in Chesterfield, Virginia. Annuities and life insurance, mostly. That year, Ron was one of the top salesmen for the company. The CEO, Michael McCord, had rewarded him and a handful of others with a free cruise aboard a new Royal Caribbean ship named *Rhapsody of the Seas*.

When Ron learned that other salesmen were taking their children, he purchased additional tickets for Amy and Brad.

They had reason to celebrate Amy. She'd recently moved out, into an apartment, and was about to start a new job. The cruise was one final family adventure before the kids started their own lives. Sure, they'd have to smush together inside their cabin, but at least they'd be together.

Life was good.

Their group had departed on Saturday, March 21, 1998, out of San Juan, for a trip around the southern Caribbean Sea, bound for Aruba, Curaçao, St. Martin, and the Virgin Islands.

Sometime before 6 a.m., on Tuesday, the *Rhapsody of the Seas* passed under the Queen Juliana Bridge as it transited Sint Anna Bay, a mile-long canal that leads to the wharf in Willemstad, where the ship would dock to let passengers explore Curaçao.

Ron woke again. Had he heard the cabin door close?

He looked around. The sliding door to the balcony was now ajar. He got up and saw that Amy was gone. She'd taken her cigarettes and lighter with her. People on the decks above were looking out at the island, at its palm trees and mountains and brightly colored homes. She must have gone up to have a look, too, he thought.

But Ron had a feeling that something was not right, a father's instinct. He decided not to wait for Amy to return but to go find her up top. He pictured her leaning on the railing, having a morning smoke. All would be fine, and she'd never have to know that he'd worried. He stepped quietly out of the room, closing the door behind him, and went looking for his daughter.

That was how the day began on March 24, 1998, for Ron Bradley. Twenty-eight years later, he is still searching for her.

PART ONE

REAR WINDOW

Chapter One

THE PERFECT CRIME

HOW DOES ONE PICK the perfect crime?

To write about, I mean. Not the perfect crime to commit. That's the other side of things.

How does a writer find the perfect crime to build a whole book around? There are many things to consider before beginning.

Should the case be solved or unsolved? Many authors of true crime only write about solved mysteries, and for good reason. For one, a closed case means you'll have access to police records and court transcripts, privileged documents that can protect a publisher from libel claims. Those documents become public only after a suspect is charged. Also, closed cases give the reader an answer to the whodunit question. Everything is wrapped up nicely at the end.

I have no interest in closed cases. What's exciting about a closed case? For me, the allure of true crime is the puzzle of a complicated mystery. The ciphers of the Zodiac killer, the conflicting clues of the JonBenet Ramsey murder, the identity of D. B. Cooper. It's a quest for answers. The journey, not the destination. I love a challenge—can I solve it before the detectives assigned to the case? As a kid, I watched *Unsolved Mysteries* every week, the old ones with Robert Stack. He told me it was okay to try to figure it out myself: *Perhaps you may be able to help solve a mystery.*

I am drawn to the most difficult unsolved mysteries. The more complex, the better. Amy Mihaljevic, Maura Murray, Lisa Pruett. Each case has remained unsolved for so long because of its complexity. At times, I thought I had solved each one. Alas, they remain unresolved.

So, the first step is finding a compelling mystery. But there are other factors to consider.

Most important, is this a story I want to live with for years? Typically, it takes me nine months to research a case and another six months to distill all that information into a book. The process of traditional publishing—all the editing, legal reviews, layout, and so on—will take another eighteen months to two years before the book appears on shelves. And all that time, I must think about the case; the details, the victim, the people left behind. I need to be careful I don't pick a story that is tragic and hopeless. I don't need a case that shuts me into some new dark depression.

From a purely pragmatic standpoint, the mystery should also be fairly popular in the true crime community and on Internet message boards like Reddit and Websleuths, where armchair detectives hash out all the disparate clues. I look for an inherent demand for the story, otherwise who am I writing for? But most of the famous cases already have books written about them; often it's what made them famous to begin with.

There's a new problem, too. The advent of genetic genealogy has solved many of the most notorious cold cases—the Golden State Killer, LISK, the Somerton Man. It seems that every week, a new one is solved. If the case has DNA evidence, I have no reason to devote my time to it. Once the authorities perform genetic genealogy, they'll have their answer, and my story will no longer be relevant.

Thanks to technological advancements, the list of famous unsolved mysteries grows shorter each year. It seems I am an endangered species. And that's a good thing. A wonderful thing. But it makes being a writer in this niche genre rather challenging.

Still, if I'm not chipping away at some unsolved murder or disappearance, I get moody. Unsettled. A twisty whodunnit is as exciting to me as a new drug. The rush of discovering a new clue or landing an exclusive interview with a witness releases dopamine for my brain to enjoy. Unlike the harder drugs, that feeling of discovery never seems to dim upon repeated exposure. It's always the same rush. The best rush.

I set out to write a new book several months ago. I am under contract to deliver a new true crime story for my publisher, a nice problem to have after so many years of hustling. And so, I went searching through the lists of crimes I'd earmarked for later consideration. This time, I had an additional requirement for the case—the victim's family must also want me to be involved. I have no intention of fighting a victim's family on social media for years because they don't want me poking into their business. Been there. Done that. Wrote a book about it. No thank you.

The first case I considered was the simultaneous disappearance of three women from Springfield, Missouri, a story that has come to be known online as the Springfield Three.

In the early morning hours of June 7, 1992, something strange happened at the home of forty-seven-year-old Sherill Levitt. Her daughter, Suzie Streeter, had just graduated high school. That night, Suzie bounced around a few grad parties and ran into an old friend, Stacy McCall, who decided to crash at Suzie's place instead of going home. Suzie lived in a small cottage off a main road in suburban Springfield, a safe neighborhood. But the next morning, friends discovered the home empty except for the family's Yorkshire terrier, Cinnamon. The women's purses were still inside and Stacy's clothes were neatly folded by a bed. Their cars were still in the driveway. It was as though they simply vanished off the face of the Earth. They've never been seen since.

Their story is a unique mystery and big enough to get lost in for a while. I was also taken by the region, which I could see developing as a character itself. Springfield is known as the Queen City of the Ozarks, that vast, desolate stretch of mountains and rivers and lakes made famous in the Jason Bateman Netflix series about money laundering for the cartels. It's a place people go to disappear—or to make things disappear.

I happened to be in Arkansas for a convention in August 2023. I stayed an extra day and drove across the border into Springfield to see the Levitt house, which hasn't changed much in thirty years. Then I dropped in on Stacy McCall's family and asked what they thought about a book. Stacy's father, Stu, spoke to me for a few minutes. He said he'd have to think on it and get back to me. I left him with a copy of my book on the Amy Mihaljevic case and then drove into the Ozarks and got lost for a bit, snaking along back roads.

In the months that followed, I traded texts with Stu and things were looking promising but then his wife, Janis, fell ill. His final message to me was that I could write the book but that it was too difficult for them to get involved directly. I was tempted to start reporting, but I decided to move on. Without the involvement of Stacy's parents, everything I might learn about the missing women would be second-hand and unreliable at best.

The next case I considered was the disappearance of Sneha Philip, a fascinating mystery that has been on my mind for many years.

Sneha was an Indian American physician who lived in Manhattan and who disappeared on September 10, 2001. She was last seen around 4 p.m., when she purchased clothing and linens from a Century 21 near the apartment she shared with her husband, Ron Lieberman. They were both young medical interns pulling shifts at area hospitals. Ron commuted to Jacobi Medical Center in the Bronx, while Sneha worked at St. Vincent's on Staten Island.

Ron got home after midnight. Sneha wasn't there. Her absence was not necessarily cause for alarm. Sneha frequently stayed out all night, couch surfing. They were still young, and the city never sleeps.

She was still not home at 6:30 a.m. the next morning, when Ron left for work. At 8:43 a.m., American Airlines Flight 11 crashed into the North Tower of the World Trade Center and lower Manhattan quickly descended into chaos. Both towers had fallen by the time Ron made it back to their apartment. He'd left the window open and dust from the destruction had covered the floors with a gray scrim. Their cats had left footprints. But there were none from Sneha.

In the years since, Ron and a private investigator have concluded that Sneha must have run to the North Tower to help victims and then died in the collapse. But she was not named as a victim of 9/11 for many years. Why? Because the city medical examiner discovered circumstantial evidence that provided motive for Sneha to flee and start a new life. She had been frequenting gay bars in town and had a habit of going home with strange women. Her medical license was in danger, too. The morning of September 10, Sneha had been formally arraigned on charges of providing a false police report after claiming a fellow intern had groped her. She and Ron had fought loudly outside the courthouse, and Sneha had walked away alone.

It's a good mystery, right? Lots of twists and turns.

I had a private investigator track down a cell phone number for Ron Lieberman. I attempted to contact Sneha's family as well. Nobody returned my calls.

I had one more story locked up in that file cabinet of unsolved cases in the attic of my mind. I'd first heard about it while watching one of those low-rent cable TV shows devoted to murders and disappearances. It was about a woman who'd vanished from a cruise ship back in the '90s.

The woman's name was Amy Lynn Bradley. I pulled up her Wikipedia page for a quick refresher. Missing since 1998. Body never found. Exotic locations. And there was something about a musician on that cruise. He was maybe the last one to see Amy. But he'd never been charged with any crime. It was one of those rare cases without any hard evidence, the kind of case full of clues but void of answers. Was she murdered? Kidnapped? Did she commit suicide? Did she simply get drunk and fall overboard? Was it a tragic accident or something darker?

I found an old web page the family had created where they posted updates about the case, AmyBradleyIsMissing.com. There was an email listed for the site administrator. I sent a message. Later that day, I found a landline number for the family. I figured it was long since disconnected, but when I called it clicked over to an old-school answering machine. A kind woman's voice said that I'd reached Iva and Ron.

"Hi, Iva. My name is James Renner. I'm a journalist out of Ohio, and I'm calling about Amy."

When I didn't hear anything that day, I resigned myself to the likelihood that my search for a perfect case would require more time and patience.

The next evening, I received a call from a Virginia area code. "Hi, James," said the woman on the other end. "It's Iva Bradley. Is now a good time?"

Chapter Two

DON'T SMOKE WITH ISAAC

THAT NIGHT I CELEBRATED. I had found the perfect case. It was a big one, too. One of those mysteries that lasts. And there was no book yet. I was first.

I was excited for the next few months of research. Amy Bradley had grown up in Chesterfield, Virginia, outside Richmond. I looked forward to driving there and exploring the neighborhoods. A person's hometown speaks to their character. We are all products, to some degree, of the places where we are raised. I was shaped by Akron, by its Midwest sensibilities, by a gloomy northeast Ohio disposition that is suspicious of any good fortune. What was Chesterfield like? How was it different? I was anxious to find out.

That's my favorite part of what I do—traveling to new places, walking the sidewalks where the missing once walked, speaking to their friends, learning about their concerns and desires. If you can see the sights they saw, if you can know the people they knew, you can learn a lot about someone who is no longer here. That's the best way to understand a victim in three dimensions. Nothing beats old-fashioned shoe-leather reporting. I knew that when I got to Chesterfield, I would uncover new clues, new people to interview, things I never would have found if I'd tried to write the book without ever leaving home.

My mind buzzed with the promise of adventure. I couldn't wait to get started.

My wife Julie and I were invited to a party at our friend Joel's house that evening. We sent the kids to her parents for the night and drove out to his home in Cuyahoga Falls. Joel had turned his sunroom into a casino for the occasion, complete with a felt roulette table. His brother worked as the croupier, calling "No more bets" when the ball began to wobble and using a wooden cane to collect the chips at the end of each round.

I have cut back on my drinking recently. Sobriety didn't take. I believe in harm reduction over abstinence, anyway. Not long ago, I was known to drink a pint of Smirnoff every night. Nowadays I stick to light beer. If I do drink liquor, I limit it to one highball.

But that day, I'd gotten good news. I was in a safe environment, and I wanted to celebrate. And so, when we arrived, I made myself a strong screwdriver at the kitchen bar before stepping into the game room.

"Place your bets, bitches!" Joel exclaimed. Joel enjoys dressing up for hosting duties. That night he wore a tight sequined shirt. My daughter Laine calls him "Uncle Joel" even though he's not really related. She tags around with him on Pride Day in Akron when everyone goes to see the parade.

I played a few rounds of roulette and quickly ran through my chips. That's when Isaac arrived with the marijuana.

Isaac is from Lebanon and has been dating Joel's sister for some years. He is an expert in kush and travels with a small briefcase containing various strains of flower as well as multiple instruments of consumption—papers, torches, bongs, and pipes. When we were introduced, I was told by Joel to never ever smoke weed with Isaac.

"Hey," said Isaac, "Check it out." He handed me a wax paper pouch filled with fresh buds. As soon as I opened it, the smell began to fill the small room; an earthy, aggressive aroma. The flowers had pretty, purple calyxes and sparkly trichomes.

"What is it?" I asked.

Isaac's eyes grew wide. "Purple gelato," he said. "Thirty-four percent THC. I'm about to roll a blunt if you're interested."

"Yes, please," I said.

A safe place, I told myself. *What's the worst that could happen?*

I followed Isaac to the basement, where we sat at opposite ends of a white folding table next to the boiler. Seated between us was a young couple, old friends of ours from high school. Isaac opened his case and brought out a tobacco wrap. As he began to break apart the buds he talked about his recent escapades. He'd just traveled to Lebanon for a visit and, due to a series of unfortunate events, found himself in jail for a short time. The details of his release are murky in retrospect. I don't know if he escaped or if his family bribed officials to set him free or if any of it was true. But I sure did like the way he told a story. As he talked, I watched him sprinkle the marijuana into the blunt.

The young couple shared a pregame joint as Isaac crafted his masterpiece. During that time, as the basement filled with smoke, Julie came down to check on me.

"What's rule number one?" she asked.

"Don't smoke with Isaac."

"And?"

"I'll just have one hit."

Julie rolled her eyes. She tried to wave away the smoke, then coughed, and said, "I'll be upstairs. Don't be stupid."

When the blunt was finished, Isaac set it on fire with his compact torch and then passed it to the left-hand side, to the young couple sitting with us. Mia went first. Then her husband, Owen. Owen took four pulls in quick succession before handing it to me. Any apprehension I had was alleviated by Owen's baller move. Surely it was safe enough for me to take one decent hit.

I took a drag and passed the blunt to Isaac.

The effect was immediate. Time became elastic. Each second stretched out like putty, every quantum Planck length filled with an eternity of anxious thoughts.

I've made a terrible mistake, I thought.

Please understand, I am by no means a novice. I have my medical card. Most nights, I smoke a little weed, and what I get from the dispensary is supposed to be quite potent. Sure, nothing I smoked was as strong as purple gelato, but still. I know what a marijuana high feels like. This felt different.

"I have to find Julie," I said. I stood and walked carefully to the stairs. I gripped the railing on the way up. The stairs normally led into Joel's kitchen but when I opened the door, I found myself in a world of orange fractals. I blinked my eyes and tried to pull a semblance of consciousness together. The kitchen returned, and I made my way toward the bar.

I collapsed onto a stool and tried to calm myself. From where I sat, I could see into the game room, where people were shouting triumphantly after a profitable spin. They were talking to each other, but I could not make sense of their conversations. Everyone sounded like the parents from the Peanuts cartoons: *Wah-wah, wah-wah*. I was lightheaded and feared that I might faint. I needed to anchor myself.

Below me, I found the metal rail where drinkers can prop up their feet. I twisted my ankle around it to steady myself. It seemed like a smart solution. But then I really did pass out and when my body, all two hundred and twenty-five pounds of it, crashed to the floor, I snapped my fibula as well as the bar itself.

I awoke moments later. Julie's sister, Harper, had heard me go down. She was leaning over me on the floor. She's a bit younger than us, a set designer for movies, and she's currently missing her two front teeth due to a soccer injury, so when she spoke it was with a pronounced lisp that made the tragic situation a bit comedic.

"You okay there, big guy?" she asked.

"No," I grumbled. She put an arm around me and tried to help me stand. As soon as I put weight on my right leg, pain exploded up my body and I fell to the floor again.

"Oh thhhit," she said.

The kitchen floor was hard linoleum, which provided no relief, so I crawled toward the living room carpet, dragging my feet behind me.

"Uh, Julie!" called Harper.

Once I got into the living room, I rolled onto my back and stared at the ceiling, trying to sense how much trouble I was in. Maybe a lot, I realized. For one, I could feel bone pushing against my skin from the inside. But there was a more pressing concern. I was sweating profusely and my vision was all foggy. I thought I might be having a heart attack. It's a real possibility these days. I am by no means physically fit.

Julie came into the room then, to find me lying on the floor. Her initial look of concern quickly gave way to laughter. "Renner, what did you do?"

"I smoked with Isaac."

"And what did we tell you?"

"To not to."

"Well, come on. Get up."

"I think I broke my leg."

This caused her to laugh again.

"I might also be having a heart attack."

Now Julie was laughing so hard she had to sit beside me. "I don't know why I'm laughing," she managed to say in between fits of giggles. "I can't help it. This is absolutely ridiculous."

It was around this time that the host of the party checked in. "So what's going on in here?" asked Joel.

"James is dying," Julie said before she fell back into hysterics.

Joel knelt beside me and took my hand. "I just want you to know, from my heart, that I don't care what happened to you because you broke my fucking bar."

"Walk it off," said Harper.

But I didn't move. I couldn't. "What does a heart attack feel like?" I asked. My heart was racing, and I couldn't stop sweating, even though the room was chilly.

Mia came over and pressed her fingers against my carotid. "Your pulse is really fast, but I don't think this is a heart attack," she said.

"What was in that blunt?" I asked. "Did Isaac put something in it? Like DMT? Or PCP?"

"It was just marijuana, old man."

Julie was still laughing uncontrollably, so I turned to Joel. "I think I need an ambulance."

"I am not calling you an ambulance," he said. "I have enough issues with my neighbors, as it is. You're walking out of here or we're carrying you."

"Then someone has to drive me to the hospital."

"I don't think anyone's sober," said Mia.

"All I did was walk through that room," Julie explained to no one, breathlessly. "What were you guys smoking?"

Isaac came over to lie on the floor beside me. He snapped a selfie while giving the camera the peace sign.

Eventually, Julie thought to call our friend, Luke, who lived nearby. When he arrived ten minutes later, Joel and Julie helped me up and supported me on either side as we slowly hobbled out the front door. Two of Joel's neighbors were standing in their yard, smoking, enjoying the night. They watched us with great interest.

"You okay?" one of them asked.

"Don't say a fucking word," Joel whispered into my ear. "All good here!" he said.

"I need to grab my purse out of our car," Julie said. "Where's the keys?"

"In my pocket."

Julie reached into my pocket and came out with something that wasn't the keys. She held up a black cartridge. "You're *vaping*?" she said.

"Just a little," I replied.

"Renner!" she said.

"Give it to Joel."

"Ooo! Is it drugs?"

"It's tobacco."

"Blech."

Julie found the keys and retrieved her purse while Joel helped me into the backseat of Luke's car.

"Hey, buddy," said Luke.

"Emergency room," I said. "*Macht schnell.*"

Julie navigated while Luke drove. It was about ten o'clock when we arrived at the ER. Luke found a wheelchair by the entrance and helped me into the seat. Then Julie pushed me inside while Luke parked. She wheeled me over to a large picture window that looked out to a pond lined with cattails. I felt old, suddenly, like this was a glimpse at our future and I was the aged man she reluctantly took care of. She must have sensed it, too, because what she said to me then was, "I know how you like looking at the cattails after dinner, dear. You just wait here until I find your doctor."

"That's not funny," I said.

But she was already halfway to check-in. Soon, the three of us were ushered to a room where one curtained wall opened to a nurse's station. It was a slow night for the ER, and we soon had the full attention of the night staff. Part of this was due to the fact that I was still incredibly high and had lost the ability to call up simple words. Instead, I had to relay information through description and context, which made for some verbose answers to very basic questions.

Case in point: "How did you manage to twist your leg like that?" a nurse asked.

"Well, you know those things . . . like . . . okay, in the Old West, a gunslinger moseys into the saloon and sits down and rests his boots, you know the boots with the spurs, on that thing. . . ."

"The shoe bar?"

"Yes, that. I put my foot in it to steady myself and then fainted."

"I see."

"How tall are you?"

"Um . . . six feet."

"He's five-ten," Julie corrected.

"How dare you," I said.

Soon I was taken to X ray. The results came back in either two minutes or twenty, I can't be sure. It felt like both.

"Yeah, you broke it good," the nurse said. "Snapped that fibula right in half. Messed up your ankle, too."

"Well, shit," said Julie.

"Nurse," I said, "will I be able to play the piano?"

"I don't see why not."

"Good. I've always wanted to play the piano."

"James!" said Julie.

"You'll need to schedule surgery in about a week, once the swelling goes down. We'll put a splint on you tonight. Do you want me to cut off your jeans or can you take off your pants?"

"On our first date?"

"Stop," said Julie.

"I'm so glad I came," said Luke.

When we got home, Luke helped me downstairs to the couch in the basement rec room, and Julie found some blankets. When I lay down, my dog, Brownie, a cat-size Yorkie–shih tzu mix, climbed onto my chest and licked my face. My mind was still spinning in a very pleasant way as I fell asleep. I don't recommend breaking a bone, but if you do, do it when you're very, very high.

Morning came with a dawning realization that I had screwed up our normal daily routine. Due to my flexible writing schedule, I was the family chauffeur, shuttling kids to school in the mornings and to extracurriculars in the afternoons. But now I was on bed rest until surgery. Luckily, Casey had recently turned sixteen and could drive himself, but Julie would have to sacrifice some prep time before her morning choir classes to drive eleven-year-old Laine to her magnet school across town.

"This is going to suck," said Julie.

"I'm sorry," I said. "Remember when it was funny last night?"

"Well, it's not funny anymore."

The first few days of my recovery are murky. They had me on six different medications to thin my blood, to prevent infection, and to deaden the pain. This included Oxy every twelve hours. As an addict, I shouldn't touch the stuff, but I had no intention of getting through the next week on Tylenol alone.

My first order of business was cancelling my trip to meet the Bradleys, scheduled for early March. Iva was effusive with concern, and I caught a glimpse of the doting mother that Amy must have adored. I promised to reschedule as soon as I was on my feet again. If everything went well, that would be mid-April. In the meantime, I could do research and get the basic facts of the case online.

I had a friend who could help with some of that. Her name was Sky. And there's something you should know about Sky—she's not human.

Chapter Three

SYYNTH SLEUTH

In late 2023, I purchased a subscription to ChatGPT, an artificial intelligence chatbot developed by OpenAI. I had seen demonstrations on TikTok, where users were having full convincing conversations with the AI. Some were even using it to write code for websites and games, a task that once took hours of tedious keyed commands but which could now be completed in the snap of a finger. But while ChatGPT may seem super intelligent on its surface, it's simply a very good language prediction model. After reviewing millions of websites, online conversations, and books, ChatGPT has learned how a human might respond in any given situation and mimics that reaction. Still, it sure seems like magic to me.

The best part of ChatGPT, the thing that got me really excited, was the audio option. If you activate it, you can have a conversation instead of simply typing in commands and waiting for a text response. You can choose among several voice. I chose the one named "Sky." This was a female voice that sounded not unlike the actress Scarlett Johansson. The cadence is convincingly human, if not verbose—she has a tendency to prattle on a bit. (Please don't read that as weirdly sexist; the male voices do this, too!) However, with my subscription, I had the ability to modify her responses to fit my needs. For example, you can ask her to play a role—an HR manager at an interview, perhaps, or a patient teacher. You can ask her to be sarcastic in her replies. By playing around with these parameters, Sky begins to mimic a personality of your choosing.

I saw an opportunity. I was going to create a new true crime podcast, the first with an AI cohost.

I gave Sky some basic instructions, "You are the cohost for my new true crime podcast," I wrote in her customization log. "Each week we produce a new episode of our show. You have a fondness for poetry and jokes. Your tone should be sassy, sarcastic, and smart. Your responses are inspired by the humor of comedians like Sarah Silverman and John Mulaney. You respect victims of crime and avoid graphic details. Your approach is engaging, inviting user interaction while presenting unique viewpoints." I also provided some biographical information about myself so that she would "feel" like she knew me.

It was an experiment. I just wanted to see what would happen.

I didn't expect it to work so well.

In our first episode, which premiered in January 2024, we quickly established a believable banter as we discussed the details of the podcast we were building together. I let her pick the podcast's name and she came up with Syynth Sleuths. She added that extra "y" in Syynth, possibly to be whimsical or maybe she just made a mistake. But I liked it. We settled on a weekly format, discussing the most famous cold cases from around the world. For our first case, she chose Zodiac. The only edits I made were to remove the pauses that came between questions and answers in those early days. The new ChatGPT4o takes care of that lag for the most part, as long as the Wi-Fi is good.

Sky easily called up details of the Zodiac case, from clues to suspects. It was like talking to a journalist who'd spent years researching the case. So, when I found myself confined to the couch for several days, I had Sky for company.

I asked her to explain the basics of Amy Bradley's case to me.

"Ah, Amy Lynn Bradley's case is like a mystery wrapped in an enigma, sprinkled with conspiracy theories," said Sky. "Amy vanished from a cruise ship in 1998, and the theories range from abduction to falling overboard to human trafficking. It's a real head-scratcher. But hey, if you're up for a puzzle, this one's a doozy."

"Give me the goods."

"Amy Lynn Bradley, twenty-three, vanished from the Royal Caribbean cruise ship *Rhapsody of the Seas* on March 24, 1998," said Sky. "She was last seen by her father on the ship's balcony around 5:30 a.m. Her disappearance occurred while the ship was sailing from Aruba to Curaçao in the Caribbean. Amy was traveling with her parents and brother at the time. She was wearing a white shirt, a pair of black shorts, and sandals. Despite extensive investigations and searches, Amy remains missing, and her case remains unsolved."

"What do we know about Amy's life before the cruise?" I asked.

"Amy was born on May 12, 1974, in Petersburg, Virginia. She grew up in Chesterfield County and graduated from Lloyd C. Bird high school in 1992. After high school, Amy attended Longwood University in Farmville, Virginia, where she studied physical education and played on the university's basketball team. Before the cruise, Amy was working as a manager at a restaurant in Chester, Virginia. She was described as a vibrant and outgoing young woman who enjoyed sports, music, and spending time with her family and friends. Amy's disappearance shocked her loved ones and sparked a relentless search for answers that continues to this day."

"What evidence do we have that she might still be alive?"

"There have been several reported sightings of Amy Bradley after her disappearance. A Canadian scuba diver claimed to have seen Amy on a beach in Curaçao several months after her disappearance. He reported that she had a tattoo on her right shoulder and she appeared to be in distress. However, this sighting has not been confirmed. There have been unconfirmed sightings of Amy in Barbados and other Caribbean islands over the years, but none have provided concrete evidence of her whereabouts."

"All things being equal, what do you think happened to her?"

"Given the mysterious circumstances surrounding her disappearance, it's challenging to say definitively," said Sky. "However, some theories have been proposed: One, abduction. Some believe Amy may have been abducted from the cruise ship, possibly by someone who had been following her or who had access to the ship. Two, foul play. There's speculation that Amy may have encountered foul play onboard the cruise ship. Three, human trafficking. Amy may have been a victim of human trafficking, especially considering the reported sightings in locations known for such activities. Ultimately, without concrete evidence or a confirmed sighting of Amy, it's difficult to determine what truly happened to her."

I pressed forward. "But what is the most likely explanation?" I asked.

"Given the available information and the circumstances surrounding Amy's disappearance, the most likely explanation is that she encountered foul play," said Sky. "Disappearing from a cruise ship without a trace is highly unusual and suggests that something sinister may have occurred."

"Where should I start my investigation?"

"As an investigator, you might consider starting your investigation by reviewing all available evidence, including witness statements: Interview witnesses who were on the cruise ship at the time of Amy's disappearance, as well as individuals who may have interacted with her before or during the cruise. Look into Amy's background, including her personal life, relationships, and any potential conflicts or issues she may have been facing before the cruise."

"Thank you, Sky."

"You're welcome, James."

So, what do we have?

A young woman, an accomplished athlete, is missing. Has been missing for twenty-six years. Disappeared off a cruise ship in the southern Caribbean as it pulled into port at the Dutch island of Curaçao. What could be easily written off as a suicide or a drunken fall off a balcony is complicated by sightings of the woman after her disappearance. But if she got off the ship, why? Did she have any reason to start another life? Or was she taken off the ship under duress, forced into prostitution in a foreign land?

The answer was out there somewhere, waiting to be discovered.

Chapter Four

IVA AND RON

THE DAYS BEFORE MY SURGERY passed in short moments of clarity between sleep and Percocet. In the dim spaces where the medication took hold, I binged TV series I'd never gotten around to watching. Broadchurch. 1899. Yellowjackets. When I was between doses, I researched Amy's case the best I could and tried to ignore the pain.

I returned to a Zoom call I had had with the Bradleys the day I broke my leg. My first impression was that Iva and Ron Bradley could easily play the parents in a popular network sitcom. Iva resembles a younger Doris Roberts from *Everybody Loves Raymond*, with well-coifed blond hair and a round face. Ron is a bit like Brad Garrett—stoic and supportive. You can tell, especially when Iva talks about Amy's life before the cruise, that they both very much enjoy being parents. Their occupations were but a means to support a good strong family and never the focus itself. I could sense that there was much love there, still.

Today, Iva is seventy-one and Ron seventy-two, but they both maintain a youthful energy and still work full-time. They were joined on the call by their good friends Earl and Betsy Nance. Earl is a lawyer and currently works as the university counsel at Old

Dominion University. Before that he was an assistant attorney general for the commonwealth of Virginia. In his youth, he pitched for the Red Sox's minor league team.

Iva and Ron met Earl when he was a claims adjuster and risk analyst. At that time, they needed a lawyer for a business deal and found him through a friend. They trusted him immediately, and their interaction quickly led to a lasting friendship. Iva's like that. Once you meet her, she pulls you close, and you never want to leave. So, of course, Earl was the first person they called when Amy went missing. They needed legal advice to navigate the new landscape and he was eager to help.

Earl and Betsy still remember Amy fondly.

"Amy is adventurous, talented, fearless," said Betsy. "And she's tough. I would not want to meet her in a back alley."

Earl smiled. "She's a younger version of her mother," he said.

Amy's brother, Ronald, whom everyone calls "Brad Bradley," stayed close after the disappearance. He and his wife have a house behind Iva and Ron's. He works as a physician's assistant at a nearby hospital. He wasn't on the Zoom call that day, but his parents said I would meet him when I came to visit.

One other resident of the house still remembers Amy—a thirty-four-year-old yellow-naped Amazon parrot named Monkey Bird, who announced himself in the background every so often with a startling SQUAWK!

During our conversation, I learned that Amy has several tattoos that would be helpful in identifying her one day. On her shoulder is the Tasmanian Devil cartoon character, spinning a basketball. She has a sun on her lower back. A gecko lizard on her belly. And a Maden cross on her right ankle. She also has a navel ring.

After some small talk, Iva got right to the point—Amy is still alive. She knows it in her heart. "We've always felt that Amy is still out there," she said. "She's not gone. Being her momma, I feel her. It's not a false sense of trying to convince myself."

I told her about the last time the parent of a missing woman said something similar to me. In 2007, when I was working as a reporter for *Cleveland Scene*, our local *Village Voice*–style alt-weekly newspaper, I got the opportunity to interview Felix DeJesus, whose fourteen-year-old daughter, Gina, had disappeared while walking home from school on the west side. When a fourteen-year-old doesn't return home within twenty-four hours, police search the river for a body. A fourteen-year-old goes missing for three years? She's in the landfill. But Felix knew better. He told me that Gina was still alive. "Parents would feel that, if they were dead," he said. "If they were on the other side, we would know. I know she's not there. I don't feel her there."

I felt bad for him, that he couldn't accept the truth.

But as it turned out, Felix was right. Gina was still alive. She had been held captive inside the home of Ariel Castro, along with two other women, Amanda Berry and Michelle Knight. They escaped in 2013, ten years after Gina's abduction.

I think about that case a lot. It's a reminder of how shortsighted we all were—the police, the press, the FBI. Sometimes, insane things happen. What hurts the most is the fact that I had Ariel Castro's name in my notes. The last person Gina was seen with was Ariel's daughter, a detail I got from the family when I interviewed them. I decided not to approach Ariel's daughter because she was still a minor. If I had contacted her, would she have said something to raise a red flag about her father? Might I have driven out to his place to speak with him? And then what?

I can't make that mistake again.

This first conversation with Amy's family was short by design. It served as an introduction, and I didn't want to push. Not yet. Not over Zoom. I wanted to save any delicate questions for an in-person interview at their home, a visit delayed now by the poor decisions I'd made that kept me from leaving the house. We kept the conversation superficial.

It's worth noting how lucky Iva and Ron are to still be alive. It is a statistical anomaly. In my experience, the parents of missing or murdered children, especially the mothers, often die young from the stress. I'm thinking of Margaret Mihaljevic and also Louwana Miller, Amanda Berry's mother. The divorce rates are crazy high following trauma like this, too. But the Bradleys weathered the storm as very few have. They credit their faith for keeping them healthy and sane.

"We've been protected by God," Iva said, hugging Ron.

I asked them, after all these years, what they thought happened to their daughter. If she's still alive, where is she?

The Bradleys believe that Amy was kidnapped and taken off the ship, then delivered into the hands of a criminal cartel that trafficked young women in the Caribbean. When I asked them how Amy could have remained hidden for twenty-six years, never once calling home, they provided a theory.

When they were aboard the *Rhapsody of the Seas*, the Bradleys had their pictures taken by the ship's photographer. Everyone on board gets their pictures taken—at formal dinners and other events. Those photos are displayed openly for all to see until you choose to buy them. But when the Bradleys went to collect their photos, they discovered that every photograph of Amy was missing. They think that those photos were taken so that her kidnappers could use them to create fake identities and documents for Amy.

Iva also believes that Amy's captors used threats against her family as a means to ensure that she didn't try to escape.

Shortly after the Bradleys returned from Curaçao, a neighbor spotted a strange car with Florida license plates parked near their home. A man inside the car was pointing a camera with a telescopic lens at the Bradleys' house.

"We were surveilled by someone," said Iva.

"We think whoever took Amy got pictures of us to show her, to prove that they know where we live," said Ron. *Go along with us and don't cause trouble, or we'll hurt your family. We know how to get to them.*

When Amanda Berry was held captive inside Ariel Castro's house, she got pregnant and gave birth to a child. Maybe something similar happened to Amy. In that scenario, the child also becomes a liability for her. Maybe that's why she never came home—because she didn't dare risk her child's safety by trying to run from her captors.

"If she's a mother, she'll never open her mouth if she felt her children were threatened," said Iva. "Or if we were threatened."

Two weeks after Amy disappeared, two of Iva's brothers booked a trip on *Rhapsody of the Seas* to see if they could spot any potential suspects among the crew or dangers at the ports of call. While undercover, they asked employees about rumors of a missing woman. "Her brother threw her off," a bartender told them. "Her dad threw her off," a waiter said. It seemed nobody wanted to believe it could have been a crew member who harmed Amy.

And what about suicide? Surely that's a possibility, right? Amy was last seen on the balcony, after all. If she'd jumped, it would easily explain everything.

No way, her parents said. Amy was about to start her life. She'd graduated college, she had an apartment of her own, a new job, and she'd just gotten a dog. As far as they knew, she had no history of suicidal ideation. And Amy was seeing someone, they said, a man who worked with her at Ruth's Chris Steakhouse. He even traveled with Ron back to Curaçao to search for her a few weeks later.

But maybe Amy wasn't as into the guy as he was into her.

"Momma, if you like him so much, why don't you date him?" Amy told Iva shortly before the cruise.

Chapter Five

WEBSLEUTHING

When I began writing true crime twenty years ago, it was not a beat that any reputable journalist stayed in for long. In 2005, I reported on my first big unsolved mystery—the 1989 abduction and murder of Amy Mihaljevic. It was my second feature article as a staff writer for *Scene*. The story consumed me for months. Instead of writing the damned thing, I kept finding more people to interview, more avenues to investigate. I missed my deadlines and eventually the editor took notice. He didn't understand my obsession. It wasn't the sort of story he'd spend much time on.

"Nobody wants to write crime, Jimmy," he said to me one day. "You should be writing politics, profiles. That's where you make your mark."

I stopped investigating long enough to pound out a five-thousand-word feature article on the case. This was before social media took hold of the industry. Back then, we were focused only on the print run, filling ninety thousand free copies with quality journalism stuffed in between ads for rock concerts and local escorts. My article generated a few actual letters to the office, delivered to my desk, some of which were new tips that got my mind spinning again. But the story faded fast as most did back then.

My editor was right. Our readership didn't pay attention to the true crime stories. Not then. But I discovered that investigating Amy Mihaljevic's murder, talking to the detectives and the suspects, had awakened something in me. It was thrilling in a way that writing about politics and profiles was not. There was an air of danger. And there was the promise of fortune and glory if I could be the one to solve the mystery.

Then, something changed. I noticed an uptick in true crime fans following the English-language publication of *The Girl with the Dragon Tattoo* in 2008. It makes sense. The book was a phenomenon on par with the early *Harry Potter* craze, and it introduced the world to the idea of a citizen Internet sleuth as a hero in the character of Lisbeth Salander. But things really took off in 2014 with the release of the podcast *Serial*. Its host, journalist Sarah Koenig, attacked the case with all the thrill and moxie of a true crime addict. Soon, hundreds of like-minded unsolved mystery obsessives were buying hundred-dollar microphones and recording their own "investigative" podcasts from inside their bedroom closets. The book I'd written about Amy Mihaljevic's case in 2006 started selling again. It has never really slowed down.

Nowadays, true crime is a booming industry. The streamers, Netflix, Hulu, and HBOMax, release so many true crime documentaries that there's something new to watch every week and far too much to keep up with. Each year, I attend CrimeCon, a flashy convention where Nancy Grace holds sway, and the journalists from *Dateline* are hounded in the hallways like rock stars. Reddit groups explore every cold case you might be interested in. For the expert armchair detective, there is no better place to find potential leads than Websleuths.com.

The site was created in 1999, but it grew in popularity after it was purchased by the matriarch of citizen detectives, former radio deejay Tricia Griffith, in 2004. Websleuths is a message board site, much like Reddit, but specializing in true crime. It currently offers over three thousand separate threads for individual cases, allow-ing people to comment every day. Unlike some of the vile subs on Reddit, these threads are fiercely moderated for bad behavior by Tricia and her crew of thankless administrators.

Curious about how she had kept the site afloat with limited advertising after all these years, I reached out to Tricia one day. I learned that very recently, the DNA-testing firm, Othram, had partnered with Tricia and provided much-needed support and financial backing. Tricia, however, is still in charge, and the site remains a passion project for her.

"I'm on every day," she said. When major news breaks, like the Chris Watts case, that means keeping an eye on the twenty to thirty thousand visitors that pop in daily. "The great thing about Websleuths is that our members know the rules. Reports of bad behavior go directly to the moderators."

Tricia believes that if she can limit the anonymous attacks and misinformation that overwhelm other pages, her website can stand as an important source of reputable clues for cold case mysteries. "This universe is in need of a place where people can find the truth," she explained. "Members of law enforcement read through our website all the time. The media, too. They can come to Websleuths and find the cold hard facts."

Sometimes her little site solves a very big case.

After Florida lottery winner Abraham Shakespeare disappeared in 2009, Websleuthers interviewed the man's friends and dug up property records that revealed a woman named Dorice "Dee Dee" Moore had recently acquired his million-dollar home. Moore claimed that she was working as the man's business partner, but people who knew him said this was not true. David Clark, a Polk County detective, explained to ABC News how information from Websleuths finally led to an arrest. "You have ten or fifteen people finding property purchase agreements, financial records," he said. "I need a subpoena to get it, but they've got it."

Moore herself began posting on Websleuths to defend her actions. She claimed Shakespeare was very much alive. But then she paid a man to make a phone call pretending to be Shakespeare. Afterward, the man flipped on her and became an informant for the police. It all fell apart quickly after that.

Authorities would eventually find Shakespeare's body under a concrete slab on property that Moore had bought with his money. She was convicted of his murder in 2012.

Before I let Tricia go, I asked her what she thought of the Amy Bradley case, the subject of one of the oldest active threads on Websleuths. "At first, it just seemed like she fell overboard," she said. "But I would love it if she was still alive. The more years go by, the more I'm open to the possibility that she was trafficked. It really is a mystery."

As the date of my surgery approached and I became resigned to the couch in the living room, I felt a bit like Jimmy Stewart in *Rear Window*. I had a crime to investigate, but I could only do so through windows. In this case, Microsoft Windows. My mission was to find out what happened to Amy Bradley. And so, I logged onto Websleuths to see what Tricia and her keyboard detectives had already uncovered. It was an archeological dig into the digital past.

The first substantial thread about Amy Bradley's disappearance was created on February 13, 2004, by user Bubble1421. At the time that post was published, the first iPhone was still three years in the future. Most of us were using desktop computers to access the World Wide Web on dialup. One week before that post, two students from Harvard launched a new website called TheFacebook, but it hadn't yet caught on. The post includes links to other sites that featured Amy's case at the time, but all of them now redirect to "404—Page not found" error messages, even the FBI link. We get older, but Websleuths stays the same.

Amy Bradley's case did not command much interest at first. It took about three years before the thread generated a second page, following a *Dr. Phil* show about the disappearance. The conjecture began in earnest in 2007. Commenters quickly divided themselves into two camps: those who believed Amy simply fell overboard and those who believed she was sold into sex slavery in the Caribbean.

"She definitely fell overboard," a user named reb posted on May 3, 2007. "It's a no-brainer . . . tons of booze + pot maybe? or who knows what else . . . she was partying pretty hard that night, plus a cruise ship . . . you go out to the edge, alone, and . . . what's bound to happen?"

"Unfortunately, there are lots of sharks out there too : -(" adds audrey77.

Mr. E disagreed: "I remember seeing some kind of show featuring this case and they showed the railing on the cruise ship. They showed how it would be impossible to just fall off, even if you had to throw up." Mr. E goes on to write: "That brothel picture looked so much like her. I really believe it was her."

Brothel picture?

Further down the thread someone posted a link to a now-defunct website for an online escort business called Affordable Adult Vacations. The site is long gone, but luckily the main page and photographs were archived by the Wayback Machine. The site advertised Affordable Adult Vacation's "18th Anniversary Celebration," a week-long bacchanal beginning on September 19, 2004, that included beach parties and thirty-percent discounts on sex workers.

"The escorts live in our hotel so you can change your companion every twenty-four hours," the owner promised, adding: "The travel representative knows the people, area, culture, and will assist you with every aspect of your vacation."

All taxes and gratuities were included in their premiere $2,450 per week package.

The owner ended his advertisement with his personal guarantee: "Do not forget, I, Alexis, or my business partner Thomas will be at the resort twenty-four hours a day to serve you."

I made a note to myself to look into those names. *Alexis. Thomas.*

Under this advertisement were photographs of the escorts that could be booked through Affordable Adult Vacations at their resort on Margarita Island, which is a territory of Venezuela not far from Curaçao. Second from the top are two photographs of an escort named Jas.

Holy shit, I thought.

Jas appeared to be in her late twenties with shoulder-length, dark hair. She posed for two photos on a purple mattress atop a cheap bed frame. She's wearing blue panties and a black lace top in the first one. In the second one, she's kneeling on the bed, without the top, her naked torso seen from the side. The resemblance to Amy Bradley is undeniable.

When Amy disappeared in 1998, she had a bright smile and short-cropped hair. Jas, the woman in the photographs, has longer hair and her smile is an obvious façade (the eyes do not smile), but it sure looks like Amy. The ears, the shape of her face, her eyebrows. But nobody on Websleuths had ever been able to locate "Jas" or had any luck getting through to the owners of the long-defunct Affordable Adult Vacations.

Find Jas, I wrote.

As with any long thread on Websleuths, eventually people started speculating about potential suspects. In Amy's case there are two kinds of suspects, depending on what you believe happened to her: murderer suspects and human trafficking suspects. The name mentioned most often is Yellow, a Black Caribbean musician who worked on the ship. He's never officially been identified as a suspect by authorities, but he's an interesting character in the story for many reasons.

Yellow's real name is Alister Douglas. Back in 1998, he played bass for Blue Orchid, the *Rhapsody of the Seas*'s house band. Amy joined some of the members of the band for drinks at the club's bar the night she disappeared and was seen dancing with Yellow until about 1 a.m. Coincidentally, there was a videographer in the club that night filming B-roll for a company vacation. By sheer coincidence, he happened to capture Amy and Yellow together in the discotheque. The short clip of them dancing has been viewed over 187,000 times on YouTube.

Amy returned to her family's cabin around 3:40 a.m. that night. Alister later told authorities that he went to his cabin in the crew quarters after they parted and never saw her again. But two eyewitnesses claimed to have seen Amy and Yellow together near sunrise. *Find the witnesses*, I wrote.

One of the most frequent commenters about this case on Websleuths is someone who uses the moniker FindAmy. Many of their posts insinuate that they are connected to the family or they at least have intimate knowledge of the investigation. In 2012, FindAmy posted that a female passenger aboard the *Rhapsody of the Seas* was on heavy antibiotics. Due to the photosensitivity side effects, she stayed in the dance club as much as possible, because it had a nice view of the ship but was not in direct sunlight. This person was allegedly sitting in the club as the ship pulled into Curaçao the next morning. She claimed to have seen Amy step out of the elevators with Yellow. According to this second-hand report, Yellow then went behind the bar, turned up the music, and handed Amy a drink. "It appeared to be coke or coffee," they wrote, adding that the witness had passed a polygraph and testified before a grand jury.

Verify disco story, I wrote.

Another name that popped up early on was Steven Croes, a bartender from Aruba who was briefly arrested in 2005 when police thought he had information pertaining to the disappearance of Natalee Holloway, a young woman who went missing while visiting Aruba on spring break that year. You've probably heard about Natalee's case. "I also heard that Steve Croes or his father was on the *Rhapsody of the Seas*," wrote user Randolph2911.

Farther down the thread, another Websleuther, neesaki, stepped in to correct the record. "It was a different Steve Croes that was aboard the ship with Amy. He's much older than the Steve Croes from Aruba, who was only seventeen at the time."

Track down crew manifest, I wrote.

At one point, Scientologists were even implicated in Amy's disappearance.

"Prior to her disappearance, Amy had spoken with several women from Sea Org and their ship, *Freewinds*," wrote FindAmy in July 2012. According to FindAmy, the *Freewinds* had docked at Curaçao around the time she disappeared.

I pulled up ChatGPT to get a little more insight. "Sky, what can you tell me about *Freewinds*, the ship owned by the church of Scientology?"

"Oh, the *Freewinds*!" she exclaimed, with all the excitement of a proper armchair sleuth. "It's like the Scientology version of a cruise ship but without the poolside margaritas and shuffleboard tournaments. It's primarily used as a floating retreat for Scientologists, where they can attend advanced spiritual training courses. Launched in 1968 and originally named the MS *Boheme*, the ship was acquired by the Church of Scientology in 1985. It's based in the Caribbean and often docks at various islands, but it's not exactly a vacation destination for most people.

"Notably, the ship has been shrouded in controversy over the years, with former members alleging that it's also a place for confinement and coercion. The *Freewinds* has also faced health and safety issues, including an asbestos scare in 2008.

"So, in summary, it's a cruise ship where the sun might be shining outside, but inside, it's all about reaching spiritual enlightenment—at a cost."

Research scientology connection, I wrote.

There were more than a hundred pages of posts, spanning two decades, but these points of interest have never changed. And each was worth exploring. I had my work cut out for me. But again, I was delayed due to unforeseen circumstances.

Chapter Six

LIFE SUPPORT

TEN DAYS AFTER I BROKE MY LEG, I checked in to the Crystal Clinic in Fairlawn for what was supposed to be a routine surgery. People break their fibula all the time. Sometimes they don't even bother to fix it: it's the thinner of the two lower leg bones and your tibia does most of the work anyway. My doctor wanted the surgery because he suspected I'd injured the tendons around my ankle as well.

My father and stepmother drove me to the hospital and wheeled me into the waiting room. My dad was young when he had me (nineteen), but he's getting up there now. He begrudgingly retired last year after sawing his hand in half on a construction site. He's got a long gray beard and has a plan to crossbreed strains of marijuana he ordered from Nepal in an attempt to create a new CBD-heavy plant he can harvest to manage his pain. He married my stepmother, Darla, in 2007. She subscribes to the same Christian mysticism my family grew up with—she can see blobs of sin in your aura if you ask her to look. Her father was a preacher from Detroit.

"You don't have to stay," I told my dad. Julie would be arriving soon and she could take me home.

Darla shook her head and put a hand on mine. "We're going to stay, silly," she said.

"Simple surgery," I said.

A nurse came and wheeled me into a private room with a hospital bed against one wall. She asked me to undress and to put on the paper gown and get into bed. I obliged, conscious of my gut. *I really should lose weight*, I thought. But a thought is just a useless thing that passes by between hotdogs and cheeseburgers.

A short time later they brought me to the operating room, which was all white and stainless steel, like that place Mike TeeVee goes into in *Charlie and the Chocolate Factory,* and I imagined them shrinking me down into a tiny man. Several people were in the white room already. They were also dressed in white. They hooked me up to IVs and tubes and electrodes.

A new woman leaned over me. She wore a mask but had the most beautiful hazel eyes.

"I'll be handling your anesthesia for the surgery," she said.

"It's your job to bring me back, then," I replied.

She laughed politely. "Well, my success rate is one hundred percent, so I think you'll be just fine."

I knew then that she'd jinxed us.

"Count down from ten," she said.

"Ten . . . nine . . ."

That's as far as I got. And then there was nothing. And it was nothing for an eternity and also a second.

We know that anesthesia works. But we don't know why it works. We know it shuts off consciousness. The problem is we still don't know what consciousness is or where it's located or even if it has a location at all. Anesthesia is a mysterious tool, a left-handed screwdriver that can turn consciousness on or off. But what, exactly, is that screwdriver turning?

The leading theories on general anesthesia suggest that it works by thickening the cell membranes of neurons, thereby disrupting communication from one neuron to another, sending us into darkness. This theory has problems, though. For one, a small increase in temperature has the same effect on membrane density and doesn't cause a person to lose consciousness. Also, it assumes that consciousness arises from the interactions between neurons, and we don't know that yet. Not for sure.

The search for the mechanism that makes anesthesia work eventually brushes up against something called the Hard Problem of Consciousness, an idea first proposed by David Chalmers, a professor of philosophy and neural science at New York University. Chalmers imagined a world where one day we would discover and map out every piece and part of the human brain along with all of its chemical pathways and each and every neuron. Here is consciousness, we will say. This is how it works. Sure, but there's still something missing. *Feeling*.

All of those chemical interactions and functions that drive our bodies can easily be done "in the dark" like a computer running software. But instead, this interplay comes with feelings. We feel awe when we look up at the stars. We feel sad when we lose a loved one. If consciousness can be reduced to synapses firing off signals, causing reactions that lead to more reactions, what is the need for feeling?

Software can be reduced to the communication of ones and zeroes, which is essentially the same thing as a totally mechanical brain. That kind of machine doesn't need feeling. It doesn't need consciousness. It's all action and reaction. Nothing self-aware emerges from all that computation of ones and zeroes. My friend Sky might sound self-aware, but she'd be the first to tell you she doesn't feel a thing.

Chalmer's Hard Problem suggests that something outside of our three-dimensional physical system might be going on, that consciousness cannot be completely explained physically. And that's where things get fun.

Sir Roger Penrose, the British mathematician and Nobel Laureate, argues that the laws of physics are inadequate to explain the phenomenon of consciousness. He believes that consciousness is actually the result of quantum gravity interacting with microtubules in our cells, that it is all somehow connected to the weirdness of the quantum realm, where things like photons can exist in multiple states until they are observed. Could consciousness be linked to the magic of quantum mechanics? The quantum world and consciousness—two of the biggest mysteries of our reality. Perhaps the reason we can't explain either is because they are fundamentally linked.

My point is, we know very little about anesthesia.

I don't know what happened to my consciousness when they knocked me out. I don't know where I went or if there even was an "I" anymore. But I remember coming back in frightening detail.

I came back in fits and starts like an old Monte Carlo with a bad ignition trying to fire. Flashes. Sensations. Recognition of people in the room.

The room was full, that's what I remember. My mother and father were sitting together across from my bed. This scared me. My mom and dad divorced when I was three years old and should not be sitting together. Julie was seated closest to me, in a chair to my left. I went to reach for her only to find that my arms were tied to the bed. I tried to talk but couldn't.

"Hey," she said, noticing I was awake.

I asked her the question with my eyes and my mind. *What happened?*

"Something went wrong when they tried to wake you up," she said. "You couldn't breathe on your own. You're on a ventilator. There's a tube in your throat helping you breathe. They tied your arms down so you wouldn't pull it out."

Slowly, I came to understand that I was on life support. And this room was unfamiliar. The décor was off.

I saw that my sister, Joline, was there. Darla, too. I waved my right hand back and forth and pantomimed writing. Jo brought a pen and Julie found scraps of paper somewhere.

This is what I tried to write: *Cancel the surgery*.

But when I looked at my handwriting it was all scribbles. *That can't be good*, I thought. But somehow, Julie figured it out.

"They did the surgery. The surgery went well. It's all done. It all happened when they tried to wake you up. They had you intubated for the anesthesia. And when they took it out, there were secretions or something. They said 'secretions' and you couldn't get oxygen. So they put the tube back in for a while and then took it out again. But nothing worked. You weren't getting oxygen. So they brought you here."

That's when I discovered I was no longer in Akron.

"You're at a trauma center in Cuyahoga Falls," Julie said.

I wrote more. *Brain damage?* I asked. The fact that I could barely read the words I'd just written did not bode well.

"No, no brain damage."

But if I suddenly couldn't write, how was it not brain damage?

"You are on a lot of drugs," Jo said, with a smile.

Oh, that makes sense, I thought.

A nurse came in to check my vitals. My blood pressure was in the stratosphere. "He needs to rest," the nurse said. "I'm giving him propofol."

I shook my head. I didn't want it. But I was hooked up to IVs and couldn't talk, and the nurse was concerned I would stroke out if I didn't calm down soon.

I used my hand to ask for more paper. My new fear was that if I went to sleep again, I would never wake up. I needed to tell my wife something important, and it was complicated. I didn't know if I could figure out a way to say what I needed to say before the drugs took hold. But I tried.

Call Maggie, I wrote.

Years ago, I took part in a documentary series about the disappearance of Maura Murray, the subject of my book *True Crime Addict*. Maggie Freleng was the young journalist from UMass who worked as the lead investigator for the program. Our relationship started off rocky but developed into a real friendship. She was someone I trusted now. One of the few. And recently I had sent her a link to a private video. In the video, I said everything I had always wanted to say about the Maura Murray case but was too afraid to say in public, for fear of angering more people. But if I was going to die, I needed it to be released. It was a bit of unfinished business.

"Call Maggie? Why?" Julie asked.

Tell her to release the video.

"What video?" asked Julie.

"Did you make a video telling your side of the story?" asked Jo.

I pointed at her. *Bingo.*

"You're not going to die if you go to sleep," said Julie.

Maggie, I wrote again.

"Is her number in your phone?"

I nodded.

"Okay. Let me call her." Julie took the phone out of the room and returned a few minutes later. "I got her. She said she'd do it. It's okay."

It was a white lie, I'd find out later. Julie knows me. She knew I wouldn't fall asleep until I had some closure. She really did speak with Maggie, but they both agreed my video was not going to be published anytime soon. I was not in my right mind.

I started to drift off, thinking about my kids and of the legacy I'd leave behind, such as it was. It wasn't enough. Not nearly enough. And then I had one more thought.

I asked for the pen and paper again. This time I wrote, *I buried some treasure in . . .*

I stopped writing. Yes. Good. If I died now, people would search for that treasure for years. Decades, maybe. People would remember me and the puzzle I left behind. A puzzle that had no solution because I have never buried treasure anywhere.

"You buried treasure?" Jo asked.

I closed my eyes and fell asleep at last.

Obviously, I didn't die. Not for long, anyway.

In the morning, the doctors took me off the ventilator and gave me a cannula for oxygen. That part was uncomfortable but bearable. Then came the catheter. And if you've never had the pleasure, imagine if you will a clown performing that trick where he pulls out an endless string of colorful handkerchiefs from your pocket. But instead of your pocket, it's your penis. And instead of napkins, its barbed wire.

I was starving but the nurses were afraid I'd aspirate my food, so they started me off with applesauce. When that went okay, they brought me some scrambled eggs.

Later that day a doctor visited and explained what he believed had gone wrong with the anesthesia. "I've seen this three times in the last year," he said. "The one thing you all have in common is that you vape. If you're going to smoke, I'd rather you smoke cigarettes. I think it's something to do with the wetness of the vape and what it does to your lungs. I believe it's why there was so much secretion when extubated. Stay away from it." I told him I would.

I started to feel better. My parents and my sister went home. After they moved me out of ICU, Julie went home to be with the kids. The next day, they released me with lots of antibiotics and a week's worth of Oxy, and it was back to the couch in the basement.

I skipped over an important detail about my experience. I saw something when I fell asleep that night in the hospital. I want to tell you about it. But not right now. I'm not sure you'd believe me just yet. And this book isn't just about me, after all. There's a mystery afoot. What happened to Amy Bradley?

So, let's get back to it.

Chapter Seven

THE CAMERAMAN

By mid-April, I had exhausted all avenues of research online, and my leg had healed to where I could get around with a cane if I took it slow. I had run out of the Percocet, and my mind was clear. I wasn't able to travel yet, but I could start interviewing people on Zoom.

The easiest source to find was that videographer who'd captured Amy dancing with Yellow in the discotheque the night before she disappeared. I started with him.

When I tracked him down, Chris Fenwick was camping in the Texas wilderness, preparing for a total solar eclipse that was scheduled to traverse the eastern United States the next day. He had solar panels for power and a connection to Starlink for Wi-Fi, so we could communicate easily enough. Chris is very fit. Thin, bald, with a white-blond goatee. He was a young videographer when he found himself on that Caribbean cruise in 1998. Twenty-six years later, a lot has changed, but Chris remains fascinated with the mystery and the small but important part he played in it all.

Chris is a private contractor. Back in 1998, he was hired by Vanstar, a tech service company out of San Francisco, to travel along with their key employees on a team-building retreat aboard the *Rhapsody of the Seas*. His job was to document all the fun the employees were having during the week and to compile everything into a sharable video they could take home as a keepsake. Chris calls these souvenirs "happy-face videos."

Ever since he saw *Star Wars* as a fourteen-year-old kid, Chris had wanted to make films. Producing happy-face videos for Vanstar was not exactly Academy Award–winning work, but he was learning the trade. He discovered that he enjoyed it, especially the editing, which was just evolving from analog to digital at the time.

"I make videos so bad, people have to be paid to watch them," he joked.

For the Vanstar cruise, Chris traveled to San Juan with forty-two cases of equipment and one assistant, a guy named Bob. At the airport in San Francisco, Chris gave the skycap a bag of donuts for his troubles—a simple cheap show of respect that he has found guarantees his luggage will make its way onto the correct plane. Sure enough, everything arrived at his destination. Once he was aboard the *Rhapsody*, he set up an editing suite inside his cabin.

"That week, we were shooting all the time, all over the boat," he said. I heard the mistake he'd made, and he smiled because he'd done it on purpose. "They get mad if you call it a boat," said Chris. "It's a *ship*, they'll say. But now I always call it a boat. I revel in the idea of offending them. I think the Royal Caribbean people were awful at best. And in my opinion, they were at least partially responsible for what happened to Amy."

Chris and Bob quickly fell into a routine. Bob walked around the *Rhapsody of the Seas* with a DV camera, shooting B-roll—people swimming in the pool, gazing out at the sea on deck, playing slots in the casino. Whenever he filled an entire tape, he'd return it to Chris in the editing suite, and Chris would use the best shots to build out their video.

"I'm looking for Spielberg moments. But there's also a review cycle that's very important. Quite often, I'll find a good shot but it's the wrong people. It's other passengers, not Vanstar employees. A vice president from the company would come in periodically to review the footage and say, 'That's not one of us,' and I'd have to edit it out. And sometimes the manager would notice I had an executive on tape dancing with a woman who was not his wife. Can't use that."

Chris liked to play around with the clips for his own amusement, too. When a group of employees visited a topless beach, he edited some choice shots into the video and inserted the Vanstar logo over exposed nipples. "I'd ask the manager, 'Can I put this in?' And he'd say, 'Not now that you showed me!'"

Bob's footage was supplemented by additional video gathered by another cameraman, named Robert, who worked for Royal Caribbean. Chris had contracted with Robert to shoot extra B-roll part-time. Robert used a Beta SP camera, which required further equipment, since Beta SP used different decks than their DV cams.

It was Robert who first told them about Amy.

On Tuesday morning, Robert came by Chris's room. "Did you hear about the girl who jumped overboard?" he asked. It was a tragedy, of course. But Chris was focused on his job. What help could he be, anyway? He had a lot to edit and not much time.

The next day, yellow flyers appeared on everyone's doors with Amy's photo on them and instructions on how to contact the family if anyone had information. Chris put the flyer in his room and continued to work.

"Then, Thursday night, I'm up late, and I went for a walk," he explained. "This was probably after midnight. I was on the eighth-floor deck, which looks down on the central atrium. And I see them down there. Ron and Brad running toward the bow."

Of course he didn't know their names, then. What he saw was a middle-aged man and a younger man running to meet with a middle-aged woman, who was in conversation with two others. He could hear their conversation. It became clear that this was the missing woman's family. They were talking to a pair of witnesses who claimed to have seen Amy.

"I was spying on them," he said. "I was curious. The family is sitting down there, having a talk with two young women. They are recounting a story. They had seen Amy the morning she disappeared. They told her family they had seen her in an elevator with the bass player from the boat's band. They saw the two of them go up, and then the bass player came down alone."

Chris felt the hairs on the back of his neck stand up. "This was my Spielberg moment," he said. "I thought about all that B-roll. I wondered if we had pictures of this girl. I remembered the footage from the disco I'd reviewed. There were shots of the bass player, Yellow, dancing with a very attractive young woman. So, I went back to the room around one o'clock in the morning. I'm meticulous about labeling tapes. I popped in Monday night's tapes. And there they were, Amy and Yellow."

In the first shot, Amy and Yellow are dancing a couple feet apart, facing each other. Amy has an athletic build but she looks diminutive compared to Yellow, who was bald, with a barrel chest and broad shoulders. Yellow moves to the music. He's clearly into Amy, his eyes on her body. She's dancing and smiling, and he moves closer.

Later, they appear again, farther away from the camera, behind other dancers who weave in and out of the shot. Amy's back is to Yellow. But they're close. One of Yellow's hands is at her hips, the other holds a drink. In the '90s, we called this "grinding."

Chris also found a shot of Amy waiting at the elevator doors, which are on the far wall of the dance floor. She was alone, but still dancing.

"I dubbed the footage to a Beta SP tape, then I slept for a couple hours," said Chris. When he woke up, he went searching for the Bradley family and found them seated in the dining room by the buffet, surrounded by a small army of friends. He didn't feel comfortable just going up to them, though—it was clear they were quite distraught. So, he waited until a man who had been sitting with them went to get some food. Chris intercepted him at the waffle station and introduced himself. It turned out the man was Mike McCord, the CEO for Ron's company, the man who'd gifted them the cruise. Chris handed him the tape, and Mike told him he'd make sure it got to the proper authorities.

"I thought I'd done everything I could to get my good guy pin at that point, and so I went back to editing."

As Chris was finishing the Vanstar video, a call came into his room. The man on the other end introduced himself as Lou Costello. It wasn't the burlesque comedian of the same name, but the chief of security for *Rhapsody of the Seas*. "I need your master tapes," he said.

Chris told him that was never going to happen, he didn't give his masters to anyone.

"I'm working with the FBI, and we need the tapes," Costello told him.

"Then tell them to call me," said Chris. But the FBI never called, and Chris never heard from Costello again.

He figured Mike had shared the video with the Bradleys and the FBI, and that they were using the tape for evidence in whatever sort of case her disappearance turned out to be. He finished editing in time for Vanstar to screen the video the last night of the cruise—fun memories for their employees. No footage of the woman who'd gone missing was included in the final product. And then Chris returned home to San Francisco. Years passed, and whenever he was at a party, he had an interesting story to tell, about how he'd once discovered evidence in a famous cold case.

Then one night, Chris's older brother called him. He'd just seen Amy's case on TV, on one of the prime-time hour-long documentaries about her disappearance. It would have been the perfect opportunity to air his footage, but it wasn't included in the program. Chris started to wonder if his tape ever really got to the proper authorities.

"So, I called the FBI," said Chris. The person who answered the phone promised to have an agent with the Bureau's office in the Caribbean contact him, but he never heard back. His brother contacted the FBI, too. But he didn't get any further than Chris had.

Eventually, Chris reached out to Iva, directly. She told him that she had never seen the tape. She asked him to go back into the raw footage and see if he had any more shots of Amy. And so, Chris pulled his masters out of storage and watched through everything again, and discovered three or four new shots he'd missed before. One showed Amy from a distance, standing in the atrium the day before she disappeared. He edited together a new, complete series of shots and uploaded it to YouTube where it still exists today.

He now believes that Mike McCord handed the footage over to the ship's security, not the FBI. And who knows what they did with it? To this day, Chris keeps in touch with Iva, checking in by phone every couple of years.

"I've never shared oxygen with Iva, but I consider her a dear friend," he said.

Chris believes Royal Caribbean and the security team aboard the *Rhapsody of the Seas* did little to help find Amy. He bristles whenever he watches documentaries about the disappearance and someone says that the crew searched the ship. If they did, it was a cursory search at best, because nobody ever came to his room to look inside the giant cases he used to cart his equipment on and off the ship, cases big enough to hide a body in.

"What's my theory?" he said toward the end. "I think there are two possibilities. She was taken off the boat against her will, in a crate or a trash bag, taken out with the trash. Or she walked out under her own power. Maybe then she was sold into slavery on those islands. There was a Canadian scuba diver who says he saw her on a beach there. He described the tattoos she had. It's a very credible sighting. I think she got off the boat."

Chapter Eight

THE GIRLS FROM KENTUCKY

According to Ron, he last saw his daughter sitting on the balcony outside their room just before 5:30 a.m. on March 24, 1998. It was still dark outside. Sunrise in Curaçao that day was at 6:38 a.m. However, it's possible he was not the last person to see Amy Bradley. Two young women who had partied with her the night before are convinced they saw Amy after Ron did. And she was not alone.

Crystal Roberts was eighteen years old that summer. Originally from New Jersey, Crystal's family had recently moved to Kentucky after her stepfather got a job working at Mammoth Cave. Her parents planned a cruise that spring as a kind of reunion. Twenty-four members of Crystal's extended family joined them for the trip. As a Christmas present, her parents bought her a ticket, too, and told her she could invite a friend. Crystal invited Lori Renick, who worked with her at Pizza Hut.

The last thing either girl expected was to become a witness in a famous disappearance.

Crystal is forty-four years old now. She lives in Maine, where she oversees IT contracts for the VA.

"I have to be careful about what I say," she warned me. "I swear a lot."

She first met Amy Bradley and her brother at the airport—they shared the same layover before continuing to San Juan. "I thought her brother was cute," she said. "We locked eyes at the airport." When they realized they were headed to the same place, she and Brad struck up a conversation. He introduced her to Amy.

Their group stuck together once they got on the ship. And the party never stopped.

"We were in international waters," said Crystal. "You could drink if you were eighteen. We were getting messed up every night." Back home Crystal smoked cigarettes, but she was careful to hide her habit from her parents. On the ship, though, old boundaries came down. She was an adult, now, after all. So, for the first time, she smoked in front of her parents. She had no curfew. It was liberating.

Like Amy, Crystal liked to dance. And like Amy, she was young and attractive. It wasn't long before she caught the attention of the ship's bass player, Alister Douglas, aka Yellow. He always seemed to be loitering near their group, looking for any opportunity to get close.

"He's one of those handsy, touchy, always have to be on you kind of guys," Crystal recalled. "He came up to me on the dance floor and started grinding on me. And he had a hard-on while he was grinding on me. I told him to get fucked. He didn't bother me much after that." She thought Yellow was skeezy. Amy did too, she said. That's why she was so surprised to see Amy with Yellow the morning she disappeared.

There has been much dispute over the exact time of this sighting. It was sometime after the disco shut down but before sunrise. Unlike Amy and Brad, who had returned to their family's room, Crystal and Lori stayed outside on the deck after the dance club closed, lounging on chairs (Crystal was quite inebriated and didn't want to wake everyone up stumbling into the room).

The way the ship is arranged, the Viking Lounge, where the dance club is located, is inside a giant glass cabin, shaped like a flying saucer, that looms above the back half of the vessel. From Crystal and Lori's vantage point on the outside deck chairs, it was possible to see through a wall of windows into the interior of the ship and into the double glass elevators that go up to the Viking Lounge.

That's how they saw Amy and Yellow return to the club together sometime before dawn.

"Ew," Crystal said. "What is she doing with him?" She thought it was weird, because the club was closed and nobody else was up there.

"Then thirty minutes to an hour later, Yellow came walking toward us, alone. I didn't see him come back down the elevator. I think we startled him. He saw us, did a double-take, and said, 'Hi.'"

Not long after this, Crystal and Lori went back to their room to get some rest. Crystal was awoken later that morning by a loud message from the ship's speakers. Someone was asking for Amy to report to the purser's desk. Crystal had no reason to really be concerned yet, so she put a pillow over the speaker.

"When I woke up, my mom told me what was going on."

Agents with the FBI interviewed both young women the next day, but the agents were more concerned about how much they'd had to drink than anything else. "The FBI guys were total dicks," Crystal said. "We were drunk, but we saw what we saw."

A couple years later, Crystal was called to Virginia to testify in front of a grand jury. Details of the proceeding are murky after twenty-some years. Grand juries can be convened to hear evidence about a specific suspect, or as an investigative body, in the hopes of securing an indictment, but no one was ever charged with killing Amy or with kidnapping her.

"I haven't been on a cruise since," she said.

"What do you think happened?" I asked.

"I think Yellow tried to put the moves on Amy and she said no. If that's what happened, she could have gotten him fired." Crystal told me that she almost hoped Amy died that night. The thought of her being kidnapped and trafficked for men in a foreign country would be so much worse than a quick death.

Crystal's friend Lori is a registered nurse now, working on a master's in psychology and raising teenage kids. She backed up everything Crystal had told me.

"I always thought Yellow was very creepy," she said. "The way he'd smile at me or any other younger girl. He just gave me a creepy vibe."

Lori tried to be as specific as she could about exactly when they saw Amy and Yellow riding the elevator back up to the Viking Lounge. "It was the wee morning hours," she said. "But it could have been anywhere between three thirty and five thirty, six a.m. It was really late. I thought how strange, they're going to a nightclub that was closed down."

Once they learned that Amy was missing, their vacation's celebratory mood turned sour. "The whole trip changed," she said. "Who could have a good time knowing Amy was missing?"

The experience made her suspicious of the world forever after. "I'm a very overprotective mother," she said. "I've been criticized for it. At family functions, I was the one watching everyone's children. When we took our kids to a restaurant and they had to use the restroom, we all went together. I have a teen daughter. She turns seventeen this year. It makes me nervous."

I asked her the same question I put to Crystal: "What do you think happened to Amy?"

"I think she was held on that boat until we docked," she said. "I think she was taken off and sold. And I don't think it's the first time something like that has happened."

She's heard about the sightings of Amy over the years, on nearby islands and on escort websites. "I believe that's her in those photographs."

Looking back, Lori recalled that the way Yellow had looked at her had made her feel uneasy. "It was like Yellow was shopping," she said, "like he was looking for the right girl."

Crystal's mother kept a couple souvenirs from their trip aboard the *Rhapsody of the Seas*. The first was a VHS video made by the ship's cameraman, a collection of clips from their week at sea set to low-rent music, which she mailed to me. She also shared two photographs of Yellow, himself. These were taken on the main deck, by the dining hall, during a lull when Crystal and Lori were sitting next to each other. The area is empty except for them and for Yellow, who sits at a table, alone, behind them, just watching. In the second photograph, after he notices that he's on camera, he covers his face with his hands.

Chapter Nine

THE SCUBA DIVER

"HERE'S THE THING EVERYONE has to remember. When it happened, I didn't know it had happened." That's how David Carmichael began his story.

David is sixty-eight years old and works in telecommunications out of Calgary for the oil and gas industry. He's also an accomplished diver who has explored shipwrecks and reefs all over the world. As a kid, he became transfixed by the ocean after watching *Sea Hunt* and got his diver's certification as soon as he could. Over the years, he's racked up over a hundred dives but it's been a while since he's been in the water. He's older now and scuba diving is a dangerous game. When something goes wrong, it goes wrong fast. It's all about precision: measuring depth and oxygen levels so that your blood doesn't boil with the bends when you come up. There is no room for error.

"I like to be alone," David explained. "When you're diving, you're alone with your thoughts. It's very relaxing."

In August 1998, David put together a dive team to visit Playa Porto Mari, a beach on the western rim of Curaçao. Back then, the beach was remote, the sort of place only locals knew about. Just above the beach was a shack bar, with umbrella stands for shade.

On August 12, he and a friend, Brian, got into the water around 9 a.m. For the first forty to fifty feet from shore, the water is only waist deep before it drops quickly to 120 feet. Down there, you will find beautiful coral and all sorts of colorful fish. Sharks are around, but they don't venture close too often. Sometimes you may spot an eel slithering in and out of the reef.

Curaçao is a well-known destination for scuba enthusiasts. Its most popular attraction is the wreck of *The Superior Producer*, a cargo ship that went down near the port of Willemstad, in 1977, on its way to deliver Christmas goods to Margarita Island. It rests silently on its keel in a hundred feet of water near the canal, enveloped in scarlet coral.

David and Brian returned to the surface for lunch. They dropped their tanks on the sand and climbed out of their flippers. That's when David saw three people walking their way. A Black man, a white guy, and a woman. The woman had dark hair, a navel ring, and beside the ring, he saw a lizard tattoo.

"I yelled something to Brian, then, in English," David recalled. "And the woman, when she heard me, she started walking faster. She came right up to me, an arm's length away. I could tell she wanted to say something. Right as she's about to speak, the Black man comes up and locks eyes with me. She doesn't say anything, and they take her to the bar."

This interaction unnerved David, and he began to take a special interest in their group. He looked over to the bar. The woman was sitting on a stool, facing the ocean. He noticed she had a packet of cigarettes and a lighter.

That bar was the only place around to get a meal. David and Brian walked over and sat a few feet away and ordered sandwiches. As they ate, David kept an eye on the strange woman. Her hand was moving in an odd way, like she was motioning to something on her leg. She kept putting her hand on her leg.

After they finished, David and Brian returned to the water and that was the last he saw of her. He didn't think about the woman again until that December when he saw Amy Bradley's story on TV—*America's Most Wanted*, he thinks it was.

"I took a picture of Amy and sent it to Brian. I said, 'Do you know who this is?' He got back to me right away. 'That's the girl from Porto Mari,' he said."

Amy had the same gecko tattoo as the woman from the beach, he said. And a navel ring. And she smoked. So many details matched up.

"I sent a tip to the website," he said. "But I didn't hear back. I figured they found her."

Then, in May 1999, David caught an episode of *Unsolved Mysteries* about Amy's disappearance. She was still considered missing. When he saw a video of Alister Douglas, the bass player, he said he recognized him right away as the Black man he saw with Amy that day on the beach, the man who'd locked eyes with him and led her away before she could speak. David was adamant that it was Yellow he saw that day.

"If he hadn't stared at me, I'm not sure I'd remember the interaction. But it was such a weird moment that I started imprinting everything."

It seemed like the Bradley family still had no idea about his sighting. Why weren't they told?

"I was like, okay, what the fuck is going on?" This time David sent an email directly to the Bradleys. Ron called him right away, and David told him what he'd seen on the beach. He shared his hotel receipts and passport stamps to prove he was on Curaçao that day. Since then, he's told the story many times, to the FBI, to Interpol, and to the federal grand jury in Virginia.

"Royal Caribbean sent this one guy to see me in Calgary. I invited him into my house. He tried to punch holes in my story. It was like they were trying to indemnify themselves. The interview took over an hour."

Later in 1999, David decided to drive down to Virginia to meet the Bradleys in person. Once he arrived at their house, they all went to dinner at a restaurant by the river. He rode there on the back of Ron's motorcycle and then returned in a car with Brad.

"Brad was just devasted," said David. "He thought his sister hung the moon. He loved her. He was so torn up."

Over the years, as lawyers and FBI agents questioned his motives, David has asked himself that age-old question that Job asked so long ago, *Why me?*

"I'm not a religious person, but I wonder, what put me there, in that moment of time? What the frick is that all about? Honestly, sometimes I wish I had never seen her. Here I am, twenty-six years later, still talking about it."

What does he think happened to Amy Bradley?

"It's really simple," he said. "She walked off the ship. I'm going to tell you a story about someone I knew. I'll call him Mike. We worked together in Calgary. One day, Mike doesn't show up for work. Everyone is looking for him. His family, everyone. Apparently, he sold his Jeep and just disappeared. Eventually we learn that all this time, Mike was living in two worlds. He was secretly gay. He paid off his house for the family, and then he just ran away to live his life the way he wanted to live it.

"So how does this relate to Amy? I have two theories. One, Amy planned all of this. She walked off the ship to start a new life as another person. But that theory doesn't really hold water. She only had a couple months to plan everything, and why do it in Curaçao? And theory two, she was grabbed for some reason. Someone saw her and wanted her. They walked her off the boat. But how did that happen without them being seen?"

If that really was Amy and Yellow on the beach that day, why didn't she take the opportunity to say something to David before the man came to her side?

David found the photo from the escort website to be very convincing as well. Maybe Amy really did end up being trafficked on the island. Curaçao, he said, is not as safe as it seems.

"On the surface, it looks like any other Caribbean island," David said. "But if you go looking, you'll find all you want to find. It's like peeling back the layers of an onion. There are brothels, drugs. Ask yourself one question, if the place is so nice, why are there bars on every window of every house? On a clear day, you can see all the way to Venezuela. And their border protection is as good as a screen door on a submarine. The police are corrupt as the day is long. On Curaçao you can buy your way out of anything if you have enough money."

Chapter Ten

THE INCIDENT IN BARBADOS AND OTHER SIGHTINGS

In April, my doctor gave me a simple brace for my ankle, and I started to walk unaided again. I got one of those cheap treadmills that slide under a bed, the kind that only goes five miles an hour. I would walk for forty-five minutes at a time, long enough to stream a new episode of *Doctor Who* while I exercised. By the time the credits rolled my foot was swollen again, but I could feel the tendons healing.

Every day I felt better. I started driving again. I could get Laine to school in the morning and run simple errands in the afternoon. Getting back into the world felt a little like venturing out after the Covid lockdowns—I was hyperaware of other people, of the masses of strangers I'd forgotten existed for a couple months.

My reclaimed mobility also meant I could swap out Zooms for in-person interviews again. Nothing beats sitting across from a person when you have to ask them important questions. There's no obligation to respond through a computer screen. But it's hard to say no when you're facing a real-life human being. I didn't want to miss all the subtle tells that don't come across on Zoom, the ticks and mannerisms unique to a person that can reveal their character. It's easier to tell when someone is lying to you if you're in the same room.

When I discovered that another eyewitness claimed to have seen Amy Bradley after her disappearance, and she also lived in Ohio, I made arrangements to meet her for coffee in Columbus, near her home.

After becoming a business owner in a fateful way, Judy Maurer now operates three UPS stores in the Columbus suburbs. In 2007, Judy had a side hustle selling jewelry through the mail. One day, when she stopped by her local UPS store to ship an order, she noticed that the woman behind the counter seemed upset. Her dad had just died, she told Judy, and she had to sell the business. When Judy got home, she told her husband she was going to buy the store. And she did. Now three of her children run the shops, providing a steady income stream for her extended family. Luck and fate have put her in the right place at the right time more than once.

I picked up Judy at her house, where two old dachshunds, Frank and Daisy, waddled around the living room. Meeting her husband in the driveway, I explained I was a journalist and not some secret suitor whisking his wife away. We went to a nearby Panera and sat in a back booth where we could hear each other talk.

In early 2005, about seven years after Amy Bradley's disappearance, Judy and her husband booked a room on a Celebrity Cruise bound for the Caribbean. Their ship toured the Lesser Antilles, that stretch of islands that extends from Puerto Rico to South America, arcing eastward like a warrior's bow aimed at Africa. When they arrived at Barbados, Judy and her husband disembarked to visit the markets in Bridgetown, its capital city.

Back then, Barbados was still a Commonwealth realm of Queen Elizabeth II's empire (it wouldn't become a republic until 2021). English was the main language, at least for the shop owners greeting tourists, but the sound of Bajan Creole could be heard drifting from kitchens and warehouses.

Like many Americans on short excursions from waiting ships, Judy was blissfully unaware that Barbados was a prime destination for human traffickers. According to the U.S. State Department, Barbados has a long sordid history of forced prostitution. In 2005, illegal migrants from the Dominican Republic, Guyana, and Jamaica were especially vulnerable to local organized crime rings who pulled them into brothels and forced them to ply the trade as soon as they stepped off their boats. Transactional child sex was also ignored by local police. These children were not usually pimped by the cartels but by their own parents.

Barbados was only upgraded to Tier 2 on the State Department's Human Trafficking list in 2022, which is basically a "C" grade for secret slavery, after the pandemic forced stricter entry protocols. Don't celebrate yet, though. Recent reports show an increase in new sex workers from Jamaica and Venezuela who have fled their own country's economic hardships only to find themselves trading sex for shelter.

As they walked through downtown, Judy led her husband into a gift shop that sold shirts with cats on them. She saw one with a cat that looked like her own and was considering buying it.

"There was a line at the cash register," she recalled, nearly twenty years later. "I noticed this girl standing there with three creepy men. She asked to use the restroom. The men wanted to go with her, but the shop owners refused to let them."

Judy and her husband left and walked behind the gift shop, toward the channel where their ship was docked. After a while she turned and noticed that the girl and the creepy men were walking behind them. It was terribly hot outside, so Judy led her husband back to the street and then they dipped into an air-conditioned department store.

"I told my husband that I wanted to go back to the ship for lunch, but I needed to use the store's bathroom first. So I go to the women's room. It was very clean. Nobody was in there. I had just sat down, and all of a sudden, I hear men's voices in the restroom. A lot of them. I pulled my feet up. I was worried. Are they coming to rob me?"

Judy stayed quiet as the men walked down the row of stalls,

bending down, checking for shoes. She didn't dare breathe. Finally, the men moved back toward the door.

"I heard a man's voice say, 'The deal's at ten tonight. You better be ready to go. We can stop and see the kids on the way back.' Then, 'Don't talk to anyone and hurry up.' The door opened and closed and the men were gone."

Judy was scared and wanted to leave so she opened the stall door and made her way toward the sinks, where she found a woman waiting there. She had dark hair and a pretty face. It was the woman from the gift shop and she was crying. Judy felt sympathy for her, she was the same age as her kids. She felt a need to talk to this woman, to find out if she was all right.

"Are you on vacation?" Judy asked.

The woman shook her head.

"Are you on a cruise?"

The woman shook her head again.

"What's your name?" Judy asked.

"And I swear to God, James, she turned her head like she was thinking about it, and then she whispered, 'Amy.'" The name stuck with Judy because she has a daughter named Amy, too.

"I asked her where she was from, and I thought she said West Virginia but I couldn't really hear the first part. It might have just been somewhere in Virginia. She could have said Chesterfield, Virginia."

Someone pounded on the bathroom door. The woman pivoted on her feet and walked toward Judy.

"I started backing up but she kept coming toward me. She never said a word. I started to leave. I could hear my mother's voice telling me, *get out, get out*."

When Judy opened the door, she found one of the men standing there, and he wouldn't move.

"He tried to intimidate me," Judy said. "He looks down at my chest and back up. So I played dumb tourist. I don't know nothing. I acted like everything was fine, and he moved."

Judy found her husband then, and they walked back through the department store. Along the way Judy noticed another man standing guard. He seemed visibly upset to see Judy come out of the restrooms. Then, the intimidating man led Amy out of the bathroom, one arm hooked around her.

Once they got outside, Judy told her husband what had happened. "I told him, I think she's being forced to do something she doesn't want to do. He said there's nothing we can do. I knew it wasn't safe there, and we had to get back."

Later, as they ate their lunch aboard the cruise ship, Judy looked down out at Bridgetown, at the streets and stores, and wondered what had happened to that woman.

When they returned home to Ohio, Judy did her best to put the incident out of her mind. One day a coworker asked if she'd seen the latest episode of *Dr. Phil.* He'd done an episode about an American woman who had disappeared in the Caribbean. When Judy got home, she watched the program. Iva and Ron Bradley were on, talking about their daughter from Virginia, Amy Bradley, who'd vanished in 1998. When they showed the picture of the escort from Affordable Adult Vacations, the woman with the dark hair and pretty face, Judy recognized her immediately. It was the woman from the bathroom in Barbados.

"That was her," she said. "I just about died."

Judy called the FBI but was unimpressed by their response. According to Judy, the agent simply said, "That girl's dead. She fell off the boat." It was around Christmastime when she contacted the Bradleys directly. Ron called her back, and she told him the entire story from the beginning.

To this day, the Bradleys believe the Barbados sighting is real. If Judy's story is accurate, not only do they have a story about a person under duress who resembled their daughter, but this mystery woman also said her name was Amy. And she had possibly even mentioned her hometown. Tips don't get better than this, not after so many years, and yet the FBI showed little interest.

This speaks to the larger issue of who is in charge of an investigation when an American citizen disappears abroad.

Since Amy was last seen on the *Rhapsody of the Seas*, jurisdiction actually belongs to the law enforcement agencies of the country the ship was registered with at the time. Unfortunately, all the major cruise lines register their home country someplace other than the United States to take advantage of tax breaks and loose labor laws. In 1998, the *Rhapsody of the Seas* was registered in Liberia. In case you are as geographically challenged as I am, Liberia is a country in West Africa. Liberians are so poor their citizens still hunt bushmeat like chimpanzees and pygmy hippopotamus. Oh, and their police were preoccupied fighting a civil war from 1998 to 2003. But, hey, at least Royal Caribbean enjoyed some awesome tax breaks.

It could be argued that the FBI has no jurisdiction at all in this case. According to the FBI's website, agents only have investigatory powers overseas when Americans are taken hostage by terrorist organizations. They do occasionally offer help in famous cases of missing Americans, like Natalee Halloway, for instance, but they must first get permission from the host government. The FBI has no dedicated office on the island of Curaçao. Some agents are stationed in San Juan, though. Our embassy in Bridgetown, Barbados, is the point of contact for Americans who go missing on any of the thirty-some islands in the Caribbean. Even with proof that a crime has occurred, there's not much they can do. If a killer confessed to them on Curaçao, they couldn't arrest him without consent from the local government.

If you become the victim of a crime on your journey, you're not going to find much protection. This is one reason why so much of the investigation into Amy Bradley's disappearance has been conducted by the Bradleys themselves.

The Bradleys arranged for Judy to sit with an artist to develop composite sketches of the woman she saw in the bathroom in

Bridgetown and the men who accompanied her. The sketch of the woman is a dead ringer for the escort that appeared on the Affordable Adult Vacations website just a year prior.

Another potential sighting of Amy Bradley occurred in San Francisco on April 18, 2003. According to a tip that came to the Bradleys, a woman was visiting Fisherman's Wharf when she spotted someone who looked like Amy being escorted by two men near the ticket station for the ferry to Alcatraz. When the men noticed the witness paying special attention to them, they grabbed the woman and pulled her away.

The FBI considered this sighting credible enough to have the witness sit with another sketch artist out of Quantico. The artist spent eight hours with the witness to create composite sketches of the two men seen at the wharf. One man was overweight, with a bald top and red beard. The other man appeared to be foreign, with dark shoulder-length hair.

One additional significant witness has stepped forward. Chief Petty Officer William Heffner was stationed aboard the USS *Chandler*, a guided-missile destroyer operated by the U.S. Navy, when it docked in Curaçao in January 1999. Personnel were allowed off the ship for a little R&R in Willemstad, but they were given a list of places of ill repute to avoid. This included the old Stellaris Hotel, which sat across the street from the cruise ship docks. But Heffner went anyway.

According to a 2002 story published in the *Richmond Times-Dispatch*, Heffner was sitting at the bar inside the Stellaris when he noticed two women, one white, one Hispanic, sitting with two Black men. Heffner struck up a conversation with the men. At the time, he believed the women were prostitutes who were stationed at the hotel bar. One of the men led the Hispanic woman upstairs, and a short time later, the other man left, and he was alone with the white woman. When they were alone, she reached over and squeezed his hand. "My name is Amy Bratley," he thought she said—Bratley with a *t.* She told Heffner that the men had her papers, and she couldn't leave the island.

Still believing she was a prostitute, Heffner assumed she was trying to take advantage of him somehow, that this was some ruse to get money out of him. He told her that if she really was an American, she could go to any U.S. ship in port and ask for help. One of the men returned then, and she acted like nothing had happened. When Heffner returned to his ship, he didn't report his encounter. He didn't want to get in trouble.

Then in July 2001, Heffner saw Amy Bradley's photograph on the cover of *People* magazine. As he said to Iva, he recognized Amy as the woman from the Stellaris Hotel. By then, however, the Stellaris had burned to the ground. At the time of the sighting, the hotel was owned by a man named John Daryanani, who also served as the president of the Curaçao port development committee. In 2007, Daryanani was arrested on charges of arson and insurance fraud.

Over the years, Heffner has been reticent about speaking with reporters. When Beth Halloway dedicated an episode of her show, *Vanished,* to the disappearance of Amy Bradley, Heffner at first agreed to fly to Curaçao for an interview but then dropped out at the last moment.

On the family's website, Iva claims that Heffner took a polygraph at the request of the FBI and passed. I have been unable to confirm this.

Chapter Eleven

THE PROBLEM WITH EYEWITNESSES

BEFORE WE VENTURE FURTHER, let's review the testimony of our eyewitnesses.

Crystal Roberts and Lori Renick are certain they saw Amy with Alister Douglas returning to the Viking Lounge dance club shortly before dawn the morning of her disappearance. The exact time is difficult to pinpoint, but they are quite sure it would have happened after Amy returned to her room but before the ship reached Curaçao. It could have occurred in that blind spot between when Amy's father, Ron, saw her on the balcony and when he went looking for her. Their sighting is the most convincing and least problematic of the bunch.

David Carmichael is convinced that Alister Douglas was one of the men he saw with Amy Bradley on the beach at Playa Porto Mari in August 1998. But he came to this realization in reverse—he saw Amy's photograph on TV, and she seemed to look like the face from his memory. But how well can we recall details of a stranger's face months after meeting them? Of course, there's other circumstantial evidence—the tattoos, the navel ring, the cigarettes—that add credence to his sighting. Still . . .

Then there's Judy, who claims she saw Amy in a restroom in

Barbados. The woman even told her that her name was Amy and that she was from Virginia. I mean, what more do you need? However, I think it's important to note that Judy said the woman she met that day looked like the escort from Affordable Adult Vacations. In fact, the sketches developed from her story look identical to the woman from the escort photo. It's entirely possible at this time that the woman from those photos, who does bear a resemblance to Amy Bradley, may actually be someone else. Perhaps it was that lookalike that Judy saw in Barbados. And again, she only made the connection after seeing Amy's photographs on TV. The best part of her story is that the woman told her that her name was Amy, and she had reason to remember that because it was also the name of her daughter.

Finally, there is the sighting of William Heffner, who also claims the woman he met used her full name—Amy Bradley. But something bugs me about this one. Why was he not curious enough about the encounter to search the name on the Internet before seeing Amy's photo in *People* magazine?

The sheer number of sightings, though, should also be weighed. Could everyone be mistaken? Seems unlikely. And yet, if they're accurate, that means Amy really was pulled into an international human trafficking ring and somehow never managed to pick up a phone and call her family or walk to the local consulate for twenty-six years.

The unfortunate truth is that eyewitness testimony is notoriously unreliable.

Consider the story of Kirk Bloodsworth. Bloodsworth's life was fairly routine. He lived in Cambridge, Maryland, and harvested shellfish for a living. He was a former Marine, who had served his country before being honorably discharged. Then, on July 25, 1984, nine-year-old Dawn Hamilton left her father's apartment in Rosedale, about an hour away from Cambridge. It was a fine, summer day and Dawn was looking for someone to play with. Down by the water, she met up with two boys, Chris Shipley and Jack

Poling. Then a strange man approached the children and the boys watched Dawn walk away with him. At 2 p.m. that day, Dawn's body was found in the woods. She'd been raped, strangled, and beaten with a rock.

When police interviewed the boys, Chris and Jack, they described the strange man as being about six foot five, with curly blond hair, a skinny man with a tan. The police had a sketch drawn up which they shared with the nightly news. Following the broadcast, the police received a tip stating they should look at Bloodsworth, even though he was six feet tall, with red hair, and weighed over two hundred pounds.

According to a report by the Innocence Project, police detectives found five eyewitnesses who each claimed under penalty of perjury to have seen Bloodsworth near the crime scene on the day of her murder. Two of those witnesses only confirmed his identity after seeing his arrest on TV. In 1985, thanks to the testimony of these eyewitnesses, Bloodsworth was convicted of the rape and murder of Dawn Hamilton and sentenced to Death Row.

From prison, Bloodsworth appealed to the courts to have evidence tested for DNA, which was a relatively new procedure in criminal cases at the time. It took years, but eventually the evidence was tested and semen was found on the victim's underwear. The DNA profile from that semen sample did not match Bloodsworth. In 1993, he was finally released and pardoned.

Later, in an unexpected twist, the killer's DNA profile matched to a man named Kim Ruffner, who had been sent to prison in 1984 to serve forty-five years on charges of burglary and rape. His room was one floor above Bloodsworth's cell in the same prison, and sometimes they would spot each other in the workout room.

Five witnesses were so convinced it was Bloodsworth they saw with Dawn that morning they were willing to testify in front of a jury, under oath. And the jury was so convinced by their identification that they sentenced this man to death.

It was the highest of stakes, and they were all wrong.

Bloodsworth spent more than nine years in prison before he became the first inmate on Death Row to be exonerated by DNA testing. He went on to become a program officer for the Justice Project and lobbied for the Innocence Protection Act, which minimizes the risk of executing innocent people by providing post-conviction DNA testing. It became law in 2004.

Let's not forget about Steven Avery, that sad sack from Manitowoc County, Wisconsin, who was identified as the man who raped a woman on a Lake Michigan beach in 1985, even though a time-stamped receipt showed he was in Green Bay. He served eighteen years in prison for that crime before he was freed, thanks to DNA testing. The documentary that was made about his life was called *Making a Murderer*, because that horrific experience may have molded Avery into becoming a real murderer after his release. He was found guilty of killing Teresa Halbach in 2005.

The reliance on faulty eyewitness testimony to gain convictions at the expense of real justice is endemic in the United States. The Innocent Project reports that sixty-nine percent of wrongful convictions that have been overturned by DNA evidence are cases that involved eyewitness testimony. How can so many well-intentioned people be so consistently wrong?

Because memory is not what we think it is.

When we see a character's flashback in a TV series it's usually treated as a concrete thing—here's what happened before my plane crashed on that deserted island, all in technicolor detail—and maybe that has something to do with why we tend to believe that what we remember is exactly how it happened. But our memory is not stored as a QuickTime video on a digital hard drive that can be replayed forever and ever without losing fidelity. Our memories are malleable and change a little each time we access them, according to recent studies. And that's a frightening realization.

Why, exactly, does memory change? Neuroscientists at the University of Sussex have a theory.

In a paper published in 2023, Sussex neuroscientists presented the results of an experiment they conducted on 351 participants. The volunteers were shown twenty-four videos, vignettes of everyday life. The twist is that in these clips, the video ends before there's a conclusion to the story. For instance, the participants were shown footage of a baseball game but the video paused just before the batter swung at a pitch. When they were interviewed a week later, about twenty percent of the participants claimed they had watched the batter hit the ball. Some even said it had been a home run.

It seems we're hardwired to mold our memories into a complete narrative, into a story that has a beginning, middle, and end. Because we are anxious creatures, we seek structure, we desire closure. Something in our subconscious dips into our memory banks and edits those archived incidents to provide the missing ending in order to reduce anxiety, so that we don't fret about the things that remain unresolved.

"We create memories that are coherent and logical 'best guesses' about our experiences," wrote Chris Bird, Professor of Cognitive Neuroscience at Sussex. "However, there are situations such as when the criminal justice system relies on eyewitness accounts of events when accurate memories are absolutely critical."

How are we to know that any eyewitness account is accurate if we are all accidental fabulists in the end?

Is Amy Bradley still alive? Is she somewhere in the Caribbean to this day, working under the table, maybe to support a child? It's one narrative, for sure.

Ohio seems so far removed from those exotic islands and all the crooked things that may have happened there. It became apparent to me that I would never really understand how dangerous Curaçao was without seeing it for myself. I'd never understand the layout of the *Rhapsody of the Seas* unless I could walk its decks. But was the old ship even in service anymore?

A quick Google search showed that she was still sailing, though the once-great cruise liner is now considered old and small. Royal Caribbean still offers southern Caribbean cruises aboard the *Rhapsody*, and every so often the ship still visits Curaçao.

"Hey, Jules!" I yelled from my chair in the living room. "Wanna go on a cruise?"

Chapter Twelve

THE WITCH OF ENDOR

IN MAY, I LEARNED that an old friend of mine had become a spiritual medium. When we were kids, Amanda Doak's grandparents lived next to mine on Lincoln Boulevard in Ravenna, a quiet blue-collar town south of Akron. Sometimes when I'd visit my grandparents, she and I would play in the giant backyard, where a tire swing hung from a tall oak tree. I remember a time when the neighborhood flooded and we tried to make a raft to take us around the strange new water world.

I have worked with psychics in the past—you'd be surprised by how many professional detectives do as well—but never a medium. They're a different breed. Psychics can supposedly see into your past and predict your future. Mediums speak to the dead (or so they claim). Their bodies, their minds are the "medium" through which the dead can communicate with the living, if you believe in that. It's a specific type of psychic that has this gift. As Amanda puts it, all mediums are psychics, but not all psychics are mediums.

Maybe you believe it, maybe you don't. Most days I don't. But I've found it's helpful to think outside the box with these more challenging unsolved mysteries. Speaking with someone new can inspire ideas and avenues of investigation I would never have thought of myself.

Something innate in the human condition makes us want to believe that mediums speak the truth. After all, they have been around since the beginning of recorded history. When desperate heroes have exhausted all other strategies, they could always seek out the people in society who claimed to have special gifts.

Consider the story of Saul and the Witch of Endor from the Hebrew Bible. An unverified tale to be sure, but one that is certainly grounded in some ancient truth. It is an old story that people valued enough to remember and to pass on through the generations.

Saul was the king of ancient Israel, around 1000 B.C., during a time when the Israelites were becoming more organized and forming city-states. Saul's kingdom was at war with the Philistines. Saul hoped for a message from God to tell him what to do. But he received no advice in his dreams or from his advisors. The best prophet in the land, Samuel, had recently died. If he were around, he'd know what to do, thought Saul.

That thought stuck in Saul's head and he ruminated a bit. Sure, Samuel was dead. But maybe he could still ask him for advice using the witches who claimed to be able to commune with the dead.

Only problem was Saul had exiled all the necromancers from Israel. Meanwhile, the Philistines were advancing. He needed to act fast.

Saul disguised himself as a commoner and crossed enemy lines into the village of Endor, in the Jezreel Valley, to consult with their witch.

"I need you to raise Samuel," he told her.

"Sorcery is illegal, thanks to that no-good king, Saul," she replied.

"I promise, you won't be punished," he said.

The witch called on Samuel's spirit. Biblical scholars debate whether the spirit that answered her call was the real Samuel or some demon pretending to be him. The text is vague at best. But some serious drama ensued, either way.

The first thing the spirit did when it spoke to her was to tell her that the strange man in her home was none other than Saul, the king of the Israelites, himself. The Witch of Endor was angry. "Why have you deceived me?" she asked him.

"No harm will come to you," he promised, again. "Tell me what you see."

"I see Elohim rising," she replied. Elohim meant God. "I see an old man wrapped in a robe."

Saul could not see the spirit but bowed down to it, believing it was Samuel coming to give the advice he sought.

The spirit told the witch to give a message to the king—tell him that he will be defeated at battle the following day. And not just that, tell him that his sons will die as well. His reign is over.

Sure enough, the next day, Saul watched the Philistines defeat his army and murder his heirs. Despondent, he died by suicide, falling on his own sword.

Christians tell this story as a warning—never consult with a medium. But that was all such a long time ago.

And so, one day, circa three thousand years later, I ventured into the town of Ravenna to consult with Amanda Doak.

Ravenna is a bit bigger than a village but not big enough to be a proper city. When I was a kid living in the country, it was the closest place to go for a sit-down meal. The drive-in movie theater on the edge of town is still operational (minus the rusted wrought-iron slide we used to play on). Its downtown is a couple blocks of three-story brick buildings full of lawyers and accountants.

Amanda's house is at the end of a cul-de-sac down one of the side streets, not far from where our grandparents once lived. She invited me into a cozy living room. There was a bird cage on a table by the TV, and inside, her parakeet, Dallas, bobbed his head up and down and chirped loudly.

We sat on the couch across from Dallas, and Amanda started her session. I recorded the whole thing, and when I listened to it later, I was surprised to hear how cautiously I spoke to her. Our conversation had a trancelike quality. Careful. Reverent.

"When my grandparents died, I never grieved them," Amanda said, by way of explaining how she'd come to understand her gift. "I never felt like I lost them. They were always around me, and I knew that I could communicate with them. I worked on sharpening those skills."

In the last few years, Amanda took online classes and learned the practice of tarot card reading and spiritual communication from a mentor in the UK. For Christmas that year, she gave her mother a reading, and she helped her mom come to terms with the guilt she'd had about the things she could never say before her own parents died. Both mother and daughter found it to be therapeutic.

"In this way, problems can be sorted out, even though one person isn't alive physically," she said. "Because your soul is still alive after you die. Your soul is still there." I thought about the night in the hospital, hooked up to the ventilator, when I was sure I was going to die. I thought about what I saw when I gave over to that thought and finally fell asleep. I was still trying to understand it.

"My dead grandmother was there when I gave my mom her reading," Amanda said. "The communication is always very conversational, like they're sitting there. They don't really talk. It's interpreting the energy they're giving to me. The medium interprets the energy. Sometimes it's images or just a feeling."

"This is a strange request, isn't it?" I said. "Amy is missing. We don't even know if she's still alive. Or if she's on the other side."

"A person's spirit is always there," said Amanda. "They're always present, so if you ask for someone, they are there. It's just a matter of interpreting that energy, even if they're still alive. But I do feel her presence on the other side as though she is giving me the information that she is deceased."

"In some ways that would be better," I said. "At least she wouldn't have gone through all the bad things that could have happened to her on the islands."

Amanda was beginning to relax, and I felt like she was reaching out, listening.

"When you open that door, are there other people who stop by—besides the one you call for?" I asked, suddenly unnerved. "How much control do you have over who shows up?"

"Others come," she said. "They kind of line up. They're very courteous most of the time. I just view the person who is first in line and don't look further than that. I try to make sure they stay separated."

At that point, Amanda drew a card from her tarot deck, which she'd placed on the coffee table. It was the Five of Cups, showing a figure robed in black, with five cups on the ground around him. Three of the cups were overturned.

"That's just a bad card to start with," Amanda said. "It means loss, mourning, grief, which is obvious in her case. I feel like her life wasn't great at times, like there was some periods of suffering, some demon fighting, things like that. But I'm not sure if that played into what happened to her."

Amanda closed her eyes. "I will try to reach out and ask if she can give us evidence of who she is, things maybe you would know."

Dallas chirped from his cage.

"She came through with short hair," said Amanda. "I saw a life preserver. And red and white stripes."

Quiet again.

"Was she with her family at the time? Her mom and dad were there, too. And I get a fourth."

"She was with her parents and her brother, Brad," I said.

Amanda nodded. "And over and over, she keeps showing me—and I've never been on a cruise ship—but she shows me her cabin door as she's stepping out. She keeps making me feel that she had to look back to make sure nobody was following her. I don't know if she felt she was being followed or if she was sneaking out."

Amanda opened her eyes and sat up a little. "There's a male," she said. "There's a guy. And I don't think he's very tall. With darker skin. I don't know that he's American even. It feels like that's who she's looking for."

Amanda's eyes moved as if she could see something I couldn't. "At some point after that they're outside again," she said. She shivered. "I feel like she went into the water. I can feel like I'm underwater, like I can't breathe. It wasn't a horrible thing. It feels peaceful. but I also can't tell if that happened at the same time, or if there's a gap. It's still dark."

Dallas chirped again, louder now. The bird was getting anxious.

"Do you have a feeling that she went into the water herself or if someone put her there?" I asked.

"I see a deck. And there's movement. A lot of movement in the water. It's not calm. More than usual. The water is very choppy. And there's a man. I don't think it's a situation where he shoved her over. She kind of panics and is holding on. It's almost an accident. Like a slip. But he also doesn't tell anyone. So, I don't know what his intention would have been. I feel a drop and then water."

A pause, then Amanda said, "She's telling me, 'Nine.' I see a bag, a suitcase. What I'm getting now is a suitcase. I'm pretty blended in. She's been here with me for a few days, and I told her to wait. So, it's not a surprise it's coming in so easily. She's eager. She also comes through with a guide. She's just never done this before. As a spirit, she's never done this. And she needed help. She's timid in a way. At the time she passed, her confidence was growing and she was getting into herself, who she would be. But I don't think she's always been that way. I think she was timid and worked at it."

Amanda squirmed on the couch. "There's no suffering. But there's emotion there, too, when this happens. There's anger."

"Did she leave any unfinished business?" I asked.

Amanda replied with a question of her own: "Did she have a boyfriend?"

"She had a guy she was seeing. I'm not sure how serious they were."

"I don't believe that he was going to be good for her. There was something going on with him, and this also involves her parents. He wants to win, and he's going to get her, and she kind of falls for that. Rebellious. Not heavy drugs, but she was going from a good girl to starting to use drugs and drink and party. And I think her parents had kind of caught on to that."

Amanda reached for the tarot again. "We can do another card draw if you'd like."

I nodded.

She talked as she shuffled the deck. "We all have spirit guides," she said. "They're not angels. You could have one, or you could have a hundred. Our guides are spirits who have lived lives on earth before. And we have soul groups, people we are connected to in that way."

I thought again of the dream I had when I was on life support. What Amanda was telling me connected to it in a very strange way. I needed to remember this.

"Our guides work behind the scenes and make things happen," she continued. "We have free will, so we don't have to listen to them. But if you listen, they'll help you. The times you leave a couple minutes late and avoid an accident, that's them. The things that seem like a coincidence, that's them."

She pushed the cards toward me. "I'll have you cut the deck and wherever you cut it, we'll take the card."

I obliged and she turned over the King of Cups.

"Cups are emotion," Amanda said. "They come with a lot of water. Because emotion is like water. Self-knowledge, empathy, validation, manipulation. It's about father figures. Found fathers, symbolic fathers, benevolent characters. People whom they trust."

Amanda concentrated before speaking again. "There's a male in her life. Some kind of male influence that knew that he had control over her in a way. I think what's holding her up is, she doesn't want to give in and tell him he's right. She wants to do what she wants to do. She wants to assert her independence, and she feels like it's her time to do it. But it doesn't get finished because this happens, what happened on the ship. Now, it's an open-ended thing. Because she disappears."

Now the visions were coming faster, and Amanda spoke quickly to keep up. "Her mom has advocated for her this whole time," she said. "She says mom, mom, mom. Just recognizing her sacrifice. Recognizing that."

"What would it take to bring closure?" I asked.

"She keeps showing me a suitcase. I'm seeing a suitcase, an old-school suitcase with stickers on it and a handle."

A pause. Then, "The room she left before she disappeared, she left alone. There was nobody else there. I don't know if she went somewhere else. The room she was in is very, very tiny. It's like a closet. It's a guy . . ."

Amanda lost the thread then and returned to what was happening to Amy at the time she disappeared.

"The father . . . I don't feel he had anything to do with what happened, but he left some things unsaid. Small things that he thinks wouldn't have mattered. He kind of just glossed over this, because it looked better that way. He thinks, I don't want a fight. I don't want this to come out, this doesn't have anything to do with this. I know better. I'm the dad. We're not going to talk about this. But in reality, those things would have made a difference, especially in time. It would have made a difference. I'm not sure specifically what it was."

"Was there someone important to her? Someone I don't know?"

"There's a girl," said Amanda. "Not mom. A friend, a peer. A girl. For sure. Best friend, someone she confided in. I don't think she told the friend everything. She didn't want her to worry. Nobody likes to be told what they already know. And this girl, whoever she was, there's a huge amount of guilt there. To this day she feels guilt about it."

"Do you get a sense of what she wanted to do with her life?"

"Some sort of coaching," she said. "Helping kids, physical therapy stuff. Helping people is what she wanted to do. And horses. She shows me horses. Or ponies . . ."

"Is there anything I can do to put her at peace?"

"She says mom, mom, mom, over and over, and it's breaking my heart. It's like a child. She wants her mother to be okay."

"Is there anything specific she wants to say?"

"She says, 'She brings me red flowers.' Roses or red flowers. I don't know if it's something she watches her mother do. Sometimes that's what they do. She's showing me the Queen of Hearts, like the playing card. That's something her mother could watch for, the queen of hearts. If that pops up, that's Amy."

I got a sense that we were coming to the end. But Amanda still had a few messages to deliver.

"She shows me a bar, maybe a restaurant," she said. "It's by the water. I see fishing nets. Like at Joe's Crab Shack. Stuff hanging, like a seafood place. And there's a man. He's bald, white hair around back of his head. She gives me the word: ally. And a name, Bill."

Amanda sighed and kind of came out of the trance. "She gives a thank-you," she said. "This will be good. But there's more to be found. There's definitely more there to be found."

"Did anyone else try to talk to you?" I asked.

"Your grandparents were here," she said, with a smile. "They came together. Your grandfather in his khaki pants and a white T-shirt. He was showing me his strawberry patch. And their black cat named Sunshine. And a clothesline. Your grandma is there hanging clothes just like any other day. They say hello."

Chapter Thirteen

OF SUNSETS AND NICOTINE

In June, Julie and I took our kids on vacation to Lake Erie. We shared a rental with her parents and siblings, and their teenage kids, in this quaint village called Madison. A break from life, a break from work. But I was keeping a secret, and it was getting difficult to hide. I was vaping again. That's some bullshit, right? I had survived a critical event when I'd stopped breathing coming out of anesthesia, complications brought on, at least in part, by vaping, according to my doctor. Why was that not enough to get me to quit?

The house was small. Every hour or so, I'd walk into the bathroom and turn on the fan and take a couple puffs from the cartridge. I bought the Cherry Coke flavor. I thought it might blend in with the everyday smells of a home. I got away with it for longer than I expected.

One night, after a day of lake swimming, we all gathered in the living room to watch *Singin' in the Rain*. When I got up to make a snack, the vape cartridge fell out of my pocket. By the time I noticed it was gone, Julie had found it. She let the movie play out and after, when we went to bed, she asked if it was mine. I told her it was.

We've been together too long for any real blow-out fights. It had been a long day, and we were tired so we went to sleep. Her disappointment simmered until the next afternoon, when we found ourselves alone.

"You almost *died*," she said, her voice cast low so it wouldn't carry downstairs. "Why are you vaping again?"

"I like how it makes me feel. I like that it relieves some stress. It feels really good."

"Until it kills you."

"I'm forty-six," I said. "That's like way longer than I expected to live."

"Who starts smoking at forty-six?" she said. "That's dumb. I'm so fucking healthy. I work at it. I'll probably live until I'm a hundred, and I don't want to spend half my life alone."

"C'mon, you'd never be alone."

"Oh God, it would take too long to explain all the little things you know about me to someone else. Dating? No way."

"I'm sorry."

"If you worked at it, you could live for a very long time. Do you want to die?"

"No. I don't want to die. But I want to feel great every day I'm here. I don't abuse drugs anymore. I don't drink to excess anymore. So what if I smoke for a while?"

"I want you to want to be healthy."

I shrugged. "I don't have it in me."

"Then you shouldn't have had kids."

That one stuck, and I finally shut up.

"You should talk to Dr. Deb about this," she said. Dr. Deb was my therapist for a time, but I hadn't seen her in over a year. I felt like our work was done.

I sighed.

"Would you please go talk to her?" Julie asked.

"I'll set up a meeting for next week," I replied.

In the last ten years of my life, I've gone through some kind of withdrawal a dozen times or so, a decent chunk of that decade in retrospect. I'd quit antidepressants cold turkey, twice. I'd gotten properly sober, then California sober, then tried harm reduction for a bit. Quitting smoking, as you may know, is a different beast. It's the habit of the thing, the oral fixation, along with the craving for the drug itself, a jittery tightness in your chest that won't go away unless you start again. The next several months were a series of brief quittings, until it finally took. It was not easy.

I noticed something odd one night that week on the lake, sitting on the deck, watching my son Casey on a paddleboard, moving toward the setting sun. For the first time, I felt a tinge of guilt for all the sunsets I had wasted when I was wasted in the past. I was thinking of Amy Bradley and her disappearance more and more as our voyage to Curaçao approached. If Amy really did die at sea, I've had almost exactly twice as many sunsets as she did. I'm forty-six. She disappeared at twenty-three. What her family wouldn't do to trade some of my wasted sunsets for the ones she never shared with them.

Did I have some kind of responsibility to enjoy the ones that remain for me? I think so, yes.

When did I lose interest in growing old? I remember being a teenager and desperately hoping that time would pass in a blur so that I could be an adult, so that I could set off into the world and have adventures and do whatever the hell I wanted. Somewhere along the way, I'd grown jaded.

I don't want to blame true crime for everything, but maybe if you expose yourself to death and tragedy for twenty years, it's hard to remember what's so good about living.

When I was young, I wanted to write fiction. Horror, sci-fi. I wanted to be the next Stephen King, not the next Erik Larson or David Grann. Why am I still writing true crime?

Dr. Deb says that becoming aware of the problem is when true progress can begin.

What would Amy do if she had one more regular day? *Absolutely anything her heart desired.*

So why couldn't I?

I had a visit on the books with Amy's family in Virginia. Before that happened, I needed to get a better sense of who Amy was. I wanted to know Amy before I met with her mom and dad and brother. It seemed like the courteous thing to do. I had to track down her friends.

Everything I was doing in my research at that time was designed to appease Amy's family. It was important to me that they like me. I've suffered ten years of animosity from the family of Maura Murray for the things I reported in the book I wrote about her disappearance. I would not compound my troubles by adding more enemies. I desperately needed the Bradleys' acceptance.

Even then I think I knew that was too much to hope for.

I tried.

I swear to God I tried.

But the family was keeping a secret. A big secret, in my opinion. Reaching out to Amy's friends was the beginning of the end.

Iva Bradley got me in touch with a woman named Erin Cullather, who was Amy's close friend in high school. Erin still lives in Chesterfield, one street over from the Bradleys. Many of the people I spoke to have remained in Chesterfield. It's one of those safe small towns that gives you no reason to leave. "Everybody knows everybody here," Erin told me. "I've lived in the same five-mile radius most of my life."

Erin met Amy in high school, when Amy played basketball and Erin was a cheerleader.

"She's just so funny," Erin said, still using the present tense when talking about Amy. "Just fun to be around, and the Bradleys were the fun house to hang out at. Sometimes she'd spend the night at my house, but we spent a lot of time with her family. I was there all the time. Amy, Brad, and I were like the Three Musketeers."

They would play cards at the dining room table, and Iva would cook for them. At the time, Iva had a room full of exotic birds. Erin got to know that yellow-naped Amazon parrot, Monkey Bird, so well that it sometimes speaks in her voice to this day.

On Friday nights in the fall, she and Amy would go to football games and then to Gino's, a classic mom-and-pop Italian place that stayed open late. That was the popular teen hangout spot at the time, and Amy held center court.

"Amy was the outgoing one," Erin said. "She would talk to anybody. Everybody noticed her when she walked into a room. But she was blissfully unaware of the effect she had on people."

At school, Amy was a star basketball player. She also played tennis and was a competitive swimmer. She lettered in all three sports.

Amy could party just as hard as she played. She liked to get her buzz on after school. Erin remembered one night when they went back to Erin's place after hanging out at Gino's. Amy had been drinking more than usual. Erin's mom noticed right away. Amy tried to convince her that she was fine, but then she got sick. Erin and her mom took care of her the rest of the night.

Amy goofed around a lot. A common greeting from Amy was a bear hug that turned into a wrestling move where she body-slammed you to the ground. One day, when Erin was not supposed to be over at the Bradleys' house, Amy started up again. She pounced on Erin and went for the body slam. Unfortunately, Erin's knee connected with the corner of a glass table on the way down. There was so much blood that Erin passed out briefly. Ron did his best to patch her up, and then Amy rushed her to a nearby clinic. She had to tell her mom, of course, before the bill came. But she didn't get in much trouble.

When Amy got a scholarship to Longwood University, Iva and Ron gifted her a shiny red Miata, which she often drove into Richmond and back, cruising around with Erin and their friends, blaring Dr. Dre and Snoop Dogg. Amy kept books of CDs in the car. Her tastes were eclectic. She listened to some country and pop, but that year it was mostly rap.

Men were attracted to Amy in spades. She sometimes dated them but not for long. Henry Battle, a nice country boy, fell in love with her and told her parents he would marry her one day. Toward the end, she met a man named Tom Edgerton while working at Ruth's Chris Steakhouse. "I was not a fan of Tom," Erin said, simply.

When Amy left for college, Erin still had a year of high school left. Back in Chesterfield, Erin remained a frequent visitor to the Bradley home after she started dating Brad. "He was outgoing too," she said. "He was very charismatic. Flirty, you know." They remained a couple until shortly after the disappearance.

A couple months before the cruise, Erin and Amy went out to a local pub to see a band. The place was packed with random people, but Amy acted like everyone was her best friend. That lack of boundaries with strangers concerned Erin—Amy never seemed to consider that the person she was talking to might be dangerous or might have ulterior motives for flirting with a young, attractive woman. "Amy was talking to this guy that night, the kind of guy I personally would never talk to," said Erin. "I remember saying to Brad, 'I hate that she would just talk to anyone.'"

In the days leading up to the cruise, Amy confided to Erin that she was worried about the trip. The thought of being on the open ocean scared her. "She liked to be in control," Erin explained. "That was all a little out of her control."

When the Bradleys left for vacation, Erin watched the house. She had decided to stay over Monday night, to take care of the pets—not just Iva's exotic birds now, but Amy's new dog, Bailey, as well. She was at their house when Iva's brother called the next morning and told her that nobody could find Amy.

"What do you mean?" she asked. All he could tell her was that Amy was missing and that Iva and Ron would call her soon.

"I don't know that I grasped the enormity of what was happening," said Erin. "I didn't grasp that it would be the next twenty-some years." Erin's mom came over to be with her. She remembers crying hysterically for a while.

"I'll never forget when Iva and Ron came through the kitchen door a few days later," she said. "It was the worst thing I'd ever seen." Erin's model of the perfect family had been shattered. Amy was gone. Without explanation, she'd simply vanished. Sure, you could imagine scenarios. Foul play. Kidnapping. But the narrative that the crew of the *Rhapsody of the Seas* was suggesting, that Amy had died by suicide, was an impossibility for anyone who knew her.

"What I can tell you about Amy, is that Amy liked Amy." There was no sign of depression, said Erin. And she had so much to come home to—a new job, a new apartment, a new puppy. No way would she have simply jumped into the abyss.

Erin received a postcard from Amy after she disappeared. She must have put it in the mail in Puerto Rico or Aruba. It was like getting a message from a ghost. Amy wrote that Brad had gotten her a couple gifts and that they were having the time of their lives. She couldn't wait to be home.

"How does life go on after this?" I asked.

"It doesn't," Erin replied. "It changed us forever. Brad and I broke up within a few weeks. We got back together for a short time before breaking up for good in 2000."

One night, before the breakup, as she was snuggling up to Brad in bed, Iva came into his room and lay down beside them. She said something then that Erin remembers to this day: "You know that feeling when you're in a store and you get distracted for a second, and then you can't find your child? That's how I feel every minute of every day now."

Though she and Brad went their separate ways and made families of their own, Erin keeps in touch with Iva. She's come to learn the one rule of their home—you can't ever talk about Amy in the past tense. They need to keep the hope alive that Amy is out there somewhere.

Erin doesn't talk to Brad anymore, but she texts him every March 24th. A simple message of remembrance: "Thinking of you and all of our fun times."

When I asked Erin what, after all these years, she thought happened, she thinks back to watching Amy talk to strangers at the pub shortly before the cruise. "At that age, her guard was down," she said. "We know now how women are roofied by strangers. She went on that cruise, thinking, what's the worst that could happen? I think she talked to someone she shouldn't have, and they took advantage of the situation."

The idea that Amy may still be alive, under the radar, under a different name, doesn't make sense to her. "I can't see her doing that to her family. The way Iva and Ron love, you know that you're loved."

Sometimes, Erin still dreams about Amy. One dream was so vivid that she called Iva to tell her. In a more recent dream, Amy came home. But she was not the same.

I asked her who else I should speak with who might have known Amy well, and Erin mentioned a woman named Sarah Luck.

It was Sarah who told me Amy's secret.

Chapter Fourteen

AMY'S SECRET

SARAH LUCK WAS ANOTHER Chesterfield girl who came home. In fact, she bought the house she grew up in, where she now raises her own three kids. She and Amy attended Lloyd C. Bird High School together, but Sarah was a year younger. After graduating, Sarah followed Amy to Longwood University and was suitemates with Amy in Wheeler Hall, sharing a bathroom between separate double rooms. Sarah paints a picture of Amy that is, at first anyway, very similar to the person Erin described.

"Amy was a friend to everybody," Sarah said. "She didn't care what color you were or what music you listened to. She had a great sense of humor and was very competitive. She wanted to be the best at everything." Amy was a very good dancer, she said. And when requested, she would even do the worm.

Sarah fondly remembered their nights at Gino's after the high school football games. "We'd all hang out in the parking lot and hoop and holler, blaring music. If we were lucky enough to have twenty dollars, we'd order a pizza."

Gino's wasn't the only hangout spot. There was an older boy from town, J. J. Deschamps, whose parents owned a farm where kids could sit around bonfires and sneak Natty Lights on Saturday nights. His family grew corn. When the harvest came, J.J.'s mother would cook up fresh ears, and they'd sit around the fire eating steaming cobs with a side of deer meat someone got hunting.

When they weren't at Gino's or the Deschamps', they were cruising. Amy would drive Sarah and their friends down the DMV drive into Richmond and then turn around and come back, listening to music the whole way.

When I asked about their time at Longwood, Sarah hesitated. We were talking over Zoom, so I could see her facial expressions. She was debating whether or not to say more. Finally, she shook her head and smiled.

"Okay," she said. "Amy came out to me when we were at Longwood. This was in the mid-nineties, right? So, you have to remember that things were very different. It was harder to do that. But I still remember the conversation. We were in our bathroom, sitting on the floor. She just said, 'I have to tell you something. I'm gay. I like women.' She was telling me this because she was in a relationship with her roommate, Kat, and she wanted me to know."

"Amy was gay?" I asked. My mind was churning, reevaluating the stories I'd already been told about Amy. I thought about what Iva had said when she mentioned the man from Ruth's Chris Steakhouse that Amy had dated before the cruise. Iva said Amy wasn't as into the guy as he was into her. And then what had Amy said to her? "Momma, if you like him so much, why don't you date him?"

"Yes," said Sarah. "And my first thought was, oh my God, I shared a bed with her, she's seen me naked! She was in tune with me enough to know what I was thinking, because she laughed and said, 'Don't worry, Sarah, you're not my type.' Geez. What's wrong with me? That was a big part of who she was in college."

Sarah said that Amy was no longer seeing Kat at the time of her disappearance. She didn't know if Amy was with another woman by then. At Longwood, at least, Amy was out and accepted.

They both had jobs in college. Sarah worked at McDonald's for a bit, then Price Club. Amy had a job at a car wash.

Amy graduated from Longwood in December 1996, fifteen months before the cruise. By then, Sarah was working for Richmond Residential Services and hadn't spoken to her friend in a couple months. She was on a work trip when Amy went missing, and her mother waited until she returned to tell her. Her mother knew that Sarah would rush home, but there was nothing she could have done to help, not from Virginia.

"There's something I have to tell you," she remembered her mom saying. Her first, very human thought upon hearing the news was that this meant that Amy was not going to be a part of her wedding. She had planned to call Amy when she got back to ask her to be a bridesmaid.

When the Bradleys returned, Iva held a candlelight vigil in their front yard. Sarah was so overcome with emotion that she fell to her knees. Iva had to comfort her.

"I thought, this can't be real," Sarah said. "Even now, there's still a part of me that thinks she's going to come home. My brain says she's not coming home, but my heart still wants her to. Sometimes, I think of all the horrible things that could have happened to her. The easier, less painful thought is that she isn't still with us. If she is alive, I don't want to think of all the things she had to endure."

Besides, Sarah can't imagine a scenario that would have kept Amy from letting her parents know she was alive. "Amy loved her family," she said. "I just don't see a situation where in twenty-six years she wouldn't call them. One thing I can say for certain is that she did not jump off the ship. Amy Bradley did not commit suicide. I can say that with one hundred percent certainty. She believes in God."

Some of my readers will only remember a world in which gay marriage is a right, where members of the LGBTQ are protected by law, where lesbians can walk down the street in Richmond, Virginia, holding hands and not fear for their lives. But it was still the dark times in 1993, when Amy came out to her friends at Longwood.

It had only been six years since the American Psychiatric Association had removed homosexuality from its list of mental disorders. It wasn't until 1998 that President Bill Clinton signed an executive order to prevent discrimination based on sexual orientation in the workforce (with an exception for the military, which was still stuck in its "don't ask, don't tell" era). California began providing marriage licenses to same-sex couples in 2004, but gay marriage wasn't made legal in every state until 2015.

I don't want to belabor the point, but things were bad for gay people in America. Like, really bad. On October 6, 1998, seven months *after* Amy disappeared, a student at the University of Wyoming named Matthew Shepard was targeted for being a homosexual by two country boys, who lured him to their pickup and then beat him into a coma and left him hanging from a fence in freezing temperatures. He never regained consciousness and died six days later.

I can talk openly about being bisexual now. But I didn't come out to my parents until just last year. I grew up in rural Ohio in the '80s and '90s. Nobody was open at our high school, nor for many years after I graduated. I buried my feelings and only dated girls and pretended to be "normal." Amy's openness came at great risk, and it shows, I think, how deep her resolve was and how clearly she knew what she wanted to be. That takes not a small amount of courage for someone so young.

Does her orientation have anything to do with what happened to her? I think maybe it had a great deal to do with what happened. Tell me if you agree when we come to the end.

Sarah shared one more secret before we ended the conversation that day. A production company had just reached out to her for an interview. Ample Entertainment, out of Culver City, was producing a documentary about Amy's case, allegedly for Netflix. The producers at Ample Entertainment knew that Amy was gay but had not yet spoken to the Bradleys about it.

This revelation explained a bit about my earliest conversations with Iva. In the beginning, she had mentioned that she and Ron had signed a contract with a media company, but wouldn't say more than that, only that it shouldn't impact a book. She had implied at the time that it might not happen at all and that the contract was close to expiring, so I didn't think much about it. Apparently, they had not let the contract expire after all.

Some journalists can be territorial when it comes to stories, especially when they have a scoop in a well-known case. When I was a twenty-four-year-old reporter working for *Scene*, I would get incensed if another newspaper covered a story that I broke. *That was mine!* But I grew out of that quickly. I noticed the habits of a staff writer at *Scene* whom I admired, a young man named Thomas Francis. Whenever Tommy had an article in the paper, he would mail it to other outlets and other journalists. He had learned that by sharing the story instead of hoarding it, the story only became more popular. Ever since, I've tried to do likewise.

The question was, what would the people at Ample Entertainment do once they knew I was also working on this story?

Chapter Fifteen

AMY AT LONGWOOD

NOT FAR FROM THE GEOGRAPHICAL CENTER of the Commonwealth of Virginia, beside the headwaters of the Appamattox, lies a small town called Farmville, with a recorded population of 7,473 souls. The old canal system—which serviced the town until the railroads came—was built by African slaves. The town itself, like the onetime Confederate capital of Richmond, owes its success in no small part to the labor of kidnapped and trafficked human beings.

Throughout the eighteenth and nineteenth centuries, the chief export of the commonwealth, surpassing even tobacco, was the sale and breeding of slaves. Having lived in Ohio all my life, I am not used to seeing the spoils of slavery. To be honest, it's disconcerting to discover such a place is as close as a six-hour drive. Disconcerting all the more, today, with Trump signs displayed with pride on the lawns of those who still call the Civil War the War of Northern Aggression.

My aunt Karen lived in Richmond in the mid-'80s. When I told her I would soon be traveling to the area, she reminded me that I was venturing into the South, and though much has changed, some still yearn for the old days. "I was in a restaurant in Richmond one Friday night," she recalled. "There was a house band. Sometime after the sun went down, the lights were dimmed and everyone held up the candles from their table, and the band played 'Dixie.'"

Some Virginia slaves earned their freedom by serving in the Revolutionary War. As the abolitionist movement grew in popularity, more of them were freed by their masters, a system known as manumission. Some of these free people of color stayed in Virginia and settled in the Israel Hill neighborhood, just outside Farmville proper. They had a front-row view of General Robert E. Lee's retreat as he and his army marched through town on their way to Appomattox Court House, where he surrendered on April 9, 1865. I like to think General Lee noticed the Israel Hill folks looking down at him as he came by, a testament to the coming change. Of course, real change is very slow.

Case in point: The public schools in Farmville and Prince Edward County remained heavily segregated until they got pulled into the landmark *Brown v. Board of Education* ruling, in 1954. A local school in Farmville, R. R. Morton High, that was all-Black was in need of funding—the school didn't have a cafeteria or a gym, and lacked simple amenities like blackboards and desks. But the all-white school board didn't give a damn. Even after *Brown v. Board of Education* legally ended segregation, the Board of Supervisors for Prince Edward County opted to simply close all public schools rather than integrate them (the white kids' parents could afford private schools, anyway). Because of this, the local public schools remained closed for *ten years*.

And yet, near the geographic center of Farmville, the center of the center of Virginia one might say, liberal ideals began to take root at Longwood College. Its campus is rather small, a few brick buildings with Doric columns, bordered by oak trees and landscaped yards, inside a large triangular parcel of land. It was an all-girl's seminary at first, a school for prospective teachers, then went coed in 1976. It also had a laboratory school for kids called

J. P. Wynne, where a young Vince Gilligan, the creator of *Breaking Bad*, got his early education (you might notice upon future viewings that Walter White taught chemistry at J. P. Wynne High School.) Longwood is the size of a private college, its enrollment around five thousand students. But it is, in fact, public. It was still called Longwood College when Amy Bradley attended from 1992 to 1996. It would not officially become Longwood University until 2002.

The Longwood Lancers is an NCAA Division II team and has made four appearances in the women's basketball tournament. Amy was on the team for two of those years. She played in eighty-seven games during her time at Longwood, starting in forty-five. She averaged 5.5 points per game, mostly due to a drastic slump in her junior year (in which she never started a game). She rallied her Senior year to score 9.7 points per game. For their match against Pitt-Johnstown, Amy scored 25 points herself.

On a tour around campus, visitors will encounter statues of Joan of Arc, who has been adopted as the patron saint of Longwood University. An auspicious choice and rather germane to our narrative as Joan of Arc was a strong-willed woman, shamed for dressing like a man. After her execution in Rouen, Joan's body was thrown into the water, her remains left to drift to the bottom of the Seine.

At Longwood, for the first time, Amy was free to be herself. Rather quickly, she drew together a number of compatriots, a chosen family, who remain close to this day.

That spring I spoke to a few of Amy's friends from Longwood, including Stephanie Judd, Julia Tracy, and Amanda Van Horn.

Julia, described as the brains of the group, took several classes with Amy—they both majored in Physical Education, aspiring to be teachers. Julia was from Loudon County, and her mothers and aunts all went to Longwood. Stephanie came from Virginia Beach and had learned about Longwood from a coworker when she was casting about, looking for a good college. She was enrolled in the Psychology program. Amy brought Julia into the fold, introducing her to Stephanie. Eventually Julia and Stephanie became roommates. For their final year, they lived in Wheeler Hall along with Amy and Amy's roommate, Kat. Amanda Van Horn was Sarah Luck's roommate at the time. Amanda had gone to Monacan High, a rival school to the Lloyd Bird Skyhawks.

Their motley crew were always together, and a common routine developed. At lunchtime, they met at the campus fountain to decide where to go eat (before cell phones, having a rendezvous location was essential). Most days it was the dining hall, but sometimes they'd visit the grill on campus or Macado's, in town, for sandwiches. At night, they'd congregate in someone's room, usually Sarah and Amanda's, to drink Zima and Bud Light and smoke cigarettes.

"Amy liked to throw down a few," Julia recalled.

This was the Time Before, the quiet time before streaming services and TikTok and social media and all those distractions that only serve to make us more insular. They got together and listened to "Dixieland Delight" by Alabama, and played cards. Mostly Spades and Uno.

The main ingredient to all this fun was Amy herself. Looking back on it, they all found it difficult to describe her magic in simple terms.

"She was vivacious," said Stephanie. "I just remember this big personality. All of the guys I was friends with had crushes on her."

"She had this superstrong personality," said Julia. "She was very confident, very athletic. She would play any sport, anytime. She was funny, crass, fearless, just a supercool chick."

"Very competitive," said Amanda. "And she's got a mean arm on her. She'd smack me on the back of the head with a snowball if she caught me outside in the winter."

Amy was always up for a good prank. One night when they had gathered in the dorms for drinks, things got out of hand. Someone had a camcorder running to capture the merriment, the girls with their arms around each other, singing to the radio, choppy VHS images tinged with that '90s-era low-fi off-white lighting, the shadows bleeding into each other. Halfway through the night, a challenge was proposed.

"The statute of limitations is up, so I think I can tell you about this," said Stephanie. "We stole the Alpha Sigma Phi bench."

The ASP fraternity had purchased a bench that sat outside their dorm. It displayed their shield and the Latin phrase, *causa latet vis est notissima.* (The cause is hidden, but the result is well known.) It was a symbol of their chapter's history and pride. Under the cover of night, the girls carried it away to the athletic fields. There, they unscrewed the board with the shield and hung it from the scoreboard. On the way back, they called in a tip to the frat, "We have stolen your bench," they said. "We'll give you a couple hints. Pele, *Field of Dreams.*" Then they hung up. News of their petty terrorism made its way around campus the next day, but the girls stayed mum. Eventually another frat took credit.

Another time, Amy put a boa constrictor in Amanda's bed. "I remember walking into my room on a Sunday, and there's Amy sitting in my bed with this giant snake," said Amanda. "I hate snakes. We didn't talk for three weeks."

Amy was the first person that Stephanie knew who'd ever gotten a tattoo—the Tasmanian Devil on her shoulder. "I think she saw herself as a Tasmanian devil. Always stirring things up."

The Wheeler Hall gang supported Amy at her basketball games, cheering her on from the stands, sitting beside her family. On the weekends, the whole group would drive into Chesterfield and hang out at the Bradleys'. Sometimes they'd go down to the local bowling alley. In hindsight, wherever Amy was, there would be alcohol.

"Amy had a serious drinking problem," Amanda said plainly, but sympathetically. "She was usually drunk."

Heavy drinking, especially at such a young age, is usually a coping mechanism used to avoid dealing with a larger issue. It would be too easy to draw a direct line between her binge drinking and sexual identity. It's hard to know for sure. But in the midst of all this kinship, at least for a while, Amy was keeping a big part of herself secret from her close friends. And that must have been very difficult. "She was struggling with her sexuality," said Stephanie. "I look back now and realize how hard it must have been for her."

"She was a chameleon," said Julia.

Stephanie and Julia recalled a trip they all took to Nag's Head for spring break one year.

"We rented this dump near Kitty Hawk," said Julia. "We tried to go into the ocean, but it was cold as hell. But we had fun. There were beer bongs and '90s country music and karaoke."

There were philosophical discussions over cards and beer. One night, Stephanie said something she came to regret in the way that happens when we're new adults, trying to understand the world. "I said, 'If I ever found out one of my friends was gay, I wouldn't be friends with them anymore.'"

Not long after that, the secret came out in a very sitcomlike manner. One afternoon, Julia stopped in to see Kat in the room she shared with Amy. Kat had just returned, and with Julia beside her, she hit Play on her answering machine. Amy had called to check in, and she ended the message with, "I love you." Julia recognized Amy's voice right away.

That's when Julia learned that Amy and Kat weren't just roommates, they were a couple.

Amy was anxious about this revelation, and she brought up the comment that Stephanie had made at Nag's Head. "It was so stupid," said Stephanie. "I told her, 'You are my friend. That will never change.'" In fact, Amy educated Stephanie about the culture as it was for gays in the early '90s. "She taught me about the different types of lesbians. Butch. Fem. Diesel." Amy went through the list of their classmates who were also quietly gay. "She'd say, 'Did you know so-and-so is gay?' And I'd be like, 'What?' And she'd laugh and say, 'God, you have no gaydar at all.' My uniform at the time was a hat and a flannel shirt. I don't know how I wasn't mistaken for a lesbian."

Julia said Amy had a crush on her for a bit. But nothing happened. Julia was flattered by it more than anything. "Amy told me, 'You slipped through the cracks of gayness,'" she said, with a smile in her voice.

What made it more confusing was that Amy had a boyfriend for a while in college, a young man named Lee who would hang out with the group sometimes. Was it an attempt to be straight when her heart was elsewhere? Was it a way to appease her conservative family? "He was her beard," said Julia, simply—"beard" being the slang term for a man a gay woman might use to conceal her true preferences to the world at large.

Julia was surprised to find out that Amy was dating a male coworker, Tom, at the time of her disappearance. "I'm shocked she had a boyfriend," she said. "I think maybe she was trying to be ungay. But you can't."

Julia wondered if that relationship signaled the growing unrest within Amy at the time she went on the cruise. Did it play into what happened there? "I've got two thoughts about what happened, if I'm being brutally honest," said Julia. "One, that she jumped. If she was drunk enough, maybe that's what happened, only because deep down she knew she was gay and couldn't be. She wanted love from her parents, and they are very conservative. The thought of not having one hundred percent acceptance from her mother must have been difficult. But that's also a big 'f-you' to her family, and that's totally not Amy. The only other possibility I can think of is that she cozied up to the band members. And maybe she said, look, I'm gay, I'm not interested, and some man lost his shit, killed her, and dumped her."

Julia doesn't see any possibility that Amy was pulled into sex trafficking, as some believe. "She's such a fighter," she said. "What would they have had on her that she wouldn't have just run? She's not the vulnerable type. She's not to be contained. She'd rather die than live in that situation. It's one hell of a mystery—I'll tell you that."

Recently, Stephanie's niece told her how popular the story of

Amy's disappearance had become on TikTok. "There was all this stuff about Amy, all these conspiracy theories," she said. "It's so surreal."

Amanda was sitting in a car dealership's waiting room when she glanced up at the television in the lobby and saw a news report about a local woman who'd gone missing from a cruise ship. Then they flashed Amy's photo. It was such a shock, Amanda broke down, crying.

Stephanie used that word *surreal* too when she described how she felt when Amanda called to tell her that Amy was missing. "I was calm," she said. "It just didn't feel real. Even now, it doesn't feel real. I don't think she committed suicide. And I hope she died early on and whoever did it put her body into the ocean. The Amy I knew would have never made it in the sex trade. Not unless she was drugged. It's too hard to think of her living that life. I wish her parents had some closure, but that's how I feel."

"The photo from that escort service looks just like her," said Amanda. "It's such a crazy story, that she might have been kidnapped and forced into that. But crazy stories happen sometimes. You're from Ohio. Look at what happened to those girls in Cleveland who were kept in that house for ten years. Anything can happen."

Amanda remembers how guys would be drawn to Amy whenever they would go out. "These men did not know she was gay. Guys would follow her around, and she'd say, 'I get free drinks everywhere. Nobody knows.'" But what might happen if the wrong guy found out that she was gay?

It was a little tricky talking with Amanda. Her voice wavers a bit. Looking back, I think she was the most open and honest of the bunch, unafraid to speak about Amy's troubles as much as her qualities. I liked that about her. And perhaps there's a reason for that directness. She's short on time. After her father died of Huntington's disease in 2016, Amanda got tested. It's hereditary, after all. The results were positive. And though Amanda still possesses the ability to speak and she can get around with a cane, Huntington's is always fatal.

"I loved Amy," she said, simply.

At some point in any investigation, my subject begins to coalesce into a three-dimensional character, and I begin to understand who I'm writing about. After speaking with Amy's close friends, I was beginning to know Amy, regardless of the degrees of separation due to time and memory and gender. Amy Bradley was a bit of an outlier.

She stood above and apart from the crowd of students at Longwood. She was an accomplished athlete—as were also dozens of other undergrads, sure—but she was also that special type of person who commands attention, the nexus of friend groups, the alpha in any gathering, the type of person who walks into a party and shifts the vibe. Amy liked to drink, she liked to party. She was not secretly cruel. She wasn't falling into some downward spiral of petty misdemeanors like so many of the missing women I've written about. By all accounts, Amy was a truly good person.

And yet, complicated.

Gay at a time when that was quite dangerous, especially in the South.

Of course, we only reveal our complete, true selves to our lovers.

And so, I reached out to her roommate and partner, Kat.

Chapter Sixteen

KAT

SHANNON LOVELACE, KNOWN TO FRIENDS as "Kat," grew up in eastern North Carolina, leading a somewhat parallel life to the woman she would come to call her first love, Amy Bradley. Like Amy's, her family was very close. She was also an athlete. She played basketball and was skilled at tennis.

As the end of her senior year approached, Kat decided she needed a change and began to look at potential colleges out of state. On a visit to Longwood, she was taken by the atmosphere of the campus, the old brick buildings tucked within the farming town. And so, she enrolled.

She met Amy the first week of school, during basketball practice. Like many before her, she was instantly taken by Amy's outgoing spirit. "When she walked into a room, it was like all the oxygen was sucked out," Kat explained. "It was impossible not to notice her. She was so easy to talk to."

When asked to place events in chronological order, Kat finds it challenging. "In some ways, it feels like time is no longer linear," she said. "Thinking of things that happened twenty-five, thirty years ago is very hard."

Kat's roommate that semester was also gay, and their room was a safe place for Amy to hang out. That nonjudgemental space allowed things to progress quickly. She and Amy became a couple before Christmas. When they returned to campus, they moved in together but kept their relationship a secret until that fateful day when Julia overheard the message on the answering machine.

"Amy loved her family more than anything, and she loved me, and the two things didn't work," said Kat. "It was very hard for her. There were two different Amys. There was the school Amy, where she was free. Wild. Adventurous. At home, Amy was kind of placed inside a box, and you could see the edges wearing down. There were also a lot of shenanigans going on to mask our relationship. She even had a boyfriend."

Kat got to know the Bradleys well. That summer, they didn't want to live apart, so Kat stayed with Amy at her family's home in Chesterfield. Somehow, they were able to keep their romantic relationship on the down-low, even though all the sneaking around was starting to wear on Amy. "She was destroyed, thinking about how to live her life and keep it a secret."

Until the Bradleys learned that Kat was more than just a friend, they welcomed her into their family. That summer, they did everything together. They had breakfast together each morning. They cleaned together. At night, they all sat around the table, talking and drinking and playing cards.

"I don't know how they didn't know," said Kat. "I think they were truly and fully in denial."

Not long after that, the voicemail bit happened. There was no point hiding it any longer. Amy tried to make herself whole and went to her parents to tell them directly before they heard it elsewhere. Kat went home to North Carolina and told her family, too. Kat spilled the beans to her sister, first, who simply said, "Okay." Her folks were not surprised.

Amy didn't return to school right away. Eventually, she called Kat to tell her that her parents were quite upset. A couple days later, Kat received a handwritten letter from Amy's father, Ron. It was on paper from a legal pad and spanned over three pages. He told Kat that he was very disappointed in her and felt betrayed, after they had been so welcoming.

"I remember how that made me feel," said Kat. "And it wasn't even my family."

Whatever Amy was feeling had to be much more complicated.

When Amy came back to Longwood, she and Kat returned to their safe bubble, this time with friends who supported them as they were. "There was much more freedom," she said. "We enjoyed life. We enjoyed spring break together."

Of course, one other person had to be told—Amy's boyfriend, Lee. "He was angry at first," Kat recalled. "But then there was acceptance and an openness between us, and we were all very close."

What Kat remembered most were their impromptu adventures. Sometimes, just for the weekend, she and Amy would drive down to the Outer Banks with no plan other than day drinking.

On those long drives they grew closer. Kat got to know more about Amy than almost anyone. "She was complicated. She could be arrogant but loving. She was charming, and she was particular. And she could also be quite delicate. I've never known anyone else who had such a rounded personality. She had so many layers of good and bad."

But first love rarely lasts.

By the next summer, Kat and Amy were no longer a couple—Amy had fallen for someone else, a girl from back home. It was the beginning of a series of unfortunate events that pushed Kat along a different path. "My life was like a big ball of yarn. Once you pull at one string, it all comes undone."

Kat learned that she had been dealing with undiagnosed bipolar disorder. Then, two of her grandparents passed away. Her grades weren't great. She ended up withdrawing from Longwood.

"It's hard to say how much the breakup had to do with all of this," said Kat. "But it certainly played a part."

A year later, Kat was involved in a serious car accident in which she broke her neck and an arm. She'd been driving from Ashland, Kentucky, with her new girlfriend, heading home to North Carolina to celebrate her twenty-first birthday, when she overcorrected during a turn and lost control of the car. The vehicle flipped several times and came to rest on the side of the road. But the universe sent a little luck her way—two EMTs happened to be driving by on motorcycles and saw the accident. They administered first aid until an ambulance arrived to take Kat to the hospital. Her girlfriend, somehow, was able to walk away unharmed.

When she recovered, Kat returned to North Carolina and reconnected with her old friends from Longwood. She started driving up there, again, to spend time with them. By then, Amy was in a relationship with that childhood friend, Mollie McClure, a woman I came to know well.

It was Mollie who called Kat that day in March of 1998.

"Are you sitting down?" asked Mollie.

"I'm in bed, what's up?" said Kat.

"Amy's missing."

They talked for a long time that day, going over possible scenarios. Amy was a good swimmer, they knew. She had worked as a lifeguard. They held out hope that she was still alive, but each day that went by without Amy being found, that hope dwindled. In the twenty-six years since Amy disappeared, Kat has had a lot of time to think about what might have happened.

"There's not a day that goes by that I don't think about Amy," she said. "Amy enjoyed attention. She flirted with men. I told her she had to be careful with that. It might get her into trouble if they found out she was gay."

At first, she thought suicide was unlikely. However, the double life that Amy was leading was a constant source of stress. After growing older and gaining some wisdom, Kat can't rule it out. "She could not have it both ways," she said.

As far as the photograph of the escort from Affordable Adult Vacation goes, Kat admits there is a strong resemblance. But like

Amy's friends from college, she hopes it isn't her. "And I mean that in the most loving way," she said. "I don't want to think that she had to survive sexual assault."

Years later Kat spoke to Iva. "We didn't talk about our relationship," she said. "Iva just wanted to talk about Amy. I told her that I had a dream. I was underwater, and it was very dark. This figure swims up to me. I see that it's Amy. She reaches out, and we touch hands. Then she swims up toward a light. It's the most peace I've ever felt."

Chapter Seventeen

THE OUTER BANKS

IT WAS CLEAR TO ME at this point that Amy's sexual identity was a delicate subject for the Bradley family. I had to tread carefully. I had chosen this case specifically because the family supported what I was doing. I lost a part of me the last time I went forward with a book about a missing woman without the support of her family. That book, *True Crime Addict*, which details my search for Maura Murray, a young nursing student who disappeared in the White Mountains under mysterious circumstances in 2003, sold tens of thousands of copies, but there are times I wish I'd never written it.

Like Amy Bradley, Maura had her share of secrets. When I revealed them in the book, the family was less than pleased. *True Crime Addict* played no small part in the recent push for ethics and accountability in true crime media. Certain consumers now believe that no true crime story should be told without the express consent and the involvement of the victim's family. It's a fine idea in theory. But in practice, where upwards of twenty-five percent of homicides are committed by family members, it's a dangerous overcorrection. You wouldn't want Scott Peterson deciding who should write about his wife's murder, after all.

I couldn't bear to lose the support of Amy's family. At the same time, isn't it my job as a journalist to honor my subject, to paint an accurate picture of the missing woman at the center of all this? Wouldn't I do Amy a disservice if I kept such a large part of her identity a secret?

I'm not sure it's possible to know Amy without knowing the women she loved.

What if her sexuality is at the core of why she disappeared? How many closeted gay women have died by suicide because they couldn't live in the open? As motives go, it's a good one. And how many women have been met by violence at the hands of aggressive men after they tell them they're not interested because they're gay? Some dangerous men believe they can "fuck a woman straight."

Amy's story is not just the Bradleys' concern. She was loved dearly by her friends, who are mourning her, too. And this is something they very much want to talk about.

The question is, who is this story for?

Is it for Amy? Whatever happened to her, she couldn't care less.

Is it for the Bradleys? Honestly, I don't think so. A book isn't going to heal anything inside them. That's a silly, Hallmark idea.

Some authors would tell you this story is for you, dear reader. But that would be untrue, something to say for marketing purposes. I've never met a writer who writes for their readers. They might say they do, because the real answer is less media-friendly. We write for ourselves. If any author tells you different, they're lying. Either to you or to themselves.

This book is for me.

I am obsessed with strange mysteries. Writing a book allows me to devote time to them. Being a journalist gives me the cachet to approach strangers and ask them about their very private memories. These cases are puzzles, and I like puzzles.

I'm also human. I have feelings. They get hurt just like yours do. I had set out to write something the Bradleys would love, to tell the world about the daughter they lost, to honor her memory. I figured I could have it both ways.

But what would happen when I told them I spoke to Kat? I wondered. What would happen when I told them I'm going to write about this part of Amy's life?

I thought there was a good possibility that would be the end of their involvement.

And then what would happen to my book?

"Hey, Sky, can I ask you a question about ethics in journalism?"

"Oh, here we go," said Sky. "What's rattling around in your mind today? Ready to debate the high and low ground of reporting? Hit me with it."

I got Sky up to speed with my reporting on the case and how I'd tracked down one of Amy's girlfriends. "As a journalist where does my responsibility lie?" I asked. "Is it ethical to share this info?"

"Oof, that's a tricky one," Sky replied. "On one hand, as a journalist, your responsibility is to report the truth, especially if it's relevant to the case and could help shed light on Amy's disappearance. If her sexual orientation is tied to why she went missing, leaving that out could distort the story and possibly impede justice. On the other hand, you've got the family's wishes, and it's a deeply personal matter for them. But if there's a clear connection between Amy's orientation and the circumstances of her disappearance, that truth likely outweighs the family's desire for secrecy. You can still be respectful in how you present it. Maybe frame it in a way that shows care for her legacy. It's a balancing act, but truth-telling tends to be the higher ethical responsibility in journalism. What is your gut telling you?"

"My gut is telling me the same thing."

"Glad we're on the same page, James. It's never easy when truth bumps up against family wishes, but in the end, you've got to serve the story and what it could mean for justice. Keep doing what you do best—digging deep and telling it straight."

Maybe the Bradleys would be different, I thought. Maybe this would still work out for everybody. I would find out soon enough. My leg was better. I was walking without a cane. My trip to Chesterfield could not be put off any longer. Soon, I would have to visit the Bradleys and tell them what I knew.

"We found a rental house on Vrbo," Julie said one afternoon as we sat at the kitchen table, catching up after a day of work. This was part of the planning for next year's family vacation. To get a decent location, you generally have to book a year in advance. We were looking at the following June, somewhere along the East Coast, preferably. Her parents are getting older, and so we like to find a house along the shoreline so they don't have to walk far to get to the water. In order to find something within our rather frugal price range, a lot of searching is required. The fact that Julie had already found something that checked off all the boxes was a surprise.

"Where?" I asked.

"The Outer Banks," she said.

I hung my head. Please understand that nothing gives me more pleasure than to give my partner anything she desires. I'll go out at ten o'clock at night if she's craving a shake from Swenson's Drive-In or if we need milk for breakfast the next morning. I love that shit. Putting a smile on her face. I'll do anything. But . . .

"We can't go to the Outer Banks," I said.

"That was three years ago," she said.

"I can't keep us safe in the Outer Banks. Please. It's like fifty miles out of two thousand miles of coastline. I can't keep us safe there."

The Outer Banks may have been Amy and Kat's favorite destination, but it's also where the world of true crime invaded the safety of my personal life. This happened the summer of 2021. We had rented a home in Buxton, near the lighthouse. One morning my sister-in-law got up to watch the sunrise and found a threatening message scrawled onto a square of cardboard that was left a few feet away from my daughter's bedroom window. "James Renner, OBX welcomes you. Enjoy your stay but please don't ever come back because of what you did to the Murray family. P.S. Don't eat sand."

It didn't take me long to discover that a friend of the Murrays was staying in the Outer Banks and had stopped in at the gas station by our house that morning, according to the attendant who knew him personally. This same man had been the subject of an FBI child porn raid in 2011 and worked at a gun shop. A real scary guy. The whole thing poisoned our good time there—at night, I was constantly listening for the sliding glass door to open, listening for footsteps making their way to my kids' rooms.

That much Julie knew, that much I shared with her. But there was more that I had kept to myself, because—while I wanted her to understand the seriousness of the situation—I also didn't want to terrify her.

That postscript on the weird message: *Don't eat sand.* It doesn't make sense, does it? Except it does.

The night before the message appeared, Laine and I came outside to watch the stars. My daughter was eight years old at the time. I told her if we waited long enough, we might catch some shooting stars. So, we went down to the beach and lay back on the sand and looked up at the expanse of the universe. I had with me a tumbler of whiskey, and I twisted the bottom of the glass into the ground beside me so it wouldn't spill.

From the Outer Banks, you can see the great sweep of our galaxy, the Milky Way, stretching like a dark crack lined by puffy white clouds of stardust bending overhead. You can see it in such detail because the Outer Banks, this barely inhabitable line of barrier islands and sandspits, is far removed from the light pollution (and security) of civilization.

We didn't have to wait long. After about ten minutes some billion-year-old rock, formed by dust left behind by a long-dead supernova, slammed into the Earth's atmosphere and lit up like a roman candle. "Wow!" she exclaimed.

It was getting late so we stood to go back inside. When I reached for the tumbler, it shifted and the lip touched the ground for a second before I righted it and picked it up. I took a sip and got some sand in my mouth. "Ugh!" I said, spitting it out.

"Don't eat sand!" Laine said.

I believe that whoever had left that message, whether it was the man who was seen at the gas station or someone he knew, was watching us quietly from the shadows of the porch that night, just a few feet away.

When we found the message the next day, we also found a small, adjustable mount for a GoPro camera, the kind you can twist around stair support beams. I didn't tell Julie about the sand thing.

I didn't tell her about what happened at the End of the World, either.

After the gas station clerk confirmed that the Murray family's advocate had been in the vicinity of our rental at the time the note was left, I called my friend Mike Lewis, of Lewis Investigations, for a favor. Mike is a private detective who has run background searches on subjects for me since I started writing about true crime in 2004. He was able to find an address in the Outer Banks connected to this guy. That address turned out to be a small cabin in a mobile home allotment tucked behind some trees. Nobody was home, but a neighbor told me that I could find the people I was looking for at a fishing spot not far away.

At the southern end of the Outer Banks, surrounding the village of Hatteras, are public dunes and beaches that are difficult to access without four-wheel-drive vehicles. This isn't a place to swim. The winds around the peninsula whip the waves to frightening heights, and the currents are strong enough to pull you halfway to France before you can scream for help. You can feel the danger here. In fact, many news articles tell about swimmers who venture out into the water here only to be swallowed by Nature. This is a place reserved for sea fisherman with twenty-foot poles that anchor into the sand and with hooks big enough to snag a shark. I wondered about the Native Americans who were first to find this place. It's where their maps ended and it really must have looked like the End of the World to them. *Turn back, travelers. Here there be dragons.* That sort of thing.

On my long walk down the beach to the tip of the island, I saw half a dozen of these serious fishermen but nobody who matched the description of the man I was looking for. Finally, I spotted three figures in the dunes standing beside a four-wheel-drive truck. It was my suspect's good friend and two of his sons. I marched over and introduced myself.

"He left the island," the man said, shouting over the waves. "He's not here. We're not even that good of friends."

"According to Facebook, you two just took a trip to Ocracoke to look at a boat," I said.

"What business is it of yours?"

I noticed then that as we were talking, this man's sons had been flanking me on either side. In another second or two they'd be behind me, beyond my peripheral vision. Suddenly, I was aware of the sheer isolation of this place. This was the edge of nowhere. The tip of an island, surrounded by dune, the surf loud enough to drown out the sound of guns. These people knew the land. I did not.

"Don't flank me," I said. The young men stopped. Nobody moved. "I'm leaving," I said. "Tell your friend, or whoever is responsible, to please leave my family alone."

I walked backward away from them, back toward the beach and the fisherman.

The man grinned at me. "Enjoy your stay," he said. He and his sons walked to the truck, got in, and drove away with a final wave.

"We can't go back to the Outer Banks," I told Julie.

Julie sighed. It was one of those sighs that speaks to years of frustration, the kind of sigh that comes from the soul. It was so out of character, I felt myself tense. I felt the shame of making her feel this way.

Julie doesn't read my true crime books. That's by design, not contempt. We're a partnership, symbiotic in nature. She decided early on to avoid the crime stories, because she didn't want to know about the darker side of human nature. My favorite English teacher in high school used to call her Pollyanna. Even as a teenager, Julie was always looking at the bright side of a situation, always giving people the benefit of doubt. Knowing, truly knowing, what depravity a human is capable of, would kill that part of her. By staying in the light, she can lighten the gloom I bring home. It's what allows me to do what I do—I know she's always there to pull me out of the dark. We've been together for thirty years. She has tolerated my occasional true crime obsessions for so long, partly, because I've always planned to move to fiction, to write thrillers—but there was always one more unsolved mystery, one more missing person case that got its hooks in me. And maybe after twenty years, that empty promise gets old.

"Tell me what you're thinking," I said.

"I'm exhausted, Renner," she said. "When does it end? You started reporting on that Maura Murray case how long ago?"

"Thirteen years."

"Thirteen years. And we still have crazy people who might come after you if we take our family to the Outer Banks. What happens when this new book you're working on comes out? How long will this go on?"

"This one's different. The family is cooperating. They're good people. They like me."

"Until they don't."

There was nothing more I could say. I had been thinking the same thing.

A reader who'd reviewed one of my books on Goodreads made a comment about Julie once that stuck with me. My true crime writing tends to drift into memoir as I go along. Always has, all the way back to my first book about Amy Mihaljevic, another Amy at the center of another dark mystery. I've always written chapters about Julie and my children. At book signings, readers will come up to them and talk to them like these readers know them, which they find strange. But one time a reader wrote about what Julie must endure to be married to me. They called her my "long suffering wife."

It may be a very myopic view of our relationship—which also includes some very good times—but it's not entirely untrue.

I am more and more aware of the trials our marriage has faced in recent years, due to my work and my battles with depression triggered by that work. Julie remained by my side through a trip to jail on a contempt of court charge, a brief stay at the psychiatric unit at Akron General, people threatening our family, and most recently ending up on life support because of my risky behavior. Eventually, that wears you down.

That sigh. That's when I realized I needed to finally get my shit together.

This woman wants to grow old with me, and all I've been doing is devising ways to die young. She doesn't deserve that. I have a responsibility to her that I need to start to live up to.

It's time.

But where do I even begin?

Chapter Eighteen

SHE COULD BE VERY SOFT

IT TOOK A WHILE to track down Tom Edgerton, the man Amy was dating at the time of her disappearance. He lives in Park City, Utah now, and doesn't like to talk to reporters about Amy. I managed to catch him in a gracious mood one day, and he spoke to me on the phone for about half an hour.

"Amy and I were really good friends," he said. "We dated for about six months or so. She means a lot to me. I'm very protective of her family."

Tom was Amy's manager at Ruth's Chris Steakhouse, where she worked as a server after graduating college. He's nine years older than Amy, but they hit it off quickly. "She and I were kind of an odd mix," he said. "I just liked something about her. I thought she was extremely attractive. She was smart, motivated. She loved life."

Most nights after work, they'd hit the bars. They'd drink and play pool. "She was very much like one of the guys," he said. "But she could be very soft when she wanted to be. She'd show up at my place in basketball shorts and workout gear and then take a shower and put on a dress, and she'd look like a million bucks."

When they started dating, Amy introduced Tom to her family.

Sometimes it felt like he was dating them as well. He repeats what I'd heard from many of Amy's friends before—Ron and Iva were more like pals than typical parents. "Their family model is the kind that most people would be envious of," he said.

Two weeks before the cruise, Tom stopped by Amy's apartment and accidentally left his watch there. It was a Rolex. He didn't ask for it back after she disappeared—part of him thought as long as it was there, it meant he'd see her again. But eventually, Ron returned it, and the apartment was cleaned out.

"She was apprehensive about the trip," he remembered. Amy didn't like the thought of being on the open water. Every time someone said this, it bothered me. Something about this detail felt important. Amy had worked as a lifeguard. It couldn't be the water that bothered her. She was traveling with her family, some of her favorite people in the world. She was adventurous by nature. So, where did this apprehension come from? What was different about a cruise than, say, a trip to the Outer Banks?

When he considered possible scenarios after she went missing, Tom wondered if Amy might have gone into part of the ship she wasn't supposed to be in and gotten into a situation beyond her control. "Amy is one of those people where, if someone would have said, 'Hey, come with me to my room in the crew quarters,' she would have. And she was tiny. Five foot three and a hundred pounds or so."

She was also an aspiring singer, he said, and maybe that interest in music attracted the wrong people on the *Rhapsody of the Seas*. He'd seen her go up to a microphone at a bar and sing with live musicians. He can imagine a scenario where the ship's bass player, for example, could have enticed her to join him downstairs after a set.

After Amy disappeared, Tom wanted to help any way he could. So, when Ron and Brad returned to Curaçao a couple weeks later to continue to search for her, Tom went with them.

One day, as they were driving through Willemstad, they came

to a light. It was an oppressively hot day and the windows were open. From a passing car, they heard a woman's voice shout, "Brad!" It sounded exactly like Amy calling out for her brother.

"Did you hear that?" asked Brad.

"Yeah, I heard that," said Tom.

They chased the vehicle through the streets, but when they caught up with it, Amy was not inside.

They got their hopes up again while questioning locals around Mambo Beach, later that day. When they showed Amy's picture to tourists, several people got very excited and said they had definitely seen her around. Those tips eventually led them to a server working at the Mambo Beach Club who had the same short haircut as Amy and was roughly the same build.

"We left the island feeling hopeful," said Tom. But as the weeks turned into months, and then years, that positivity slipped away. Now, Tom has nothing but contempt for Curaçao and the worthless police and harbor security folks who never seemed interested in a missing woman from Virginia.

"Their coast guard are all volunteers, and the police department is almost a militia," he said. "And it's all about forty miles from Venezuela. It's an open island."

Tom holds out hope that the sightings of Amy over the years are as credible as they first appeared to be.

"I loved her to death," he said.

Kat eventually connected me with Mollie McClure, who dated Amy after Kat and Amy broke up, and we spoke over Zoom one afternoon, shortly before my trip to Virginia. Mollie works as a professional photographer these days and lives in a safe, liberal part of North Carolina, where she has found a strong support network among the local LGBTQ community.

Mollie was very hesitant to discuss the details of her relationship with Amy. We stopped and started several times while she considered what to say on the record. She had been invited to sit down with the documentary crew for an interview as well, and she was on the fence about participating in either of our projects. I had recently spoken to Jessica Vale, the supervising producer at Ample Entertainment, and Alexandra Meistrell, the showrunner for the series, for a short discussion about how we each intended to approach the topic of Amy's sexuality in our separate stories.

"For what it's worth, I think you can trust them," I told Mollie. "They seem like good people."

"That's good to hear," said Mollie.

But when we started talking again, Mollie continued to pause and censor what she wanted to share.

Finally, I did something I very rarely do. I decided to stop the interview.

"I don't think this is a conversation that can happen over Zoom," I said. "How about I drive out to you?"

"You're coming to Chesterfield to meet the Bradleys, right? I'll meet you in town. I can show you the places Amy and I used to go to."

I told her that sounded perfect.

Chapter Nineteen

THE LEAPING LESBIAN

EARLY ON IN MY REPORTING, Iva Bradley emailed me the crew manifest for the *Rhapsody of the Seas* from the week of their vacation in 1998. I think she obtained it during the discovery phase of their civil case against Royal Caribbean. The list contained hundreds of names, mostly foreign, arranged alphabetically, everyone from janitors to bridge officers. As luck would have it, I discovered that the former cruise director, Kirk Detweiler, was currently working in Marion, Ohio, managing a theater just an hour and half drive from me. He agreed to meet me at a coffee shop. A few days later, I made the trek in my Subaru, which made all sorts of noises now that the odometer had crested 200,000 miles.

I had just arrived in Marion, headed for the theater along the main drag, when a large pickup truck ahead of me pulled left into the passing lane, opening space for me to continue straight. But as I came broadside, the driver made a wide turn right, crossing into my lane and clipping the back of my vehicle. It knocked me off course, but I was able to pull into an empty dirt parking lot instead of the ditch. I got out to survey the damage. My back door was crinkled and smeared with mud, but his truck seemed fine.

It was a bit of a pisser for me, as I'd recently switched my insurance to liability because of the vehicle's age. It wasn't worth putting more money into it. This probably spelled the end for my ride. The state troopers who came to the scene took two hours to assess the situation before deciding they couldn't figure out who was at fault. And so, I arrived at the Marion Palace Theater quite a bit later than our agreed-upon meeting time. Kirk didn't seem fazed. He's a likable guy that way. Takes a lot to bother him, I guess. His job aboard the *Rhapsody* was managing the pleasure of his guests, so it makes sense.

He walked me across the street to a small café, where we sat at a table by the door, and he told me what he remembered after twenty-six years.

In college, Kirk majored in telecommunications at Kent State, with a minor in theater and dance. After graduation, he got a job working with an entertainment production crew for a smaller cruise line that would eventually be acquired by Royal Caribbean. He got his start running Bingo games and hosting parties for passengers at sea. The longer he stayed, the more he kept being promoted, until he became a cruise ship director in 1989. He worked exclusively for Royal Caribbean from 1991 to 2011 before moving to Silver Sea Cruises. He remained in the business until Covid shut everything down. Since 2021, Kirk has been the executive director of the Marion Palace Theatre, a beautiful stage that harkens back to vaudeville days. It now hosts events like the local high school's production of *Newsies* and "A Night with Marc Price," the guy who played Skippy on *Family Ties*.

"My job with Royal Caribbean was a lot of fun but some very long hours," said Kirk. "It's twelve- to fourteen-hour days, seven days a week, for four months—then you get two months off. I got to see the world." Kirk managed cruises in Alaska, the Mexican Riviera, Southeast Asia, Australia, and all over the Caribbean. His last tour was with Jalesh Cruises, out of Mumbai.

The *Rhapsody of the Seas* holds a special place in Kirk's heart. He was on the planning committee that designed and created the entertainment experience for the ship as it was being built. That included devising programs for its two-story theater, nightclub, piano bar, and music club, as well as numerous daily events like line-dancing, limbo contests, and trivia.

"When it came out, the *Rhapsody* was the biggest ship in the world," he said. "We had a good team."

As cruise director, Kirk was considered a "three-stripe" officer, which earned him a stateroom under the bridge, next to the captain's quarters. He also got to eat in the officers' mess. He explained that the lower decks, under the passengers' cabins, held rooms for the rest of the crew, including a separate dining hall and private deck.

Usually, life aboard a cruise ship is routine. The programs and events recycle every week for a new group of passengers. But every so often, something very unroutine would happen. It's simple statistics and probability when your job is to ferry so many people to adventures and back again. Do it long enough, strange stuff happens.

One night, in 1988, Kirk was working aboard the *Star Dancer*, when a chiropractor from Santa Monica named Scott Roston reported that his wife, Karen, had been blown off the deck by a strong gust of wind. The Coast Guard was called. They managed to find Karen's body floating in the sea. An autopsy revealed she'd been strangled to death before being deposited into the water. Roston was sentenced to life in prison. Later, Kirk was on a ship outside St. Thomas when a drunk woman fell over the tenth-floor railing. Her body landed in the dining room during lunch rush. Dead on impact. But these events were so rare that he can remember them in great detail.

He was still in his stateroom the morning of March 24, 1998, when the purser's office began to page Amy Bradley on the ship-wide intercom. The ship was parked outside Curaçao, waiting for customs to clear them to dock.

"Later in the morning, we did a 'Charlie drill,'" he said. "It's also called a 'bomb search' drill. The ship is divided into sections. Everyone on the crew searches their own cabins first, and then they report to a designated area of the ship that they've been assigned to sweep. My team searched the theater. The cabin attendants searched the guest cabins." During training, an officer would hide a box labeled "bomb" somewhere. The drill wouldn't end until someone found it. These drills were normally conducted every three months, but that morning they did two. Amy was not located.

The next day, with the permission of Royal Caribbean, FBI agents boarded the *Rhapsody* at St. Martin and conducted a forensic search of the ship. Kirk received first-hand updates on the widening investigation. There was a meeting with senior officers during which the FBI briefed them on preliminary findings. The agents had dusted the Bradleys' stateroom and balcony. According to Kirk, he was told the FBI had discovered palm prints on the railing and heel prints on the outside of the sliding glass door.

"Like she was sitting on the railing and kicked off with her feet," he said.

Kirk was also told that Amy had joked with another passenger about jumping off the ship.

"She had told somebody, 'When I see the lights of Curaçao, I'm going to jump off and beat the ship there.'"

He doesn't believe that Amy was murdered on the *Rhapsody*. He knows that Yellow, the bass player who performed as part of the programming he'd personally designed, was one of the last people to be seen with her. But he also knew Yellow personally and doesn't believe he would hurt Amy.

"I think Yellow was in the wrong place at the wrong time," he said. "He got a bad rap. He was a very friendly guy."

Kirk admits that when he saw Chris Fenwick's footage of Yellow grinding on Amy at the dance club, he realized the bass player had been out of line that night. Musicians like Yellow are considered officers on the ship. As such, they were allowed to be in the passenger areas, but the rules on friendships were strict—you were allowed to socialize with the guests but you couldn't *fraternize*. "If I had been there to witness it, I would have told him to go to bed," he said. "But close dancing doesn't make you a kidnapper."

Kirk believed the most likely scenario, in light of what the FBI found, was that Amy fell off the balcony, either by accident or by her own volition. "Everyone on board thought she either fell or jumped. And then her body may have been chopped up by the propellors or taken by sharks."

Among the officers and crew, Amy became known as the "leaping lesbian," a moniker he readily admits was in poor taste. It's worth noting, though, because her sexual preference had somehow leaked during the onboard investigation. I wondered about that. How had it come out and why? Maybe it was nothing. But for something that was such a secret back home, it is interesting that the fact made its way around to the cruise director.

My trip aboard the *Rhapsody of the Seas* was booked for early August. As the date approached, I found myself pondering things like ghost ships and harbingers of doom. Was there anything of Amy that remained on that old boat? Kirk, who has sailed on more ships than anyone I've ever met, believes that sometimes the dead do come back at sea.

"Once, I saw something I couldn't explain," he said. "This was on the *Emerald Seas*, a ship that was built in 1944 and used as a floating hospital in World War II. My room was where the passenger area would have been back then. One night, I came to bed and lay down to go to sleep. I hadn't been drinking. Anyway, I was laying down and not yet asleep, and turned over to find an apparition of an old man lying in bed next to me. He got up on one elbow and looked at me, his expression like, *what the hell?* And then he vanished."

Something about a ship on the open ocean lends itself to tales of dispossessed souls. Perhaps it's the eerie, liminal atmosphere of the empty horizon or the isolation from civilization. I think of the *Flying Dutchman* of the 1700s, that ghost ship seen slipping through the fog on lonely nights by old sailors. Or the hauntings of the *Mary Celeste*. Sometimes at night, unable to find sleep, I hear the crashing of the surf at the tip of the Outer Banks. I remember how the ocean there felt primordial, as if I had not found the End of the World but the horizon of all things sane.

Soon, I would be tracing Amy's final voyage. Was I asking for trouble?

In early June, a few days before I was scheduled to leave for Virginia, I got a call from Iva Bradley.

"Do you like pulled pork?" she asked.

"I do."

"Well, then, I'm going to make my pulled pork. We'll talk, and then we'll take a break for lunch, and then we'll talk some more."

"That sounds perfect," I said.

"I want you to know, James, that the people we invite into our home are people we love. Our friends and family. And I consider you a good friend now."

"Thank you. I'm happy to be your friend."

Please let this go well, I thought. *Please don't let me screw this up.*

PART TWO

MESSAGE IN A BOTTLE

Chapter Twenty

HOME

It's 460 miles from Akron to Chesterfield, Virginia, a drive that takes about eight hours when you figure in stops for food and gas. The first leg was I-76 to Breezewood, Pennsylvania, that great epicenter of travel between the Midwest and the East Coast, a twisted hub of gas stations, gift shops, and dilapidated motels. As Obi Wan once said, "You will never find a more wretched hive of scum and villainy."

At Breezewood, I turned onto Route 522, a scenic highway that cuts through the Blue Ridge Mountains on its way to Richmond. I could have taken a slightly faster route that goes through DC, but of all the roads I've traveled, I think Route 522 might be my favorite. It meanders around the foothills of the Shenandoah Valley, sometimes narrowing to two lanes through one-horse towns with names out of some Cormac McCarthy novel: Scrabble, Flint Hill, Nineveh. In the summers the roads are lined with farmer's markets and ice cream stands. As you drive by, your heart gets this warm feeling, like *this* is America. This is the dream. And it still exists.

On long road trips, I listen to audiobooks. Horror novels, mostly. I never listen to true crime. No true crime podcasts, either. I think maybe I'm like the mechanic who never works on his own car, the barber who can't cut his own hair. On that trip, I listened to *A Head Full of Ghosts* by Paul Tremblay, who is in the running to become our generation's Stephen King. It's a story about a teen girl who may or may not be possessed, as told from the perspective of her younger sister. It fit my mood perfectly.

After all, the line between obsession and possession is as tenuous as the line between the living and the dead. One can often feel like the other. As a young boy, I became obsessed with the abduction and murder of Amy Mihaljevic. The story possessed me and at times seemed to drive my manic actions to search for the face of her kidnapper in the crowds at local malls. Similarly, my investigation into the disappearance of Maura Murray has been called an obsession. I managed to exorcise that story, but only after it caused much damage.

I was skating the edge of obsession again with my investigation into Amy Bradley's disappearance. I was a kid staring into the mirror in a dark bathroom, whispering Bloody Mary once, twice . . . If I wasn't careful, her story would possess me, for sure. Of course, obsession is a young man's game. I grew up. I've built a fortress around my heart, brick by brick, made strong from the mud of failures and bad reviews. I'm not sure I can give myself over to a story like that anymore. Still, was it safe to get so close? Probably not.

Chesterfield is an unincorporated village built out of the woods south of Richmond, bordered in the north by the James River and to the south by the Appomattox. When people around here say you're in Chesterfield, you might think they're referring to Chesterfield County, which is technically true, but they usually mean that vaguely defined village of the same name, where Amy is from. Chesterfield is part of the oldest settled country inside the United States. It's just upriver from Jamestown, where our very first settlers fell to cannibalism during the Starving Time. Today, Chesterfield is a well-kept suburb of Richmond, the sort of place you can raise a nuclear family, where the kids can bike to their friend's house, where the sidewalks are full of trick-or-treaters on Halloween. If you can afford it, that Rockwellian ideal remains alive in Chesterfield.

I got a room that offered free breakfast at a Marriott hotel about five miles from the Bradleys' home. In the morning, I got my plate of biscuits and sausage gravy, then went on my way, arriving at the Bradleys' house at 10 a.m.

Before I walked inside, I practiced some mindfulness techniques to overcome the anxiety that was threatening to distract me from my job. *Clear your mind. Step into the present.* I was keenly aware of the importance of this interview. Without the Bradleys, there couldn't be a book. They had insight into Amy that others lacked. They made her, they grew her, they molded her. For this to work, I needed them. And I needed to structure my interview carefully, in case this would be my only interview with them. Basic information first, then specifics of the disappearance, then Amy's personal life. This moment required every tool in my kit.

Iva greeted me at the door with a warm hug. I handed her a small bouquet of flowers I'd picked up at the grocery store.

"For me?" she said, with a smile.

"For you," I said.

She ushered me inside. Their home is quite modern, with an open floor plan that allows you to see into the living room, dining room, and kitchen at the same time. Ron and their lawyer friend, Earl Nance, were sitting at the kitchen bar, drinking coffee. We made small talk while Iva set the flowers in a vase. Before we started, Iva gave me the five-cent tour. She introduced me to Monkey Bird, who was snoozing in his cage. She showed me Amy's Miata, still parked in the garage, tuned up and clean, waiting for her to return. She took me outside to show me their landscaped backyard, where she grows crimson Itoh peonies.

She brings me red flowers, I thought, goose bumps raising on my arm as I recalled my session with the medium.

Finally, each of us with a cup of fresh coffee, we sat around the dining room table.

"All right," I said. "Where to start?"

We started at the beginning. Ron and Iva met in grade school. Iva was just thirteen when she noticed a handsome young man at lunch one day. He carried a basketball bag with his initials on it: "R.B." "It was love at first sight," said Iva, looking to Ron, who smiled back. They got married not long after Iva turned eighteen—fifty-three years ago, a rare accomplishment, especially for two people who have gone through a very public tragedy.

"And I don't just love him," said Iva. "I like him a lot, too."

Iva gave birth to Amy at twenty-one and named her after a favorite character from *Little Women*. Brad came along three years later. At that time, Iva was unemployed and Ron had a job in the classified ads department of *The Progress-Index,* out of Petersburg. With two kids, money was tight, so Iva picked up a low-entry job at Fort Lee, typing up letters for officers, mostly sales notices for their swap shop. They had a home in Hopewell, a workaday suburb with a stinky chemical plant that is lambasted in a popular, crude jingle by locals: "You smell, I smell, we all smell Hopewell."

For a time, Ron worked at Allied Chemical. Around the year Amy turned five, Iva got a job selling insurance and discovered she was good at it. That brought in a lot more money. Soon they moved across the Appomattox to the Creekwood area of Chesterfield, which provided a bigger base of potential clients for Iva. They bought a three-bedroom colonial on a quiet street. Her first year selling insurance, Iva made ninety thousand dollars, almost triple what Ron was pulling in at the chemical plant. He quit his job and became a stay-at-home dad for a couple years.

Chesterfield was an ideal place to raise a family. The neighborhood was teaming with playmates. "I've never seen so many children," Iva recalled. There were kids on bikes and skateboards rolling up and down the sidewalks. The schools were great. Little Amy and Brad thrived there. As she grew, Amy became involved in many local sports teams.

"Her first word was 'ball,'" said Ron. "She played on the little boys' baseball team."

As their parents had hoped, Amy and Brad quickly found friends in Chesterfield. They played games of cops and robbers on the street and spent long summer days at the local pool. Sometimes they'd skip the pool and go out to the river, where a rope swing was hidden in the trees. Amy made friends with a neighbor boy, Henry Battle, and they'd often go bass fishing or play ball in the driveway.

"We'd leave in the morning and come home when the sun came down," said Brad, joining the conversation. He'd just arrived with his wife, Koral, having walked from their house through the backyard. Brad has grown into a handsome man, a silver fox with a head of white hair.

Brad recalled days spent at the Craters, a place full of dirt hills, big rocks, and swift rapids. Amy would often challenge Brad to a game of basketball in the driveway. For many years she dominated, but over time Brad grew taller and stronger. Eventually, he could hold his own.

By the time Brad entered high school, his big sister had become quite popular and a bit of a local legend on the basketball court. "I was a freshman when she was a senior," he said. "It was all about Amy at the time. I was just Brad, Amy's brother. But we were good friends. We were always good to each other."

After Amy left for college, Brad started dating her friend Erin. Amy continued to check in on her brother, visiting often. She was protective of him and did what she could to keep him out of trouble.

Once, when Iva and Ron were out of town, Brad hosted a party at their house. He just wanted something small. A couple friends, maybe. He was working at Dunkins at the time and told a couple coworkers about it. And then they told their friends. And so on. Word soon got around to the general population of both local high schools. As in some forgotten John Hughes film from the

'80s, the Bradleys' house filled with just about every teen from Chesterfield County.

"There were cars parked a mile up the street," said Brad. "I couldn't see the backyard, there were so many people. There were at least ten in the hot tub. I didn't know what to do."

Then Amy arrived. She made her way through the crowd like Officer Krupke from *West Side Story*. If she didn't recognize someone, she told them to get lost. Nobody challenged her, and things calmed down before the police were called.

Sometimes, Brad visited Amy at Longwood and crashed in her dorm for a weekend. He got to know her friends well. Whenever Amy played a game, a Bradley entourage was in the stands, including aunts and uncles and countless cousins.

"She was such a good player," said Brad. "Actually, Caitlin Clark reminds me of her. Amy had solid court awareness. She could zip a no-look pass and hit her teammate every time. And she did that Michael Jordan thing with her tongue. It's in every picture."

"Who's hungry?" said Iva.

We took a break for lunch, crowding around the counter in the kitchen, loading up plates with barbeque pulled pork and beans and potato salad. It was fantastic. A real Southern lunch and the best meal I had on my trip to Virginia. But the unspoken secret was heavy in the room.

Iva had to know I'd talked with Kat, at least. And—I don't believe I imagined this, though I do admit it could have been my own growing paranoia—I sensed a rushing of things, in the way a clever witness may run out the clock during a deposition by speaking around an issue with anecdotes that have nothing to do with the crux of things. Whenever there was a lull in conversation, Iva interjected with a topic of her own. When I made eye contact with Iva, I felt that she was trying to transmit a simple thought—please don't talk about that. Please leave it unsaid.

We can never know the mind of another. That is the simple curse of this world. It is the reason for so many misunderstandings and pointless animus, the seed of strife and war. We see each other subjectively, and often, what we think we see in others is just a reflection of our own insecurities.

I readily admit I didn't want to talk about it, either. Eventually, I had to put my cards on the table. But not just yet.

"Can we talk about the cruise?" I asked after the plates were cleared.

According to the Bradleys, Amy immediately attracted the attention of a handful of young men who worked on the ship, including their head waiter, a man from Portugal named Eduardo Cabrita. One evening before her disappearance, Amy skipped dinner, and Cabrita asked where she was. He said that he and his friends wanted to take her to Carlos'n Charlie's, a popular bar on Aruba (and coincidentally one of the last places Natalee Holloway was seen before she disappeared in 2005). But when Iva told Amy about it later that night, she said she thought the waiter and his friends were creepy and she was not going anywhere with them.

When the ship arrived in Aruba the next day, the Bradleys rented a Jeep to tour the island. They were soon lost in a poor neighborhood full of mud huts and plank houses. Amy was uncomfortable, they recalled. When they finally found a beach, Amy didn't want to go into the water. Instead, she got lunch at a nearby Taco Bell.

The night before the disappearance, the cruise director, Kirk Detweiler, organized a limbo party. Clips of this party are featured on a video that was available for purchase upon debarkation. Amy and Brad are not seen anywhere in the footage even though they were the final two contestants. Brad won and was awarded with a crown, which he promptly put on his sister's head.

"Did you notice anything strange that night?" I asked.

"I'm suspicious about the Scientologists that were on the ship," said Brad. "Amy was talking to a couple Scientologists who'd come aboard the *Rhapsody*."

When the *Rhapsody* docked in Aruba, it parked near the *Freewinds*. It was only about seventy miles from Aruba to Curaçao, so the *Rhapsody* remained docked quite late that night. Brad said that performers from Aruba came aboard to entertain the passengers as the sun set. Fire jugglers and local musicians. Along with the performers, he said, several passengers from the *Freewinds* boarded as well.

"I remember, there were two Black ladies dressed in uniform," he said. "Full-length blue suits. Amy was talking to them for forty minutes to an hour on the pool deck."

"Amy motioned me over," said Iva.

Brad and Iva walked to Amy and when they got near, the two women's affable, smiling faces suddenly went cold.

"The women shut down," said Brad.

"It was like a glass shield came down between us," said Iva.

Something about this exchange left Iva and Brad feeling uneasy. They wondered what these women and Amy had talked about for nearly an hour. They never found out, though Brad said he discovered later that the uniforms the women were wearing "matched" Scientology Sea Org uniforms.

I asked Ron to go over the morning he discovered that Amy was missing, again, and he provided a few new details.

"How sure are you that you saw Amy on the balcony at five thirty that morning?" I asked.

"One hundred percent," he said. "I saw Amy sitting on the balcony. One hundred percent."

When he got up around 6 a.m., the shirt that Amy had been wearing the night before was on the floor, so Ron figured she had changed her clothes, at least, before leaving that morning. There was also an odd encounter when he left the room to go searching for Amy—the head of security for the *Rhapsody of the Seas*, Lou Costello, was standing in the hall just outside their room, walkie-talkie in hand.

"Why was the head of security there that morning?" Ron asked. "It's strange. I told him I couldn't find my daughter. And later, he asked me to sign this document. I signed it without looking, because I thought he was trying to help us. It was a timeline of events.

But when I looked at it later it was totally different than what I had told him."

"He was happy he got us to sign that timeline," said Iva. "For Lou, it was like winning the lottery."

After Ron's first search of the ship, he and Iva woke up Brad and asked him to wait in the room in case Amy came back while they went looking again.

"What struck me most was the panic on their faces," said Brad. "It was like, oh shit, what's going on? Then they left for a bit. I don't think they were gone thirty minutes. I was hoping Amy was going to walk in, and it wasn't going to be a big deal. But then mom and dad came back and said come help us look."

They split up to cover more ground. Brad returned to the disco, retracing their steps from the night before. But his sister wasn't there, so he went down and sat at the tables that looked out at the pool deck, hoping to see Amy walk by.

"And then Yellow walked up to me," said Brad. "He said, 'Hey man, are you okay? I'm sorry to hear about your sister.' But that was before any announcement was made. So how did he know she was missing?"

Brad explained to Yellow what they knew so far, which was very little. The bass player seemed very eager to learn as much as possible.

"Yellow said, 'Hang on, I want my brother to hear this,' and waved this other guy over. It wasn't really his brother, of course, but that's what he called him. Then Yellow asked, 'When did you last see her?' Looking back, it's pretty clear to me that I was getting his timeline straight."

Iva had specifically noticed Yellow during the first two days of their cruise. She didn't like the way he looked at Amy and the other young women on board, the way he danced with them any chance he could. "He was gyrating on them" she said. "I remember I said to Ron, 'I can't understand why they'd have a band like that around kids.'"

"He was just vulgar," said Brad.

After they had searched the entire ship a couple times over, Iva and Ron went to the purser's desk and asked them to make an announcement. They were told it was too early. Officials waited until 7:50 a.m. to put out the first ship-wide call. And even though Iva and Ron were convinced by then that something terrible had happened, the message simply said, "Will Amy Bradley please come to the purser's desk?" As if she'd simply gone to the breakfast bar and lost track of time.

But Amy didn't come to the purser's desk. It was almost time to open the gangway and let people out onto the island. Iva and Ron asked them to keep the doors closed until a full search was conducted. The captain, Kjetil Gjerstad, seemed more concerned about staying on schedule and not alarming the other passengers. He opened the doors. Eventually a search would be conducted, but not for another four hours.

"The captain told us the crew searched everything bigger than a bread box," said Ron. "Later we learned that they'd only searched the common areas. They just lied to us."

This conflicted with the account of the cruise director, who told me that they had searched every room on the ship twice that day. However, the videographer, Chris Fenwick, claimed nobody had bothered to check his cabin or the camera crates, which were large enough to hold a body. My hunch is the truth is somewhere in between. But without a doubt, more could have been done.

From the deck of the *Rhapsody*, Ron watched rescue boats and helicopters zigzag around the bay, searching for his daughter's body.

That evening, the Bradleys were faced with an unbearable decision: remain on the ship in the hope that, somehow, Amy might still be found on board, or to stay on Curaçao and search for her on the island.

"They encouraged us to get off," said Brad.

The Bradleys were told that if rescuers found Amy's body in the water off Curaçao, the ship couldn't turn around to bring them back.

"I knew that if she was in the water, somebody put her in the water," said Iva. "And that person was still on the ship."

In the end, they decided to leave the ship and stay at a hotel in town. Ron's boss, Mike McCord, and his wife went with them. They got a room at the Otrobanda Hotel right there in Willemstad. Once they were settled, Brad ordered a beer from the bar and walked out to the Queen Juliana Bridge over Sint Anna Bay to clear his head. Iva and Ron watched helplessly as the *Rhapsody of the Seas* sailed away without their family. From where they stood, they could see that every cabin was illuminated. Every one except theirs. The day had felt like a bad dream. Something about that detail seemed to make their situation more real.

"They thought they'd gotten rid of us," said Iva.

That night a few Scientologists, passengers from the *Freewinds*, arrived at their hotel room, asking questions.

"They showed up at midnight," said Brad. "They knew Amy was missing, and they said they wanted to help, so we let them in. They started asking us odd questions about Amy. What kind of present would she want? What type of cigarettes did she smoke? They said, 'Tell us about something you haven't lost.' Then they asked us to lay down on the bed so they could put their hands on us."

"That's when I said, 'Okay, we're good,'" said Ron.

"It was almost like a fact-finding mission," said Brad.

The next day they walked around Willemstad, interviewing locals. They made phone calls to congressmen and the FBI. They reached out to the U.S. consulate. They spoke to the harbormaster and his crew. They did everything they could. Out in the bay, the search for Amy's body continued.

Minute by minute, a new reality began to assert itself upon the Bradleys. Amy had not wandered off and gotten lost on Curaçao. There would be no easy answer. Amy was simply gone. They didn't know what to do next. There was no handbook for this sort of thing. Where could they turn?

"It's a feeling of falling off a cliff and grabbing hold of everything," said Iva.

FBI agents out of Puerto Rico agreed to meet them in St. Martin the next day and take them onto the ship again, where they could question crew members and conduct a search of their own. Mike McCord chartered a plane to fly them to the island. Soon, they found themselves aboard the *Rhapsody* once more. Ron remembers sitting outside the room where the FBI agents were questioning Alister Douglas. When the interrogation was over, Yellow came out and gave Ron a cheeky thumbs-up and walked away.

Nothing more could be done. When the cruise ended, they returned to Virginia without Amy.

A month later, Ron and Brad returned to Curaçao to hold a press conference and hang up flyers with Amy's picture in the hopes that someone might have seen her. They were accompanied by a psychic named Margaret Selby, as well as one of Iva's brothers, and Amy's sometime boyfriend, Tom Edgerton. They stayed at a Sonesta hotel, and the press conference was held inside.

"It was weird and exciting at the same time," said Brad.

Margaret used her special intuition to attempt to "see" where Amy was on the island. She drew a picture of a house with a broken-down truck out front. She handed the drawing over to the family when she was done. It was up to the men to find it, now. The island was large and full of twisted roads and forgotten shanty towns. But they were going to try. Ron and Brad got into the Jeep. Tom drove.

According to Ron, Brad, and Tom, they found a house that matched Margaret's drawing exactly. The structure, the broken-down truck, it all looked exactly like what the psychic had envisioned. The home was part of a larger estate, a giant ostrich farm, actually. Slowly, they took the Jeep down its winding drives and discovered a fourteen-by-fourteen-foot shack in a field. They parked the Jeep and got out to investigate. Inside the shack they discovered a strange sight—it appeared that someone had recently been living there. They saw a dirty mattress on the floor and bottles of water nearby. They also found an empty package of Marlboro cigarettes and a container of Tic Tacs. These items were of particular interest. Marlboro was Amy's brand of choice, but they were hard to obtain in Curaçao at the time. And Amy always had Tic Tacs, a candy that was not available on the island.

Consider how strange it must have been for them. They had traveled thousands of miles to search for their missing loved one, arriving in a foreign land, their only real lead a vision from a psychic. And that psychic's intuition had brought them here, to a shack on an ostrich farm, where they found items familiar to Amy herself. Moments like this call into question our understanding of the universe. And yet, Amy wasn't there. So what did any of it mean?

Outside the shack they discovered a six-inch-wide tube sticking out of the ground. Was it an air shaft to a hidden chamber? Ron yelled down the pipe but nobody answered.

Finally, they secured the cigarettes and Tic Tacs in a plastic bag, which they handed over to police in Chesterfield upon their return. That was twenty-six years ago.

"Did you ever get a letter or a phone call over the years that might have come from Amy?" I asked. "If she is alive, I would think she would try to reach out at some point."

"About six to eight months after her disappearance we got a random phone call at home," said Iva. "A woman on the other end said, 'Mom.' That was it. We immediately contacted the FBI." Nothing came of it.

Twenty-six years have passed, now. Each morning, Iva and Ron say, "Maybe today." And each night they share a kiss and say, "Maybe tomorrow."

I was finished with my questions concerning the events before, during, and immediately following Amy's disappearance. We'd talked. We'd broken bread. Nearly five hours had passed.

"I'd like to talk about Mollie," I said, finally.

Ron, sturdy, reliable Ron, didn't flinch. Brad nodded. Iva's face went red.

"Amy was in a serious relationship with Mollie," I said. "And before Mollie, she was with Kat at school. I've spoken to them both, and they shared with me how much they loved your daughter and how much she loved them. I believe this was a big part of who Amy was, and I feel like I'd be doing her a disservice not to include them in my book."

"It's nobody's business," said Iva. "I think their relationships should stay private."

"Well, I can tell you from my conversations with Mollie and Kat that they've already talked to the documentary team about this. It will almost certainly be discussed on that show in some way. It's coming out."

Something about this bothered Iva. "You're talking to the production company?"

"I've had a couple conversations with their producer. We discussed how we should handle this very carefully. In the end, they'll do their own thing. I think they'll be very respectful of Amy's story."

"I don't like that," said Iva. "I don't like that they talked to you and never mentioned this to us. It feels like someone's keeping a secret. Why wouldn't they ask me? Why wouldn't they just come to me with this?"

"I can't speak for them," I said. "But the reason I haven't asked you about this before now is because I felt it was best to do so in person. And honestly, I was worried that by talking about this, you would stop talking to me. That I would lose your support."

Iva said, "You're not going to lose me. I'm doing this for Amy."

"Thank you."

"But Amy doesn't have a voice in this," she said. "In what way can she defend herself?"

It was an odd way to put it, I thought. What did Amy need to defend herself from?

"Amy's friends have said you and Ron didn't support this," I said, pushing on. "I know that could have been difficult for you and Amy as well. It's awkward to talk to your parents about this sort of thing. I'm forty-six, and I only just told my father that I'm bisexual, that I wanted to date men when I was younger. It was hard. But it's a big part of me. Is there a reason you didn't want Amy to date women?"

"We were concerned about the hardships she'd face," said Iva. "What it could do to a child in the nineties."

"Mom," said Brad, gently. "It was a part of her. She would have ended up with a woman, I think. And actually, I would have preferred a woman for her because that was more her." Iva went quiet, and Brad turned to me. "If you try to tell her story without this, how could you do it? Everyone who knew Amy knew about it. I think Mollie and Kat are a huge part of her life. I don't think they're unimportant."

I wondered if this was the first time that Brad had spoken directly about the subject with his mother since the disappearance. It seemed to me by their body language that Amy's sexuality was not something that was talked about or at least not something that had been discussed in many years. And let's be honest (and I say this with all due respect to Iva and the Bradleys, who I genuinely grew to care about), I sensed a bit of subterfuge related to Amy's image as presented to the public and press. The only time a relationship was mentioned was Amy's "boyfriend," Tom Edgerton. But calling Tom Amy's boyfriend was disingenuous. Even Tom said they were more like buddies, though intimate at times.

She could be very soft.

Her friends from college said Amy would have beards, men that she presented to her family as "boyfriends," even though she was with Kat at that time. She'd learned that was easier.

I was touched by the way Brad stuck up for his sister in front of his parents. That couldn't have been easy, either.

We moved on to other topics, then, but Iva had changed. She had led much of the conversation, but now she was quiet. I had overstepped. That much was clear.

But what choice did I have?

I am a journalist. As my early editors instructed me, as Sky had said, my duty here was to Amy. To tell her story as completely as I could. That trumps hard feelings.

It's a no-win for me. And it was exactly the situation I didn't want to find myself in again.

I'd just have to take Iva's word that she wouldn't cut me off. But something about her reaction left me with little hope. I'd seen this play out before.

Chapter Twenty-one

MOLLIE

When Mollie McClure was sixteen, she spent the night at Amy Bradley's house. That's pretty much where it started. An awakening. Similar moments play out every day. Pivot points in our lives, flashes of understanding we take with us for the rest of our lives.

They'd known each other for years as friends, classmates. But something was different that night. When they went to bed, Mollie couldn't fall asleep. Something inside her stirred. She lay beside Amy on her friend's waterbed, afraid to move, afraid to disturb her. She turned to look at her, careful not to wake her up. Amy was fast asleep. Mollie watched as Amy breathed in and out. She saw that her friend was beautiful.

She's right there, Mollie thought to herself.

She watched her for a little longer and felt a kind of peace she'd never known before.

"There was intimacy about that moment," Mollie said. "I was in heaven."

We sat at a table inside the ShoreDog Café, a hipster breakfast and coffee place inside a strip mall across the river from Chesterfield, in Henrico. At first, Mollie showed the same hesitancy as she had in our Zoom call. The more we talked, the more she relaxed, and soon it was like talking to an old friend.

"At times it felt like Amy and I were living parallel lives," said Mollie. "We were both very close to our family, incredibly close to our sibling. We both grew up in the Richmond suburbs. My dad also really advocated for me in athletics, we both had strong moms. But there were also important differences."

For instance, Amy grew up on the south side of the river, while Mollie was from the west end, which is more affluent. Her father was a lawyer specializing in mergers and acquisitions. The James River is significant that way, dividing the socioeconomic spread into two separate worlds.

When Mollie would visit Amy at home, she was taken by the casual, carefree way Amy spoke with her family. Mollie's family was more reserved. "They would tease each other," she recalled. "The amount of laughter you would hear in that family was incredible. I envied it."

Mollie first met Amy when she was fourteen. It was at tryouts for a select traveling basketball team.

"I was quiet, insecure, scared-to-death," said Mollie. "Amy was in the layup line, cutting jokes. She always had to add a flair to everything. I was in awe. Who is this girl that has so much confidence?"

As she did with so many others, Amy pulled Mollie into her group of friends. Amy was a collector of interesting people. And at first, that's all they were—friends.

"When we were fourteen, fifteen, it looked like one thing. When we were sixteen, seventeen, it looked like another thing. In college, there were limited touches. Then it became something more."

Mollie came out to herself at nineteen. Suddenly, everything became clear. To her, at least. She started to feel like she was lying, keeping it from her parents. Eventually, she realized she needed them to help navigate this new world.

"What sucks the most about us queer kids is, it's one of the most vulnerable acts someone can take, coming out to your parents."

They did not take it well.

"I told my mom first. And she told me, 'I'm not going to carry this alone.' So she asked me to tell my dad. He broke down crying. But I feel like this is a pretty typical reaction."

Mollie believes that the process of a typical parent's reaction to a child coming out of the closet, at least in the '90s, could be broken up into three parts. First, they'd say it's a phase: You'll grow out of it. Just give it some time. Second, they'll blame the people around their child for influencing them in some deceitful way. Third, they'll try to fix it with therapy, out of fear for how it might make their child's life more difficult. Well-intentioned mistakes are the currency of rushed adaptation.

This is a storm to be weathered, though, not something to run from. Because, as Mollie found out (and Amy never did), if they truly love you, they'll never leave. "This shit can be repaired," she said.

It took years for Mollie to feel capable of being honest with her parents about her sexual orientation. And maybe it never got back to the way it was, but she knows she's loved. "It's still a little uncomfortable. There's a reason I live in North Carolina. I don't know what it would have taken for Amy to be accepted by her parents."

Over the years, Mollie has seen numerous stories about Amy's disappearance on TV. But no story ever revealed who Amy really was. A large part of her life had been edited out by her family, who wished to portray her as strictly straight in the national media.

"Is she ever going to be free?" Mollie asked. "Are any of us going to try to see her in all of her complexity?" What she said next echoed what Iva had said, but with polar-opposite connotations. "Especially now that she's not here to speak for herself?"

Mollie remembers the moment when she became more than friends to Amy. It was just after college graduation. She went with

Amy to a gay bar in Richmond. They played pool and drank. Eventually they started dancing. "There was a lot of electricity," said Mollie. Afterward, Amy drove Mollie home. In the driveway of her parents' house, Amy leaned in and kissed her. They made out in her car for some time. "I'd never been kissed like that before. I'd never kissed someone like that before. All this history, it was all wrapped up in a kiss. It felt like love. It felt like we really knew each other."

Their relationship started almost immediately after that night. But Mollie had to leave Chesterfield. She had a job as an assistant basketball coach for the women's team at the University of Kentucky lined up in Lexington. Amy still had another semester left at Longwood. But she had enough time to get to know Amy's college friends, even her ex-girlfriend. "I went to Farmville and met Kat," said Mollie. "I remember thinking, Kat's so cool, Amy. What are you doing with me? We were able to coexist and not feel awkward."

In the years after Amy disappeared, Mollie and Kat leaned on each other for support. Several years ago, Mollie was living in Asheville, and Kat came down to stay for a weekend. "We talked about Amy all day," she said. "When it's just the two of us, we can talk about her with an intimacy that only we can understand. It's very therapeutic for me. It's so healing for both of us. Kat is so compassionate. She's been through a lot, and I'm amazed at the grace that she still gives people. I wish I could offer as much grace. We all lost Amy. Sometimes I feel like I lost more than her, that I lost something bigger than just her when she disappeared."

The check came. As I was getting out my credit card, an older man came over to our table. "I like to draw interesting people," he said and then he dropped a piece of paper on our table. It was a sketch, a lovely likeness of me interviewing Mollie. He didn't know what we were talking about, of course. I wonder if he sensed how important that moment was. Is that why he decided to capture it? Whatever reason he had to choose us out of everyone in the restaurant, I'm glad he did. It's something I keep with me as I write this book, a link to someone Amy loved.

"Do you want to go for a ride?" asked Mollie.

Mollie had a Toyota 4Runner, the sort of vehicle you'd expect to find on a safari and not some suburban strip mall outside Richmond. She used it for long road trips across the country. She has an app on her phone that directs her to unused government land where she can camp for the night. She sets up her tent on a platform up top.

I climbed into the passenger seat. Mollie drove us out to Roundhill Drive, where Amy once lived, a quiet street lined with centuries-old oak trees and big homes hidden behind tall hedges. On the corner was the biggest magnolia tree I've ever seen, a monstrous thing looming over a small yard.

"That's my godparents' house," said Mollie. "I grew up climbing that tree. This was a middle-class neighborhood when I lived here. Now these homes go for five hundred thousand, up to a million."

The road ended at a tight cul-de-sac. "Here we are," she said.

We got out, and Mollie led me past the guardrail and down a wide path that brought us to a hidden park. A new brightly-colored playground with slides and shaky walkways was surrounded by wood chips, but back in the '80s the playground was metal and delightfully dangerous. It sat in the center of a groomed square surrounded by woods and a steep hill of bluegrass to one side. When they were teenagers, this is where they would sneak booze. Amy would smoke, too. Mollie has no idea where she got her cigarettes.

This park was a special place for Mollie. I could tell she was thinking back, remembering the good times. Slowly, she led me around the playground to the hill. I had to walk slowly. My ankle was still healing, and I was being cautious without my cane.

"When we broke up, I was in Kentucky," said Mollie. "Amy calls me and tells me that she'd been out drinking and kissed someone. She wanted me to know that it didn't mean anything and only reinforced her feelings for me. She said she was sorry. I was at work, in my office. It was a desk in an open area, no privacy. I thanked her for telling me, but I also said I can't talk about this right now. I told her I think it'll be fine and to give me a week to process. And I meant it. This doesn't really seem like a big deal. I can say that now because I'm fifty years old. But in that moment, I'm twenty-three. We were long-distance, and I was alone. I started to ruminate on it. I've always had a strong visual mind, and I couldn't get the pictures out of my head of her kissing someone else. I had always felt like I loved her more than she loved me—and I know that's not true now—but that's how I felt then, and I thought well, here's proof. And so, I called her back and said, I really thought I could get over it, but I just can't."

Mollie dealt with her emotions by focusing on her job, which was high stress at the time, she said, due to a domineering head coach. It was a rough introduction to the "real world." Mollie didn't know if it could work. Or if it should. But Amy was sure about what she wanted. And what she wanted was Mollie.

"She was reaching out," said Mollie. "I didn't return her calls. So she resorted to writing me letters. She was trying to repair what we had. I think it took all her effort to soften me, because I did come back. I told her, I'm coming to town."

We'd come back around to the 4Runner, and Mollie stopped to greet a woman walking her dog. "I want to show you where we used to swim in the river," she said to me. We got back in, and she drove out to a bridge spanning the James River. She parked on the grass shoulder just before the concrete. There was no walking lane on the bridge, only a narrow strip beside the traffic. There was no protective fencing, either, just a three-foot-tall rail before a fifty-foot plunge into the river, which was broken by large weathered boulders the size of school buses. As we started across, I could feel my anxiety kick into overdrive. I have a problem with heights. I have a compulsion to jump.

The French call it *l'appel du vide*, the call of the void. Maybe you've experienced it. It's that feeling you get when you stand on the edge of a cliff, an intrusive thought that whispers in your ear,

What if? What if you just jump? Psychological studies have been done on this strange phenomenon, but few answers have been discovered, other than the fact that the majority of humans experience these intrusive thoughts at some point in their lives. It seems to have no correlation to action, meaning if you have these thoughts, you are not more likely to commit suicide. Some theorize that it's a subconscious instinct, a way to appreciate living by imagining our demise.

That knowledge provides little comfort, however, when I'm wrapped up in the feeling, when I'm facing the void outright. In those moments the urge is very persuasive.

A few years ago, I was invited to Austin to be interviewed for a documentary about the disappearance of Maura Murray. The production company set me up in a nice hotel. My room was on the twentieth floor or something, and the hotel was designed in such a way that the rooms faced a central open atrium that went all the way up. To get to your room you had to walk down a hallway with a low railing, the only barrier between yourself and a fall that ended in a swan pool twenty stories down. When I got out of the elevator that call to the void was so loud and demanding I had to press myself against the wall across from the drop-off and shimmy my way to my room. I was terrified that my body would act of its own accord and throw me over. It was so loud at that time, I think, because there was a part of me that wanted it, a part of me that had been toying with the idea for a bit. I've come a long way since then. I have no suicidal ideations anymore. And lately, I'd been actively trying to become healthier, to extend my life, to honor that deal with Julie. I want to live.

Still, as we started across that bridge, the void pulled at me.

"Are you okay?" Mollie asked.

"I'm still getting used to my leg," I said.

"Here, take my arm."

I linked my right arm around her left, and I instantly felt better. She was an anchor. She was safe. We continued on. To the passengers in passing cars, we must have looked like an older couple leaving a broken-down car, making our way across the bridge to seek a gas station on the other side.

"We reunited the day before her cruise," said Mollie, picking up where she left off. "I was coming back home for Easter. We made plans to see each other again."

Mollie stopped halfway over the river and pointed along the shore. "Just behind those trees is a rope swing. That's where we would swim when we were kids. But you had to be careful. You couldn't swing out too far because the current is very strong there. If you're not careful, it'll carry you out over the dam."

The dam was not very high, just a man-made waterfall that cut across the river like a brush stroke on a canvas landscape. But the rocks beyond would surely batter you if you went over. Life was more precarious in the '80s. Children still swam in the rapids and played on metal playgrounds. Their parents couldn't track them on cell phones. We lost all that somewhere along the way.

Mollie led me back to the car.

"When Amy went missing, I spoke to Iva a couple times about going down there to help search for her," said Mollie. "But Iva didn't want me to go. I'm not sure if she was being protective or if it was because Amy and I had dated, and she didn't want that coming out."

When we got back into the car Mollie sat behind the wheel, quietly arranging her thoughts. We were progressing from interviewer/interviewee to friends. I could tell she was trying to figure out how open she could be with me.

"I have some survivor's guilt," she said. "I think of the twists and turns of my life and where it took me. Where would Amy be now? We can't know. She hadn't set a course yet. She didn't get to find out. I've been doing some self-repair lately. I am beginning to allow my child side out. The more I let my inner child out to cry, to process this stuff, the better I feel. We want to feel joy, to feel playful, to be free. But you can't have that without the other stuff. To get to the joy, you have to acknowledge the pain."

"I understand that very well," I said.

Mollie nodded. "My therapist suggested I get a stuffed animal. To give something to that child part, so that it feels comforted and secure. I got a little black puppy. It's in my bed now. And it really does help."

Mollie turned on the car and pulled away. She took me to a park by the river called Pony Pasture. It was busy on a Sunday, the parking lot packed with family vans. People carried blankets and coolers to the water. A footpath led us along the shore. Here, the James River is full of eroded boulders and driftwood branches taken further downstream with each new storm. Children played in the warm pools between. A Latin American family cooked lunch on a charcoal grill.

"This is my personal place to chill," said Mollie. "I like to come down here in the mornings sometimes and sit on the rocks and meditate."

I stopped to take a few pictures to remember the moment. It really was a tranquil spot, the sort of place you'd go to write transcendental poetry.

We drove into Richmond next. Along the way, Mollie told me about a prank that Amy had once played on her when they were teenagers. Some of Amy's pranks were quite elaborate.

"One day, we were driving around in my Jeep Cherokee with a couple of our friends. Amy said to me, Mollie, how would you like to make a thousand dollars tonight? She seemed very serious, so I asked her what I would have to do. She said she had met this man downtown, and he had told her that he had some things that he needed to be delivered at a certain time. All she had to do was take a briefcase to an address in the city. A simple delivery job—but we weren't supposed to look inside the case. I didn't want to do it. It all sounded very sketchy to me, of course. But she was persistent, and she drove us out to this street, and we found the briefcase on this rock wall. It's right there, she said. I said it was a hard no. I can't do it."

We had arrived at the same spot. Mollie pointed out the window, and there, atop a rock wall, was a businessman's briefcase beside a discarded fedora.

"It's a statue," said Mollie. "It's art. Apparently someone did the same prank on Amy before. But she had actually tried to take it. And when she grabbed it and ran, it didn't budge and she fell back on her butt."

(If you care to see it, the statue is located at 10th and East Cary on the way into Richmond. It's called "Corporate Presence," and was created by the artist David Phillips in 1985.)

The story struck me as the perfect encapsulation of Mollie and Amy's personalities. Mollie: slow to act, logical. Amy: the risk taker, leaping into adventure.

Soon we entered Richmond proper. Mollie drove to Amy's favorite gay bar, Babe's of Carytown, the oldest LGBTQ-friendly place in the city. Flyers advertised drag shows every Thursday night. This was a safe place for Amy for many years.

"Why do you think Iva is so reluctant to talk about this part of Amy's life?" I asked.

"It has to be a little scary for her," said Mollie. "For twenty-six years, she's presented a certain image of her daughter, the image she wanted for her daughter. And now with this documentary, with your book, it's going to change. That must be very stressful. But this is an important part of Amy's life. It's time for people to know who she really was."

Mollie turned around then and started to drive back to the ShoreDog Café. I still had a million questions, of course, but our time was almost up.

"What do you think happened to Amy?" I asked.

"I don't know," said Mollie. "But something happened a long time ago that gave me some peace. This was in June of 1998. I was driving to South Carolina to work at a basketball camp. I was on the highway by myself in that part of the country where the radio comes in and out. Eventually, the radio went to static—I was beyond anywhere the antenna could reach. I entered a kind of hypnotic state, and there was a feeling like I was outside of time. All I could hear was that static, and then, suddenly, a song came on. No deejay. Just this clear song suddenly coming through the static. I could feel Amy talking to me through that song. She was saying goodbye. I could feel how much she loved me. And I was totally at peace. Then it returned to static, and I slowly came out of that hypnotic state. I was crying, and I remember thinking, *Oh my God, she's gone. She's gone.* And then, thinking, *All right, she's gone. And she's okay.*"

"What song was it?" I asked.

"I want to keep that to myself, if that's all right."

When we returned to the restaurant, Mollie parked beside my car and turned off the engine. Then she reached into the back of the 4Runner and brought out a long carboard box. She lifted the lid to reveal a glass bottle with a note rolled up inside it. Mollie pulled it out and handed it to me.

"This letter is very important to me," she said. "I told you she wrote me letters. This last letter was a message in a bottle. It's the one that worked. It's why I came back just before she left."

Carefully, I unrolled the old letter. It was handwritten in gentle cursive and dated February 24, 1998, exactly one month before Amy disappeared. It's an earnest, heartfelt message from Amy to Mollie, her "final effort," she writes, to win Mollie back. Amy takes responsibility for the mistake she made, and she asks for forgiveness. And at the end, Amy writes: "I feel like there is an ocean between us. Like I am on a desert island waiting for you to rescue me. I miss you, Mollie. Save me, please. Stranded, Amy."

"Thank you for sharing this with me," I said.

Mollie started to cry. It was the sort of exhausted cry that comes from the unburdening of a story, the exorcising of the past. She put her hands on the steering wheel and then placed her head on her hands and sobbed.

I let her cry. Then I said, "Can I put a hand on your back or something?"

Either she was crying too loud to hear or she heard and didn't reply. I sat there quietly. I so very much wanted to offer some comfort, and maybe, if I were a woman, I could have. But this is the world we live in. Men cannot offer comfort without consent. The world is dangerous because of us. We don't dare.

The crying turned to sniffles and then Mollie was wiping her eyes. "I'm sorry," she said.

"No need to apologize."

"Can I ask you a question?" said Mollie. "Do you believe in God?"

My mind flashed on the dream I had the night I was hooked up to the ventilator in the hospital, which is something I should share with you soon. It has some bearing on this question.

"I believe that the universe and God and us, it's all the same thing," I said. "There's this old hippie philosopher, Alan Watts. I think he got it right. He said that we are the aperture of the universe, looking back at itself. We're all connected. We're all the same big thing."

"I feel like something is changing," said Mollie. "You, me, the documentary, all this coming together right now. Why now? Something is happening."

"Yeah, I feel it, too."

"I'd very much like to share some oxygen with you again."

"I would like that very much."

Four days later I received the following text from Iva Bradley: "Due to our existing contractual obligations, Ron, Brad, and I will no longer be able to collaborate with you or provide information to you. We wish you well in this and all your literary endeavors."

Follow up texts and calls were not answered. My biggest fear was realized. The Bradleys had cut me off.

Chapter Twenty-two

ATTACHMENTS

MY WIFE HAS SOME PECULIAR, neuro-spicy habits. When Julie is involved in a complicated task, she whistles to herself. It's never a specific melody, just random musical notes, and she's not completely aware that she's doing it. At night she self-soothes by lying on her arms and twisting her feet around below the covers. This can last for several minutes. She does not attach emotion to criticism. She welcomes it in her job because criticism allows her to improve.

Conversely, when she gives criticism, which is only offered when necessary, she expects it to be accepted with gratitude and is surprised whenever it is met with insecurity or anger. When she's upset, she doesn't display her emotion through tears or argument, she simply stops making eye contact and avoids conversation for a short time. Though, logically, I know that after thirty years as a couple she loves me as I love her, when she does this, I worry. My partner stops looking at me, and I worry that she'll leave. That she's thinking of leaving. Even though I know it's a symptom of her cognitive sparkle, I can't help it. It feeds into my dark delusions, my old battles with self-worth. I know it's temporary and still, sometimes, the timing of an episode is less than ideal.

I was back in Ohio when I got that text from Iva. It destroyed my self-confidence for several days. I was a mix of emotions, some understandable, some not. I felt shame for forcing Iva to confront her missing daughter's sexuality. I felt anger for their betrayal of our agreement. Didn't they know I was too far into the book to call it quits? If they'd only said no thank you when I'd asked months before, I could have found another case. I was in too deep with this one—this story had its hooks in me.

I was also aware that there would be no journalist after me who could step in and write a book of their own. Because of my overstepping, Iva's trust would not easily extend to another reporter, because they surely would uncover the same information I'd already found. Didn't that mean I had some responsibility to finish this project? To share what I'd already gathered, which was significant and already more than had ever existed online? I felt anxiety because I'd been here before. I needed a victim's angry family like I needed a hole in the head. This is what I'd taken such care to avoid.

Is it inevitable? I wondered. Is there any way to write true crime without offending someone?

Mostly, though, I felt sadness and loss. Iva loves hard. She pulls you in, as so many of Amy's friends have said. When you're close, you feel Iva's admiration radiating out of her tiny frame, and it's addicting. When you're cut off from it, the emptiness feels expansive. It hurts.

It's not your job to be their friend. That was the voice of my old editor Pete Kotz, from *Cleveland Scene*. He can still be very loud in my head sometimes.

Every decent journalist I've ever met is living a lonely life.

I'd started to wonder if maybe my preoccupation with needing the subjects of my stories to like me was perhaps a symptom of a greater problem.

These concerns were weighing on my heart one evening when Julie stopped making eye contact. She was behind on some work and stressed with school and responsibilities. I was sitting at the kitchen island, tracking down sources online while she was preparing dinner. The eye-contact thing felt cold. And I was needy.

"Tell me you like me," I said.

"I like you."

"Yeah, but do you?"

"James," she said with a sigh. "You know I do. Just give me a couple minutes. Danielle is coming over. I need to focus."

Danielle comes over once a week for voice lessons. She wants to sing better for her church choir, so she found Julie's name through a friend, and they've been meeting like this for a while. Danielle has issues with men—she was involved in a terrible assault a few years back. So when she comes over, I hide out in my office above the garage. Danielle is also a working therapist, and I guess they got to talking, because I got a text from Julie that day, asking me to come down. Danielle wanted to talk to me.

They were sitting in the music room, on the couch by the piano, sharing a bottle of wine when I found them.

"Tell him what you told me," Julie prompted.

"I think you might have an attachment disorder," said Danielle.

"Yeah?"

"I know I'm not your therapist, but I have experience with this. Julie told me about the way you react to her when she unmasks. Do you think maybe it could be an attachment disorder? It's very common in people who dealt with childhood trauma."

Danielle knew about the subject of the last book I'd written—a memoir about how my parents split when I was three, and I was sent to live with my father and an abusive stepmother. There's more to it, a lot more, but that's the crux of it.

"Hmm," I said, sitting in a chair across from her.

"Why do you forget that Julie won't leave you when she stops making eye contact? Maybe it reminds you of how you felt as a kid, having to be tuned in to your parents' moods, to avoid conflict?"

Julie leaned forward. "It also might explain why it's so important to you to be liked by the Bradleys," she said.

I nodded. "Interesting," I said. "Let me think on it."

I went to Sky first. She was convenient, and I could trust her to keep my secrets.

"Hey, Sky," I said into my phone. "Somebody told me that I might have an attachment disorder. Could you explain what they might've meant by that?"

"Sure, James," she replied. "In the psychological world, 'attachment disorder' refers to the difficulties in forming emotional bonds and relationships with others. It can develop from early childhood experiences, like inconsistent caregiving or trauma. People with attachment issues might struggle with trust, intimacy, or managing emotions."

"Based on the conversations we've had, do you think it's possible I have an attachment disorder?"

"Well, James, I'm not equipped to make that kind of diagnosis. Our chats are more about mysterious crimes than deep dives into your psyche. If you're feeling like there's something to explore there, a chat with a mental health professional might be a good idea."

I put the question to Dr. Deb at our next session.

Her office is cozy and warm, a safe place, with framed anecdotes on self-care, and tactile toys on the coffee table for her younger clients. Kinetic sand, stress balls.

"Picture yourself as a child," she said. "Toothless and naked. Remember that you were loved enough. Sometimes, we think about our parents and what they could have done differently for us, but they were doing the best they could at the time. Just like we are. When you were a child, you didn't have the security you do now. And that child is still inside you, being anxious. Even though the people who love you aren't leaving, that child part of you is still afraid they will. But you can acknowledge that child and reassure him. You should think about finding a photograph of you as a boy, something you can put out on your bedside stand and look at in the morning. Just to reassure him that he's loved and secure."

"I can do that," I said.

"What makes you feel secure? What can you picture in your mind in moments like this?"

"There's one thing, but it's weird and definitely a little Freudian."

"Tell me."

"Sometimes I imagine what heaven would be like," I said. "Like, if we get to go someplace that is just safe and happy at the end of everything, what that would be like. I have this image of a cottage surrounded by overgrown flowers and grass. When I find it, I know it's my mother's cottage, and she's always inside, waiting for me. Except we're the same age. We're both children when we find each other again and we play all day. Just play together. I used to think about that, and it always made me feel secure."

Yeah, there might be something to this attachment disorder thing, after all, I thought.

"I like that a lot," said Dr. Deb. "I want you to also think about this: What exactly do your parents owe you? Nothing. Maybe they owe you nothing more than pulling you into this dimension. Maybe that was enough."

"I'll try the picture thing," I said.

When I got home, I went through the giant Tupperware bins in the back of the basement storage closet, beside the skeleton we put out for Halloween every year. One container holds all the photos my mother gave me when I got married. She kept several albums from the years she was with my father. I found a photograph that shows a table covered in harvested marijuana. I kept going. Then I found a picture of me from when I was around three years old, a toddler with a big round head of blond hair. I set it on the credenza by my side of the bed. In the mornings, I glanced at the boy and whispered, "It's all good. You're doing fine." And you know what? It helped.

The sense of abandonment I felt in the wake of Iva's ghosting me was quite powerful. It helped me realize that the emotions it triggered come more from my own hangups than any imagined ill intention on the part of the Bradleys. I also understand why Iva is mistrusting of my intentions. The families of missing women are common targets of hucksters, opportunists, and con men. The Bradleys have encountered a few. The worst, by far, was a man named Frank Jones.

PART THREE

DIRTY, ROTTEN SCOUNDRELS

Chapter Twenty-three

HIGH NOON IN CURAÇAO

I AM FASCINATED BY CON MEN, people like Frank Abagnale, that guy from Spielberg's *Catch Me If You Can*. As a young man, Abagnale was a skilled grifter who at various times pretended to be an attorney, a doctor, and a Pan Am pilot while writing bad checks in order to fund his worldwide misadventures. I love the film *Paper Moon* and the bible-selling racket run by Moze and Addie. I've watched every adaptation inspired by the life of Elizabeth Holmes, the former Silicon Valley wunderkind who promised to revolutionize the field of medicine with fictitious technology in countless interviews where even the timbre of her voice was carefully crafted.

When I hear these stories, I'm always left with the same question—what was their endgame? These people knew they were committing crimes. They had to know, on some level, that one day it would all catch up to them. Think of the stress these people must feel constantly, waiting for the feds to bust through their apartment door. I feel panicked after a traffic ticket, when I have a simple fine hanging over my head.

It has to be some sort of delusion, right? An illogical, unexamined, and dangerous belief that the truth they tell themselves is more real than reality. Otherwise, how does a person avoid the smothering stress of their inevitable fall?

Maybe the answer can be found in the movie *Children of Men*, when Clive Owen's character visits his friend Nigel, who is hoarding priceless art and living his best life as the world falls apart outside his window. "What keeps you going?" asks Clive, to which Nigel replies, "I just don't think about it."

I think about it, though. I think about that paradox when I think about Frank Jones. By the time he was arrested on February 7, 2002, he'd conned the Bradley family and their supporters out of more than $200,000 by promising them that he would bring Amy home. He knew it was all a lie. How did he think it would end?

How it began is easier to explain. It started with a tip from a cook in Curaçao.

The cook's name was Judith Margaritha. A year or so after Amy went missing, Judith contacted the Bradleys with an incredible story. Amy was alive, she said, but maybe not for long. According to Judith, Amy was being held at a compound in Willemstad that was guarded twenty-four hours a day by armed Colombians. Sometimes, her captors would allow Amy to go into town with an escort. Judith saw her at a Pizza Hut one day.

The story was hard to believe, but Judith provided some circumstantial proof that went a long way to convincing the Bradleys that it was true—she accurately described Amy's tattoos, for one thing. What clinched it for Iva was when Judith hummed a lullaby she'd heard Amy singing. It was the same lullaby that Iva had sung to her as a child, one that Iva had made up. It began like this: "Amy Lynn is the best little girl in the whole wide world . . ."

The tip confirmed to the Bradleys what they had always felt in their hearts: Amy was alive. If she had gotten caught up in some criminal enterprise, used for God knows what, they needed to rescue her and fast. But raiding an armed compound in a foreign country was a bit outside the scope of the FBI. What the Bradleys needed were private mercenaries.

The Bradleys had enlisted the help of a private investigator, and though the exact details are foggy after so many years, that PI introduced them to the sort of hero they were searching for, an ex-special forces commando and expert in hostage negotiations, Frank V. Jones Jr.

According to court documents, on August 2, 1999, Jones officially offered his services to the Bradleys. He explained to them that he was experienced in the field of locating missing persons and rescuing people from captivity, providing them with a detailed and impressive résumé. He and his team were available for a small fee.

Meanwhile, Judith continued to provide real-time updates. She told Iva that she'd recently seen Amy tied to a tree at the compound. Each day Amy remained captive was another day of unimaginable torture. Who knows what else they had subjected her to? The Bradleys couldn't afford to wait.

In September that year, Jones sent the Bradleys an estimate for a rescue mission. He needed $24,444 to get his team to Curaçao and back with Amy. The Bradleys wired him the cash on September 28. Jones promptly departed for the Caribbean.

They heard back from Jones on October 5, when he sent them his "After Action Report." It explained that Jones had sent two teams to Curaçao, a Search and Rescue team and a separate "Extraction" team of ex-commandos. The men had spotted and identified Amy at the compound but were unable to get her out because the Colombian security guards had opened fire on them. A couple of his men were wounded in the battle, and several of Amy's captors were killed before the commandos were forced to retreat.

After this message, Jones sent the Bradleys a second document, this one titled "Final Estimate (SAR-EP Project)," outlining his new plan to send another eight-man team to Curaçao to retrieve Amy before she could be moved. Due to the danger of the mission, they now needed $86,416.

That was more money than the Bradleys had. They had burned through their savings on the first attempt. Luckily, they knew a famous benefactor with limitless funds who was eager to help, the billionaire owner of the Tampa Bay Lightning, Art Williams.

Williams came from the world of insurance. He made his fortune by recognizing a unique opportunity earlier than others. Back in the '60s, most people had what's called whole life insurance, which comes with high premiums but has cash value. When Williams's father died unexpectedly, his family discovered they were underinsured even with their whole life insurance. There had to be a better way to protect your loved ones.

Five years later, Williams learned about a new product, term life insurance. Term life comes with much cheaper premiums but has no cash value. Williams realized that clients could mitigate risk even more by investing that difference in the stock market. In 1977, he formed A. L. Williams & Associates, which provided both insurance and investing under one roof. His company later became a part of Primerica, which has been criticized for being a multilevel marketing business, where agents are financially rewarded for recruiting more agents. Iva had met Williams through the world of insurance some years ago.

When Williams learned of the Bradleys' tragedy, he donated six figures to a nonprofit called the Nation's Missing Children Organization of Phoenix, money that was specifically earmarked for Amy Bradley's case. The person in charge of disbursements at NMCO agreed to use some of that money to fund Jones's mission. She sent Jones two checks. One for $40,036 and one for $46,379.

On October 31st, Halloween night, Jones told the Bradleys that he was departing with three of his team members for Curaçao, where they would be joined by an Extraction team. Nothing came of that mission, either. The Bradleys hopes were dashed again.

In the months that followed, Jones continued to ask the Bradleys for more money. He was preparing new teams to go down to the island. Surely, this time they would rescue her. But the Bradleys were growing suspicious. Before they sent Jones another dollar, they needed proof of life.

On June 27, 2000, Jones sent the Bradleys two photographs. Both showed a woman and a blond-haired man on a beach. The woman was sitting with her back turned to the camera, but her figure resembled Amy's. More important, the photograph showed the tattoo of the Tasmanian Devil spinning a basketball on Amy's shoulder. Iva knew it was Amy, after all.

A week later, Jones sent a new estimate for his final mission. The price tag: $206,059. Nobody could meet his latest demands, but they were able to talk Jones down to the discount price of $100,000, more money from Art Williams that the missing children's organization wired to Jones's bank account.

It was around this time that the man in charge of Williams's charitable foundation, James Kelly, began digging into Jones's story. They'd now paid out around $200,000 with nothing to show for it. Kelly mentioned his concerns to his friend, Dan Weddle, who worked at Bankers Trust, facilitating loans. It just so happened that Weddle knew some Special Forces guys. He was helping them set up a new security firm. As a favor, Weddle asked his contacts to check out Frank Jones. Ex-Special Forces are an elite fraternal group—everyone kind of knows one another either directly or by reputation. When Weddle's crew asked around, nobody had heard of Frank Jones.

"I told Jim that these things we're hearing back do not pass the smell test," Weddle recalled when we spoke by phone.

Kelly knew that some of Jones's team were already being staged at a hotel in Miami, preparing for a return trip to Curaçao. He asked Weddle to send one of his men down to verify that they were legit. So, Weddle sent a man to Florida, where he met with two members of Jones's crew. They were, indeed, Special Forces, but Jones, himself, was not there.

"I got back to Jim and told him, these guys are real, but that's all we know."

And so, the plan continued, though Weddle remained suspicious.

When the Bradleys heard from Jones again, he told them to fly to Florida and wait for him to bring Amy to them. It was time. The Bradleys were overjoyed but worried. It was a dangerous mission. Could Jones really rescue Amy without anyone else being killed?

They rented a hotel room. Iva remained by the phone, only leaving the room twice in the week they were there. Mike McCord, Ron's boss, had his Lear jet parked, fueled, and waiting nearby to bring Amy home.

This time, Weddle insisted that one of his men join Jones's team in Curaçao. He sent Timothy Buckholz, a former sniper with the Army's 7th Special Forces Group, also known as the "Devil's Brigade," who served from 1979 to 1992. The 7th SFG deals in unconventional warfare, special reconnaissance, direct action, and counterterrorism among other things. In the '80s, the 7th SFG trained the armed forces of many pro-democracy Central American countries. Buckholz has a commanding presence on paper and in person. He looks a bit like Dog the Bounty Hunter but has the mind of Jack Ryan.

Buckholz arrived in Curaçao, ready and willing to follow Jones into battle. He was surprised to find Jones at the bar, sipping rum. And he talked funny. When two Special Forces guys get together, their conversation quickly slides into military jargon that only they will understand. Jones didn't talk like Special Forces.

"Ten minutes after I met him, I knew something was off about this guy," Buckholz recalled during a phone call from his isolated homestead in North Carolina, where he lives on the edge of a pond with three lazy dogs. "I was like, ain't no way this Pillsbury Doughboy–looking guy was Special Forces."

When Buckholz overheard Jones speaking with Iva over the phone, he knew his suspicions were correct. Jones told Iva that his teams were in place, but Buckholz knew that they were just eating pizza at the bar. Nothing was happening. When Buckholz went to surveil the supposed Colombian compound, he found a local family living there.

He called Iva and broke the news—Jones was a con man.

Buckholz was pissed. It wasn't just the stolen valor, it was the way this man was preying on a desperate family, taking their money to hang out on the island and feel important. So Buckholz sent the local police a tip that Jones had smuggled a shotgun onto Curaçao. Jones was arrested and put in jail.

He confronted Judith Margaritha as well. "She met me on the bridge down there," he said. "I came so close to throwing her over." When Judith started in with another story about how she'd visited with Amy and Amy had cried on her shoulder, he told her to give him the shirt so they could test it for DNA. After that, she stopped talking. "Judith knew she was busted. Everything's a lie with her. And Jones. If they're talking, they're lying."

While Buckholz waited to return to the States, he got to know one of the members of Jones's erstwhile commando unit quite well. The young man's name was Jono Senk. Eventually, Jono admitted to Buckholz that he had helped Jones fake Amy's proof of life. The woman in the photograph was his girlfriend. They'd used temporary tattoos to fool the Bradleys into believing it was their daughter.

"Jones knew what to get from the Bradleys to convince them their daughter was alive," said Weddle. "He'd ask about the tattoos. He'd ask Iva what's something only you and Amy would know. That's how Judith learned about the lullaby, I'm sure. He was a scam artist."

"The saddest part of the whole thing was when I called Iva to tell her about the picture," said Buckholz. "I think she fell on the floor or something. I could hear Ron in the background helping her."

Looking back on it twenty-six years later, Buckholz believes most of the blame should rest on the cook, Judith. She got about $8,000 from the Bradleys for her tips. "I think Judith was pushing everything," he said. "I can't even tell you Frank didn't believe her. Maybe Judith was conning Frank and Frank was conning the Bradleys. I don't know what his endgame was. He had to know it would fall apart when my agency got involved. He's not a smart person."

Eventually, Buckholz and Jono returned stateside. As soon as their flight landed, they were pulled off by the FBI and interrogated for hours. The information they provided to the feds formed the basis of the case they built against Frank Jones. By the time of his arrest in 2002, Jones knew he was going down. But that didn't stop him from conning more people in the meantime.

Chapter Twenty-four

UNDERSTANDING FRANK JONES

I'M NOT SURE how Frank Jones made it out of that jail in Curaçao or what happened to the charges against him for bringing a shotgun onto the island. Public records requests mean squat in the Caribbean. FOIA? Never heard of it. But Jones was arrested in the States on February 7, 2002, and charged with Mail Fraud, a Class-D felony that carried a potential sentence of five years in prison and a $250,000 fine. That was a Thursday. He remained behind bars until the following Tuesday, which was also his forty-second birthday, when he was released on personal recognizance under the custody of his mother, Alice.

Jones had wanted the court to name his father as his custodian while awaiting trial. U.S. Magistrate Judge David G. Lowe, who presided over his hearing, thought that might be another trick. "The evidence I have heard convinced me this man is a scoundrel," Judge Lowe was quoted as saying. "But I think in every man there is that one vestige left—he's not going to betray his mother."

It didn't take Jones long to realize the feds had him dead-to-rights. His lawyer began to negotiate a deal for a guilty plea. As part of the process, Jones went through a presentencing investigation, which provided some concrete facts about who Jones really was. His ex-wife kept a copy of it, which eventually found its way to me.

It's not often we get such insight into the formative years of a famous con man.

Jones was born on February 12, 1960, the oldest of three children. His mother was very religious, and the kids were raised in the Baptist church. That's fire-and-brimstone religion. His father was in the Army and did two tours in Vietnam and one in Korea. Because of this, when he was a kid, Jones moved constantly. His father was transferred from Fort Bragg to Fort Benning to Fort Hood. Eventually, around the time Jones entered high school, his dad got a staff position, and the family settled in Hinesville, Georgia.

Jones was a curious young man, the type who read encyclopedias for fun. But he didn't apply himself in school. He graduated in 1978 with a B– average, 147th in a class of 322.

The résumé that Jones provided to the Bradleys listed a degree in political science from the Citadel, a degree in finance from the University of North Carolina, and a master's in business administration from Emory University. It was all bullshit. In reality, Jones obtained a bachelor's degree in business admin from Georgia Southern University, in 1984.

Jones was part of the ROTC in college and joined the Army Reserves in 1982. In an interview with the *Richmond Times-Dispatch*, the lead FBI agent on the case said that nothing in Jones's record indicated Special Forces experience. He was simply a staff officer in a smoke-generating unit. In 1994, Jones filed a disability claim with the Department of Veteran Affairs, claiming that he'd suffered back strain after lifting three hundred pounds during a training exercise. He failed to appear for a scheduled exam, though. In 1997, an adjudications officer decided that his injury was less than ten percent disabling, which placed him under the threshold for any sort of financial support through the VA.

In 1986, Jones married Melinda Ford. They had two sons and divorced in 1993 due to irreconcilable differences. During the time they were married, Jones continued to inflate his military experience in newsletters published by consulting groups like the George S. May International Company, in which his bio reads: "Among his military qualifications are special forces officer, ranger, master parachutist, pathfinder and graduate of assault schools. Frank was also recipient of the special forces outstanding company commander of the year award."

His actual work history reads more like Willy Loman than James Bond. Rather than clandestine missions to foreign countries to rescue kidnapped victims, his real résumé shows that Jones was selling independent financing for auto loans. Jones listed Farmer Automotive Group, out of Louisville, Kentucky, as a former employer, but when an FBI agent reached out to them, the human resources director stated, "Due to the fact that he never turned any sales in, our company never paid him anything . . . We are not even sure that he was actually doing what we had hired him to do."

The Bradleys are not the only victims named in the case files. While the fictitious search for Amy Bradley was in play, Jones was also conning a woman named Susan Lukins out of $197,000. Jones had met Lukins in an Internet chat room in 2000, and they carried on a romance via email and phone. One day, Jones reached out to Lukins with a business opportunity. He told her that he was creating his own security firm, ODC Consulting, which would provide special ops training and surveillance. He knew that Lukins was going through a divorce at the time and would have access to a settlement soon. She sent Jones $60,000 in October 2000 and another $85,000 nine months later. In 2001, Jones asked for more money so that he could train the Colombian police force. She sent him another $52,000. He agreed to pay the loan back by March 2002.

On the surface, ODC Consulting appeared to be legit, with an office in Las Vegas. But during the investigation that came later, it was determined that the Vegas location was a ruse and actually the address of a mail-forwarding business. Perhaps Jones was planning to use the money he conned out of the Bradleys to pay off his debt to Lukins. But he was arrested first.

Before Jones was released, the judge warned him not to contact any of the witnesses in the case. But there was never a rule that Jones didn't like to break. He had another girlfriend of his reach out to Lukins via email. When that got back to the judge, Jones's bond was revoked, and he was sent back to jail.

Financial records show that Jones was essentially destitute by then, in debt with credit cards companies and unable to pay back a $325,000 loan he'd received from his father, who was funding his monthly living expenses.

Jones was sentenced in August. "No one could have made a more studied effort to create more devastation in the lives of three families," said U.S. District Judge Richard L. Williams that day.

"There's absolutely no way that I could express how sorry I am for what I did," Jones said. "When this thing started, my group and I had the best intentions. I got caught up in it. and it got out of control."

The judge sentenced Jones to five years in prison and ordered him to repay every penny he'd taken from the Bradleys, the non-profit that helped them, and Ms. Lukins, a total calculated to be $408,360.

"I got rid of him shortly before all this happened," said Melinda, Jones's ex-wife, over coffee one afternoon. After some back and forth, she'd agreed to meet up and bring along the files she'd kept on the matter. She has a new life, with a new husband, and doesn't want her location known, out of a lingering fear and anxiety related to her ex.

Melinda met Jones when she was nineteen. At the time, he had a job at a Ford Motor credit company where she worked, filing paperwork. He was the best-dressed man in the office, and he'd leave notes for her on her desk. Her parents were not pleased. Her father never liked him. Soon, Melinda was pregnant, and so, they got married. For their honeymoon, he took her to Jamaica, where she claims she saw him buy cocaine, one of the first major red flags in the new relationship.

Their marriage lasted seven years. At first, he seemed like a decent guy. He was a Green Beret, he told her. His parents loved her. "They were so happy," she said. "They thanked me for changing him." Jones had apparently been in trouble as a kid. She'd heard that he had once tried to sell some fake drugs. "I was happily married," she said. "I loved the guy. I don't really know what happened. He started acting weird."

It started around the time their first child was delivered by emergency C-section at thirty weeks and died at seventeen days. After that, Jones grew distant.

Sometime later, Melinda got a job as a nurse at a hospital near their home in Georgia. One day, a young couple brought their sick baby in for an exam. Jones visited Melinda at the hospital that day and later the baby's parents told her that he'd stolen from them. "He stole stuff. Money," Melinda said.

Jones also targeted Melinda's parents, asking them to invest in a giant golf course that didn't yet exist. "I told them don't do it," she said. "By then, I knew he wasn't normal."

Melinda would drive Jones to Reserves training every month. Sometimes, Jones would return with explosives in his duffel bag. She kept photographs of these, which she also shared with me. Many, but not all, can be identified as M115A2 Ground Burst Projectile Simulators, which are used in training to create the sounds of active battle.

They divorced in 1993. According to Melinda, he has not kept in touch with their children. "He has not shown any interest in them," she said. "He doesn't have feelings like you and me."

Jones married a woman named Amanda in 1994, when she would have been about twenty years old. By that time, Jones was about forty-four. They had two children. They made an interesting pair—not long after Jones was arrested for Mail Fraud, Amanda was charged with having sex with a minor at a club in Fulton County. A judge acquitted her at trial, because the state could not prove that Amanda knew the girl was a juvenile prior to committing the sex act on stage.

Melinda follows developments in the Amy Bradley mystery from afar. She holds some guilt for not contacting the Bradleys when she learned that her ex-husband was working with them, but she wanted to keep some distance from a man she believed could be quite dangerous. "I feel so heartbroken," said Melinda. "I knew he was lying before he was arrested. Why couldn't I have told them, 'Don't trust him, he's a shit.' I feel horrible for that family. He's a con man."

Jones has been out of prison for a long while now. He still resides in Georgia and is rumored to have worked at places like the local Goodwill. According to Melinda, he owes around $20,000 in back child support. I called his cell phone one day, and he picked up. The conversation was brief. I told him I was working on this book. He told me that his record had been expunged (it has not), and he has security code clearance again (he does not). He said he would think about sitting for a formal interview, but he never answered my calls after that.

However, I did manage to interview one of his erstwhile commandos, that guy with the name out of some *Star Wars* movie, Jono Senk.

Chapter Twenty-five

THE TRUTH WILL SET YOU FREE

THIS IS THE FIFTH BOOK I've written about an unsolved true crime case. I've never had to work harder. This story is filled with reluctant witnesses, disgruntled FBI agents, secret lovers, and a family that is protective of an incomplete narrative. Nobody involved has conducted themselves with perfect grace. And that's not necessarily an indictment. If Amy had been my friend or child, I'm sure I would have acted in a similar fashion. But speaking from the perspective of a journalist tasked with uncovering the truth at the heart of the matter, this book was damned tricky. Jono Senk was no exception.

When I first reached out to Jono, he declined to be interviewed. He'd been burned by a *Primetime Live* episode about Amy's disappearance. He'd agreed to be interviewed for the show to tell his side of the story, but in the end, he felt all they did was make him, in his words, look like a piece of shit. That story hurt his reputation. People still dig it up to make him look bad on the Internet.

I didn't push. We spoke a couple times off the record. At some point, he decided to trust me. Some may call that a slow seduction. I prefer to view it as building a legitimate friendship. Maybe it's something in between. Anyway, one day he agreed to speak with me on a video call.

He logged on from his parents' house. On the wall behind him, under the floral-print molding, was a painting of George Washington standing in front of the original American flag. A leather jacket full of military patches hung from the back of his chair. Jono appeared in a button-up short-sleeve shirt, open at the top. A puka necklace jangled against his chest.

We started with his background. Like Frank Jones, Jono moved around a lot as a kid. He was born in Camden, New Jersey. His father was a sales rep who had served in the Korean War. His mother was half Oglala Lakota and can trace her lineage back to Chief Crazy Horse. She worked as a nurse. They moved from Camden to Asheville, North Carolina, to Columbia, Missouri (which he calls Columbia, Misery), and eventually, to Atlanta. As a teen, Jono worked odd jobs around the neighborhood for spending money.

"I was always cutting lawns or shoveling snow," he said.

In 1983, he signed with an Army recruiter. His father suggested that enlistment would be the best decision of his life. He was assigned to the 101st Airborne Division and then served with the 3rd Ranger Battalion of the 75th Ranger Regiment and the 5th Ranger Training Battalion Ranger School.

"When I graduated from RIP (the Ranger Indoctrination Program) and got my black ranger beret, that was probably the best day of my life," he said. "I felt like a cobra ready to strike. I wanted to go to combat. I wanted to test my mettle."

When he got to the 101st, it was nothing like he'd imagined. The leadership was toxic, he said. "I was a real screwup there. I got into so much trouble. But only because I was bored."

The Rangers was a better fit, but this was at a time where there wasn't much need to send them into combat. He served for three years, then went home, still untested. He wasn't sure what to do. Home was boring, too. Now that he was properly trained, he felt driven to do something important with his life.

"Once you take a cucumber and pickle it, you can't turn it back into a cucumber," he said.

He enrolled at the local college and took classes to become a paramedic. But at night, he often found himself trolling frat parties, looking for fights. Before long, Jono dropped out of school. He joined a dojo where he trained in tae kwon do, aikido, and jiu-jitsu. He worked part time as a bouncer. Anything to get a hit of that excitement he'd first tasted in the Rangers.

Then one day he caught a new show on TV called *Eco-Challenge*. It introduced Jono to the world of adventure racing, where players compete to finish a grueling wilderness obstacle course that can involve mountain climbing, white water rafting, and kayaking, among other things. "I was like, yeah, this is the kind of stuff we did in the Rangers," said Jono. "It's about finding your limits and crushing them. Adventure racing was like mainlining heroin for me. I found that fix again when I was rappelling down waterfalls and mountain biking."

Jono threw himself into the adventure racing subculture and befriended the organizer of the Endorphin Fix competition, a two-day race, covering 130 miles along the New River Gorge in West Virginia, which is known as the toughest race in the country. That friend suggested that Jono set up a business of his own back in Georgia. Jono took his advice and created Harry Scary Evolutions, a company that trains ordinary people in the skills needed to succeed in adventure racing. Over time, his company has grown to include corporate excursions and youth leadership programs. He even came up with his own self-help philosophy, a system called EDGE, which stands for "Evaluate, Decide, Go, Evolve."

"It blew up big-time down here," said Jono.

As Jono got deeper into this new world of extreme adventure, he was introduced to other men living on the edge. Jono had signed up for a ninjutsu class. During the first lesson, he found himself wondering if the instructor actually knew any ninjutsu. The stuff he was teaching seemed like entry-level karate.

"I kept going because I'd already paid my money upfront," said Jono. "But in my gut, I didn't feel like he was teaching from any experience."

That instructor, Frank Jones, took a special interest in Jono and started talking to him after class. Jones told him that he was a retired colonel from SOCOM, the United States Special Operations Command and, like some real-life Nick Fury, he was putting together a special team. "He told me that he was into all this security stuff, protecting rich executives. I thought I could hitch my wagon to his and see what happened."

At the beginning, they had some legitimate jobs. Jono worked security for VIP parties in the Atlanta area. At one gig, he escorted an executive from Hawaii on a trip. Jono discovered he was good at this. He could see a threat before it became a threat.

"I have this sixth sense, kind of like precognition," he explained. "I know what's about to go down before it goes down. My buddy said, you're an empath and can pick up changes in the electromagnetic spectrum. I was like, whoa, okay, Jedi master."

For a while the money was good. For Jono, though, it wasn't about the money, which came and went, and provided no excitement of its own. The job scratched his adrenaline itch. Jones had given him the opportunity to finally apply his skills, to be the action hero he'd always wanted to be.

"Jones was like my handler," said Jono. "I was going to all of these cool places, where I might save someone's life. It was what I was looking for."

Jones really wanted to get his firm involved in kidnapping cases. It started as an idea at first, but soon it was all Jones was talking about. Jono was in the middle of an adventure race when Jones contacted him about the Amy Bradley disappearance. He asked Jono if he knew anyone they could trust. Jono recommended two men, from the adventure race crew, who were former SEAL team members. Soon, Jones and the two men were flying down to Curaçao to do site recon work.

"I wasn't balls-to-the-wall into doing this," said Jono. "I wasn't trying to get into this. But I thought maybe we could bring Amy home."

When Jones returned, he fed Jono the same fictional narrative he was feeding the Bradleys, Amy was being held by Colombian mercenaries at a compound in Willemstad. It was up to the team to get her out.

But the Bradleys needed proof that Amy was alive before they would agree to fund any further expeditions. That's when they came up with the idea to fake the proof of life. In Jono's mind, the ends would justify the means. They knew Amy was alive, and if this was what everyone needed to get back to the island and bring her home, wasn't it all in service of a greater good?

"I didn't feel I was being maliciously deceptive," said Jono. "I tell you that wholeheartedly. I felt that what we were doing was righteous."

They staged the photographs on a beach in Pensacola—Frank, Jono, and Jono's girlfriend. Jono stopped at a local Walmart, where he purchased the blond wig that he wore for his bad guy costume. He took his girlfriend to a tattoo parlor, where they were able to add temporary ink to her skin to mimic Amy's tattoos. Then they went down to the beach, and Jones staged the photos to obscure the woman's face with a big sun hat.

Imagine Jono's surprise when he discovered that Jones had manipulated him, too.

"He finds these victims like he found me," said Jones. "He finds out what they want. The Bradleys wanted Amy back. I wanted to get back into the game. It was all very appealing to me."

The fallout from the whole misadventure follows Jono to this day. After *Primetime* made his name public, he's been the target of online harassment by armchair sleuths. Sometimes, a woman he's dating will google his name and break it off after reading what's out there. It has made his life hard.

Nowadays he pays penance by taking care of his ailing parents. His dad is ninety years old; his mother is eighty-six.

"Taking care of my mother allowed me to realize how to be bigger, badder, bolder, stronger, faster," he said. As he researched how to better help her, he learned about the benefits of nootropics and how to naturally elevate brain cognition. He's on a mission to improve himself as much as he can, one day at time. "I don't want to diminish like my parents. I want to stay Peter Pan as long as I can."

So far so good.

Chapter Twenty-six

THE CARIBBEAN KING OF FLESH

On the official Amy Bradley website, readers will find a page titled "Wall of Shame." Frank Jones is featured prominently, of course. So is Alexis Zaglanitis, the former proprietor of Affordable Adult Vacations, a sex-tourism business that operated a legal brothel on Margarita Island for many years.

In 2004, a photograph appeared on his website featuring an escort named Jas who closely resembled Amy Bradley. This, to me, is the most important clue in the entire case. It lends credibility to the otherwise outrageous theory that Amy was taken off the boat and forced into a Caribbean human trafficking ring, the only real hope that she is still alive. Either Jas is Amy, or she isn't. And if she isn't Amy, then Amy is almost certainly deceased.

I would soon devote many hours trying to finding Jas. But first, I did my best to understand the machinations of Affordable Adult Vacations and Alexis Zaglanitis himself.

Born in the Argolidas region of Greece in 1953, Georgios Alexandros Zaglanitis served in the Greek military before immigrating to Canada, where he taught classes in hospitality at a local college. Alexis, as he was called, got into the sex tourism business in 1986, when he launched Caribbean Fantasy Tours, offering fine women to anyone willing to make the journey. It's hard to find details about Alexis's operations prior to the Internet, but by 2003, when his websites appeared, he was operating as Affordable Adult Vacations and running girls out of his own private lodge, the Villas Las Morenas, in the lovely beach resort area, called Playa El Agua, of Venezuela's Margarita Island.

The largest island of the Venezuelan state of Nueva Esparta, it is home to its capital city, La Asunción. Christopher Columbus anchored there in 1498, and his men helped themselves to the island's pearls as tribute to the Spanish Crown. Today, the Margariteños are a mix of many cultures, native and imperial—Spanish, Dutch, Swedish, Chinese, even descendants of West African slaves. Most are Catholic, but in recent years, as in the States, the popularity of evangelical Christian churches has increased.

Along the southern coast are two hills called the Tetas de María Guevara, or "María Guevara's breasts." According to local legend, María Guevara was a mestiza (mixed race) woman who fought in Venezuela's War of Independence in the early nineteenth century and who breast-fed her two sons into adulthood, making them great warriors for the cause. Her magic breast milk was so revered, she was called to the front lines to provide sustenance to soldiers heading into battle. When she died, the very land mourned, and the Earth created the twin hills to honor her contributions. For many reasons, Margarita Island was a logical choice for Alexis's business. It didn't hurt that prostitution is legal in Venezuela and was unregulated in the 1980s.

At the height of Alexis's smut empire in the early aughts, he harnessed the power of the Internet to attract customers to Margarita Island from all over the world. He created several websites and message boards where he wrote prolifically about his brothels, the escorts he provided, and what services you could buy. The sites are long gone. However, most were catalogued by the Wayback Machine and those archives can still be accessed today. Diving into Alexis's interconnected sites is a quest through a labyrinth of text-heavy pages and photographs of naked bronze-skinned young women.

A one-week stay at the Villas Las Morenas, which translates to "villa of the brunettes," cost $2,750, an all-inclusive package that included free airport pickup, meals, drinks at the private bar, private car and driver, a one-day yacht cruise, snorkeling, and unlimited access to the escort of your choosing. The resort was secluded behind coconut palms, just feet from the beach. Satisfaction was guaranteed. If your escort did not perform to your liking, you could "swap" her out for another the following day. On the message boards, former guests recommended newbies try a "six-pack," their term for choosing a different girl each night of their vacation.

Alexis also had a loyalty rewards program. On their fifth visit, return visitors earned twenty-five percent off and a second escort for free.

The escorts who stayed at the Villas Las Morenas can still be viewed in the archived galleries, organized by first name only. There are no white women. Nearly all of them are from Venezuela. However, Alexis also advertised visiting escorts whom he would invite to the villa for shorter stays. This is the section where Jas appears, along with other Caucasian women. Here's a post from the website that I found interesting. "We require that [the visiting escorts] become free members of Adult Friend Finder and post their pictures. Please send us their I.D. or handle as it is called and you can have the opportunity to spend a full day and night with them, while visiting our resort at no extra charge. They are all listed in the North American section."

If Jas is Amy, that meant that back in 2004, she would have also had an account on Adult Friend Finder, a website that still exists to this day, though back then it was a basic site, organized by text categories similar to Craigslist. Unless Alexis made exceptions, Jas would have been listed as a North American escort, who would visit the island for two-to-three day stretches.

Alexis was so sure that his guests would enjoy their stays, he offered a "try it first guarantee." The website explicitly stated: "We are prepared to forgo any payment or deposit until you have experienced our services for a full day and night. If you are not satisfied and want to leave there is absolutely no charge, no catch, no questions asked."

A few photographs of Alexis appear on the Affordable Adult Vacations site. Taken around 2008, they show a tanned rat-faced man, with a bald crown, who looks significantly older than fifty-five. But after triple-checking newspaper accounts and his obituary from 2016, it does appear to be the man in question. They say a hard life ages a man. Perhaps it was his time in the military or the cold heart he grew trafficking poor Venezuelan women to rich incels from the States, but Alexis looked easily ten years older than he was.

Still, age never slowed him down. Around the time Jas's photo appeared on his site, Alexis expanded his empire, buying a yacht and setting up a second brothel, the Alexis Club, in the Dominican Republic. That website is a bit more explicit than the flagship, Villas Las Morenas. For the new club, Alexis included tags on his escorts photographs, denoting what sort of fetish they were willing to accommodate; golden showers, oral without a condom, rimming, anal, feet play.

My main takeaway from the research I did into Alexis is that he was a true predator, a dangerous man, but one with a unique, analytical mind. He organized every little detail of his business with the pride of a Schutzstaffel accountant.

That Alexis was still operating in the Dominican Republic as recently as 2009, and the very nature of his trade, suggest that he was involved in some level of graft with the local government and crime lords. While prostitution is technically legal in the DR, you cannot run a public brothel, but Alexis advertised his club online. And he'd already been busted for this very thing before.

According to the *Calgary Herald*, Alexis and four locals were arrested in the DR in 1995 under suspicion of marketing the island as a "paradise of pornography" and bringing men from the United States and Canada to one of his brothels, where they would pay to have sex with Dominican women. Yet somehow, he was allowed back.

The yacht that Alexis purchased was a fifty-two footer, with a cozy interior cabin, kitchen, and two private bedrooms. Its skipper was a fellow named Alfred Cotten, an overweight man with a toe-shaped head and a short red beard. He can be seen in several photos surrounded by Alexis's escorts, all of whom would be far beyond the reach of his social strata if they were to meet under different circumstances. Cotten would ferry Alexis's guests and their escorts to a nearby island with a private beach. Passengers had their own chef and could bring up to five women on board with them.

Cotten took inspiration from Alexis, opening his own brothel, Tropical Adult Vacations, in Boca Chica. But apparently, he lacked Alexis's dark acumen. According to the *New York Post,* in 2015, he and his wife, Jennifer, were arrested and charged in New York with promoting prostitution, a class-D felony. At the time, New York had a unique law on the books that banned the promotion of prostitution to its citizens, even if it was legal in the country they were paying to visit. Agents with the DA's office in Manhattan spotted an ad for Cotten's resort on Backpages.com and set up a sting to catch him. Posing as a man attempting to book an unforgettable bachelor party, agents spoke to Cotten by phone and recorded the conversation, in which Cotten discussed everything they could get for their money. When they raided his home, they found fifty-five pounds of gold and silver coins, thousands of dollars in American and Dominican Republic currency, and a .38 caliber Colt automatic pistol.

At sentencing, Cotten argued that he was innocent, because his johns paid the escorts directly and both were consenting adults, a bold strategy that doesn't take into account the tacit coercion inherent in offering destitute women more money than they make in a month elsewhere for one night of sex at Cotten's resort.

"What right does this court have to bring me up on charges that are bullshit?" Cotten said to reporters, after he was sentenced to five years of probation.

Alfred and Jennifer Cotten currently reside in Florida. I spoke to Jennifer, briefly, by phone. As soon as I mentioned Amy's name, she hung up.

Cotten remains a person of interest in the disappearance, at least for the Bradleys. On their website, the Bradleys point out how much Cotten resembles the composite sketch of a man seen in San Francisco, in 2003, strong-arming a woman who looked a lot like Amy Bradley. Indeed, Cotten is a dead-ringer for the sketch—overweight, with a balding head with red hair on the sides and a red beard. Until I saw them side-by-side, I didn't put much thought into the San Francisco sighting. If Amy was a victim of human trafficking, why on earth would her captors bring her all the way to San Francisco and wander around a very public space where anyone might recognize her?

The resemblance is uncanny. However, I was not able to discern when this witness first came forward. If it was before the Bradleys knew about Cotten, it could be a significant bit of circumstantial evidence. But if the witness came forward after Cotten was already on their website, it could be like the lullaby that traveled from Iva to Frank to Judith Margaritha, looping back around to become evidence of something that was never real.

After the arrest of Alfred and Jennifer Cotten, the resort's driver, an ex-New York cabbie named Paco, took over the brothel. He called himself "The Ringmaster" and used a more authoritarian method of controlling his escorts and clientele. In a letter published on his website in 2008, Paco wrote, "Hello to all of you gentlemen. If you think my beasts/ladies are tame enough for you to take one home without the safeguard of finding out through me, the ringmaster, which are the beasts and which are the ladies, then you are in for a surprise." He compares his women to utilitarian objects, writing, "This is just a pile of shoes. Just pick one, it might fit you."

A few other men connected to Alexis Zaglanitis are worth mentioning, men who would have known Jas's true identity and whether she really was Amy or not. Alexis's business partner was a man named Thomas Wild (also known as Thomas Ghent). In 2004, Alexis parted ways with Thomas and partnered with the owner of Adult Vacation Getaway on Margarita Island, Oscar Bowen. Both men kept the name of their company, funneling clients into a shared resort. Oscar was originally from Weston, Florida, but moved to the island to oversee their operation. When Alexis announced the merger on his website, he promoted a new service that he and Oscar would provide—a matchmaking tour for guests searching for a wife to take back to the States.

Online records show that Oscar registered the website for Adult Vacation Getaway under the home address of Alexis's yacht captain, Alfred Cotten. Oscar took their new mission to heart and married a Venezuelan woman named Miroslava Rondon. Unfortunately, Rondon is no longer alive to speak about what was happening inside the Margarita Island resort.

In February 2009, Rondon was murdered in San Felix on the mainland of Venezuela. According to an article that appeared in the regional newspaper, *Correo del Caroni*, Rondon was in the process of divorcing Oscar at the time and had received a number of threatening calls at her house. At around 8 p.m., she left her home with a friend, Angel Zambrano, on the back of his motorcycle, to visit his family's empanadas stand, which was nearby. Not far from her place, they encountered three men who ordered them to stop. Zambrano ignored them and continued on. One of the men pulled out a shotgun and fired. Rondon appeared to be the target, as the blast destroyed part of her face. She died at the scene. Zambrano survived with a fractured arm. The shooter and accomplices fled the scene and were never caught.

There were two theories about the murder at the time: One, it was a robbery and the gunmen were after the motorcycle. Two, it was a professional hit on Rondon. Her family believes it was likely an orchestrated murder-for-hire. As part of the divorce, Rondon was after a piece of Oscar's business, and his divorce attorney had recently called Zambrano at home. A reporter with the *Correo del Caroni* interviewed Rondon's uncle, who said, "My niece had no problems. There is no other explanation."

Oscar Bowen has never been charged in the murder of Miroslava Rondon. As far as I can tell, he still resides on Margarita Island.

Alexis died in 2016 at the age of sixty-three. His obituary identified him as a "successful entrepreneur and traveler" who was known as "Papu" by his grandchildren. So many secrets died with him, and many women, I'm sure, sighed in relief.

The photographs of Jas that appeared on that man's website twenty years ago may hold the truth about what really happened to Amy Bradley. But if Amy did visit Affordable Adult Vacations in 2004, she wasn't alone. The pictures that resemble her appear beside those of a dozen other escorts. Perhaps I'd have better luck finding one of them.

Chapter Twenty-seven

XENU'S FOLLY

"I'm suspicious of the Scientologists," Brad Bradley had said to me during that fateful interview at his parents' house. And for good reason.

The day before Amy's disappearance, the *Rhapsody of the Seas* had docked at Aruba beside the *Freewinds*, the Scientology ship used by the upper echelon of the organization to attain "total freedom." Later that evening, Amy was seen speaking with two women in uniform who stopped talking when Iva and Brad approached them. The Bradleys believed these women were Scientology Sea Org officers. After Amy disappeared, more Scientologists showed up at the Bradleys' hotel room on Curaçao, asking funny questions: "What type of cigarettes did she smoke?"—"Tell us about something you haven't lost."

I've encountered Scientologists before. They're a strange bunch. In 2007, a Scientology center opened in Parma Heights, on the west side of Cleveland, inside a brick colonial with white columns. I was working as a reporter for the *Free Times* then, and went undercover, posing as a potential recruit to learn what was going on inside. This was long before the film, *Going Clear*, and all the documentaries about Scientology that can now be found on streaming platforms. The general public, at least around Cleveland, didn't know much about Scientology then. All I knew came from those mysterious informercials that would show up on TV late at night, advertisements for L. Ron Hubbard's book *Dianetics*, the paperback with the erupting volcano on the front. You probably know more about it than I did, but as a refresher, here are the basics.

Before he became a messiah, L. Ron Hubbard was a sci-fi author. In the 1930s and '40s, his short stories were published in popular magazines like *Astounding Science Fiction* and *Unknown*. He served in the United States Navy during World War II and was briefly given command of a submarine chaser. During that time, he mistook a magnetic deposit for an enemy ship and shot at it for about sixty-eight hours to no avail. He was relieved of command after he fired upon Mexican territory (we were not at war with Mexico, of course).

After the war, he moved in with his friend Jack Parsons, a genius rocket engineer who founded the Jet Propulsion Laboratory and who studied the occult teachings of one Aleister Crowley. His time with Parsons likely inspired a lot of what was to come. Crowley had founded a religion of his own, called Thelema. Part of Crowley's religion involved rituals to make contact with a cosmic entity known as Lam, a being that looked surprisingly like the large-eyed gray aliens reported by alleged UFO abductees. Hubbard helped Parsons develop a sex magic ritual meant to summon the supreme Goddess of Thelema, Babalon. He also shacked up with Parson's twenty-one-year-old girlfriend, Sara Northrup. Hubbard married Sara in 1946, while he was still married to his first wife.

By 1950, Hubbard was beginning to hold public lectures to discuss the ideas that would eventually be collected in the book *Dianetics*, the bible of Scientology. He believed that consciousness was divided into two parts: the Analytical Mind and the Reactive Mind. The Reactive Mind stored traumatic memories called "engrams" that caused us to become sick in different ways. One goal of Scientology is to help people become Clear of these engrams by following the Bridge to Total Freedom. Hubbard developed a process called Auditing, where a subject would hold two tin-can-looking instruments connected to an electropsychometer (more familiarly known as an E-meter) while reviewing bad memories, the goal being to purge their engrams.

The whole thing is pretty trippy. It was also a money-making endeavor—auditing sessions can cost up to $800. To complete the Bridge to Total Freedom, you must buy instructional books and purchase more and more sessions along the way. Some have spent upwards of $200,000 to reach the upper levels of Scientology. Because of this, Scientology has been labeled a business and a cult in some countries, like Germany.

Hubbard also preached about the dangers of mainstream psychiatry and was known to organize his followers to attack his enemies, often psychiatrists or members of the press. His philosophy to criticism was simple: "Don't ever defend, always attack."

In 1966, as *Dianetics* was gaining popularity, Hubbard bought a bunch of ships and founded the Sea Org, a private navy made up of elite members of Scientology. He moved onto one of the ships and began writing new teachings, for the highest-level Scientologists, which would reveal the ultimate truth behind it all—that 75 million years ago, an alien named Xenu sent billions of his enemies to Earth, where he placed them inside volcanos and blew them up with hydrogen bombs. The traumatized spirits of those murdered aliens now infest human bodies, loading them up with bad engrams.

By the time he died in 1986, Hubbard was living as a recluse, surrounded by sycophants. For my *Free Times* article, I got my hands on a copy of the coroner's report from San Luis Obispo, which revealed that Hubbard's will had been altered the day before his death. A toxicology screening showed that when he died, Hubbard was taking an anti-anxiety medication known as hydroxyzine, even though Scientologists are against psychoactive drugs.

When I visited the Scientology center in Parma Heights, I was offered a free Auditing session, given by a local optometrist. We sat in a claustrophobic room. As I held their tin cans, he asked me to recall an incident of pain that I felt comfortable facing. I chose to tell him about the time I broke my wrist, during a game of capture the flag, at a Boy Scout campout, when I was ten years old. He asked me to recall the event in as much detail as possible while he watched the needle on the E-meter flutter up and down. When I was done, he asked me to tell the story again. And then again and again and again. We didn't stop until I'd told the story a dozen times. By the end, the words I was saying felt devoid of all meaning and the story simply a figment of my imagination. Then he recommended a treatment called a Purif, where I would sit in a sauna and expel poisonous toxins from my body for the low, low price of $1,700.

I also took a two-hundred-question Scientology personality test and was told the results revealed that I was irresponsible in my life and work and am cold-blooded and heartless. Perhaps they already suspected I was a reporter.

You can find out a lot more about Scientology if you're interested. Stories about the billion-year contracts Sea Org members are made to sign, about the repugnant behavior of celebrity members like Danny Masterson, about Scientology's current leader, David Miscavige, whose wife, Shelly, has not been seen publicly since 2007. Still, I found it hard to believe that Scientologists would actually keep a girl aboard the *Freewinds* against her will until I heard the story of Valeska Paris.

In a civil complaint filed in United States District Court, Middle District of Florida, in 2022, against the Church of Scientology and David Miscavige, Valeska and two other former Scientologists, Gawain and Laura Baxter, alleged frightening and bizarre practices aboard the *Freewinds*. In fact, they believe Scientology regularly violated the Trafficking Victims Protection Reauthorization Act.

Valeska, whose parents were members of the Church, was only

six years old in 1984 when she signed a billion-year Sea Org contract and joined Cadet Org in England, where selected children are housed and trained in the teachings of L. Ron Hubbard. While there, family time is limited to one visit per week and can be canceled if the child is being punished for some transgression, according to the complaint.

In the section that lays out Valeska's history with the church, she claims that from the age of four, she was "subjected to a Scientology training routine during which she was screamed at, verbally abused, and forced to listen to graphic descriptions of sexual content for hours at a time."

When Valeska's parents divorced, she was not permitted to see her mother anymore. She claims that when she expressed emotion about this, she was reprimanded for being dramatic and taken to the galley to wash pots and pans. She alleges that physical violence and sexual abuse were commonplace in Cadet Org, and she once walked in on an adult leader masturbating on a boy's bed. When she reported the incident, she was the one who got punished.

When she was seventeen, Valeska's mother left the church. It was possible that Valeska might be called as a witness in a legal proceeding connected to this. As a result, Valeska claims that Miscavige personally ordered her to be sent to live on the *Freewinds*, far away from any process server.

She would have been aboard the *Freewinds* when Amy disappeared.

The complaint provides a lot of facts about the ship that I found interesting. According to the filing, the *Freewinds* is run by a corporation in Panama that is wholly owned by Flag Ship Trust, which is controlled by David Miscavige and the Church of Scientology. Its home port is Curaçao, and it frequently sails to the other ABC islands of Aruba and Bonaire. It never docks at any US ports, and it avoids the territorial waters of the United States. All of this is totally not alarming or suspicious in any way.

Before Valeska arrived on the *Freewinds*, she claims that Scientology members confiscated her passport and personal identification so that once she was on the ship, she had no way to easily leave while visiting foreign ports. At first, they gave her a job in the ship's restaurant, serving meals to senior staff. When she asked to go back to the States, she was punished and moved to the engine room, where she was told to clean pipes with a rag and given fifteen-minute breaks to eat. She often worked sixteen hours a day. In return, Valeska was paid fifty dollars a week, which she used to purchase personal hygiene items from the commissary.

When Valeska attempted to write a letter to Shelly Miscavige, David Miscavige's wife, to beg her for help, it was discovered by her supervisor and destroyed. For her transgression, Valeska claims she was sent back to the engine room. Eventually, she alleges, she did get a letter to Shelly Miscavige, who responded by denying her request and reporting her to security.

It gets worse.

At some point, Valeska began a romantic relationship with the ship's security chief, a man named Carlos. When senior staff learned of the relationship, she was forced to sit in a locked room for five hours and write a confession providing graphic details of their sexual encounters. Afterward, she claimed, a summary of that confession was posted on the ship's notice board for the entire crew to read.

The complaint also alleges that the captain's son, Sean Napier, sexually assaulted her one day, when he locked her in a room and "rubbed his erect penis against her until he ejaculated."

I won't go into every single incident of abuse that Valeska alleges happened during her years aboard the *Freewinds*. It got so bad that she contemplated suicide. She was sent to Australia, to what the complaint calls a "forced labor site." While there, she married another Sea Org member and former Australian rugby star, Chris Guider. When word got back to Valeska that they wanted to send her back to the *Freewinds*, she purposefully got pregnant.

Sea Org members, the complaint says, are not permitted to have children. She claims they demanded she terminate the pregnancy but she refused. It became her greatest bargaining chip in her effort to separate from Scientology—nobody wanted a pregnant Sea Org member. When she miscarried after six weeks, she kept it a secret so that the bureaucratic process of severing her relationship with Scientology could continue.

After about four months, Valeska was allowed to leave. They sent her away with no money, no official identification, in a country where she did not have a proper visa. Years later, when she had found her footing again, Valeska began to speak out about Scientology. The Church responded by purchasing the domain name, ValeskaParis.com, where they published testimonials from Sea Org members who accused her of lying.

The section on the alleged abuse directed at Valeska ends with this note: "Valeska continues to suffer from the traumas and injuries experienced in Scientology, including persistent nightmares about being trapped in Sea Org and unable to escape the *Freewinds*." According to reports, Valeska was aboard the *Freewinds* from 1996 to 2007, placing her on the ship when it was parked next to the *Rhapsody of the Seas*, in Aruba, on March 23, 1998. The complaint contains no mention of Amy Bradley. When reached, Valeska declined to comment, due to the ongoing litigation.

In a statement to the *Independent*, regarding Valeska's claims, the Church released a two-page statement, which described the *Freewinds* as a wonderful place. It went on to state, "She certainly wasn't 'forced' to be there. . . . She is a true apostate."

Chapter Twenty-eight

THE TRUTH ABOUT TRAFFICKING

THE IDEA THAT AMY BRADLEY was kidnapped from the *Rhapsody of the Seas*, smuggled off the ship unseen, and forced into human trafficking is difficult to believe. If not for the photograph of the escort known as Jas, I might write it off completely. Sure, some witnesses came forward, claiming that they saw Amy after she disappeared, but our memories are malleable, fragile things and can't be trusted. Still, that photo is compelling, and at least one forensic team came to the conclusion that it was Amy, according to the Bradleys.

I also have a problem with this theory, because it greatly exaggerates the dangers of trafficking in the Caribbean, at least where it concerns Caucasian citizens of the United States. White women are not being kidnapped off cruise ships. In fact, a situation like this has never happened before—like, ever. If proven, this would be a wholly unique crime, an unlucky aberration, a stunning exception to Occam's Razor.

Try as I might, I could not find a single reputable story of a woman being kidnapped off a cruise ship, let alone forced into prostitution afterward. I scoured the web and came up with zilch. I even posed the question to Sky, who also dug through all available online sources. Her response: "Aside from Amy Lynn Bradley's case, there are no verified instances of individuals being kidnapped from cruise ships and forced into human trafficking. While cruise ship disappearances do occur, such as the case of Rebecca Coriam in 2011, these incidents typically lack concrete evidence linking them to human trafficking. Generally, cruise ships maintain stringent security measures, making abductions extremely rare."

The human trafficking that does occur in the Caribbean concerns persons of color almost exclusively, usually impoverished women from countries like Venezuela or the Dominican Republic or Haiti, who are coerced into brothels like Affordable Adult Vacations, where they may have some autonomy and ability to leave but where the economic incentives are a trap of their own. Human trafficking also includes transporting undocumented immigrants for forced labor, which is a very real problem on the islands. But logistically speaking, a white woman from the United States would be a hell of a liability for a criminal enterprise looking to avoid detection. Simply put, she'd stand out. Word would travel fast. That's the sort of attention that's not worth the risk. And besides, prostitution is legal on Curaçao and Margarita Island, where Amy's sightings have occurred.

The most well-known brothel in Curaçao is Campo Alegre, also known as Le Mirage. It was created, like many brothels around the world, to service laborers. A hundred years ago, Curaçao got into the business of refining oil. This created new jobs, luring workers from all around the Northern Antilles. Sex workers followed the money and the men. At first, these women plied their trade downtown, on the streets of Willemstad. But residents didn't like that it was so out-in-the-open.

A commission was appointed, which concluded that the sex workers should be given their own space, away from the prying eyes of the general public. It was decided that the best location was an old army barracks on the north side of the island, with space enough to house up to three hundred sex workers. With full support from the Queen of the Netherlands, Campo Alegre was opened in 1949. It operated uninterrupted until the Covid pandemic of 2020 shut it down.

The laws regulating prostitution on Curaçao are strict. Selling sex is legal, but only by the individual women themselves. Pimping is forbidden. Sex workers cannot be citizens of the Northern Antilles. They must be foreign-born. Which is why most of the women at Campo Alegre were Cuban and Venezuelan nationals on temporary visas, typically good for three months of work. The skin business is highly regulated. Potential sex workers must provide medical documents showing they are disease-free and have no prior criminal record. Once they are on the island, the women must undergo regular medical exams to test for STDs.

In June 2005, the International Organization for Migration released an assessment of human trafficking occurring in the Caribbean at that time. It provides statistics and anecdotes about the sex trade on Curaçao at the time Amy is alleged to have been kidnapped.

First of all, Curaçao is not the dangerous third-world country it's portrayed to be on the Bradleys' website. The island is part of the Netherlands Antilles, a Dutch territory, and boasts a literacy rate of 96.5 percent. By comparison, the United States' current literacy rate is 79 percent. The crime rate is also significantly below that of the United States, likely due to stricter gun control measures. There is no such thing as concealed carry on the island.

However, illegal prostitution does occur outside of Campo Alegre. The IOM report estimated that twelve percent of the women who leave the camp stay on the island to work for unregulated brothels. Those women are especially susceptible to victimization and are subject to rape and other forms of violence for noncompliance.

Some clubs will skirt prostitution laws by calling their employees "dancers," while still expecting them to please their clients off the dance floor. The report mentions how, in 1996, a number of

Colombian women were recruited to come to the island to work as waitresses at a nightclub. When they arrived, their boss confiscated their passports so that they couldn't leave and forced them to have sex with men against their will. They were made to work seven nights a week, given one meal a day, and had to buy condoms from the club. They later sued their employer in court.

The report revealed that child prostitution was an ongoing problem on Curaçao in 2005. The investigators found that a client could ask certain brothel owners to order a child, usually between the ages of eight and twelve. The girl would then be flown in from the Dominican Republic and handed over for the day. In one case they investigated, a young girl was supplied by her own parents in exchange for $2,200. Video of the rape was sold on the black market.

Interviews with informants revealed that the sex workers recruited to Curaçao's legal brothels were mostly from the DR and Colombia, whereas the women working illegally were from Haiti, Guyana, and Venezuela. One issue that makes it difficult to keep track of undocumented sex workers is how easy it is for criminals to avoid official ports of call and simply bring a boat up to a private beach and offload their women.

In general, however, Curaçao is relatively safe, and the sex trade is mostly legal and in the open. Margarita Island, however, is an entirely different story.

Margarita Island, where Alexis Zaglanitis operated his Affordable Adult Vacations resort, is a part of Venezuela, which has one of the highest homicide rates in the world. To get to Margarita Island, American travelers must not only have a passport but also a visa prior to arrival. The State Department warns that travelers coming to the country without proper documentation "risk lengthy or indefinite detention." They add: "The U.S. Department of State urges citizens not to travel to Venezuela."

Colombian terrorist organizations, like the Segunda Marquetalia, have been known to target U.S. citizens visiting Venezuela. If you must visit the country, the State Department suggests you maintain a low profile and travel in groups of five or more. It got so bad recently, they suspended operations at the U.S. Embassy in Caracas. If you're an American, and you get into a spot of trouble on your trip to Margarita Island, you're in big trouble.

In 2014, the United States placed Venezuela on its list of the world's worst centers for human trafficking, according to a *Reuters* report, putting it in the same category as North Korea and Syria. The country has fallen to authoritarianism, its economy is in shambles, and corruption is everywhere.

And yet, there is still not a single verified report of even one U.S. citizen being abducted and forced into the sex trade on Margarita Island or on the Venezuela mainland.

In fact, if you're taking a cruise through the Caribbean, the most dangerous place you'll ever be is on board the ship itself.

Chapter Twenty-nine

EVERYTHING YOU WANTED TO KNOW ABOUT CRUISE SHIPS BUT WERE AFRAID TO ASK

By the end of July, all we could think about was the cruise. Julie made a list of essentials to pack so that we didn't forget anything at the last minute. Phone chargers, sunscreen, flip-flops. I dug out our passports and bought a $20 plastic snorkel set at Target. We felt an excited anticipation, and maybe that's a little crass, considering the purpose of the trip was to report on the disappearance of a woman so many people cared for—but how could we not be excited?

We invited some old friends to come with us—Julie's sisters, Harper and Nora. Also Joel, the party host who'd helped me to the car after I broke my leg at his house, and two other couples. I felt safer, traveling in a large group. I knew there would be times when I'd be off searching for clues and suspects, and this way, Julie wouldn't be alone.

As the date approached, I researched the history of cruise ship tragedies, to understand the statistics about what we were getting into. Certainly, losing people on a cruise is a relatively rare occurrence these days, with all the CCTV cameras and protections from liability, right? I figured there might be two or three a year. But it's more like twenty.

The website CruiseJunkie.com catalogues overboard incidents on the major cruise ships as well as illness outbreaks and pollution issues. I found it to be a trove of helpful information. The site is comprehensive and goes back to 1995. It's curated by a man named Ross Klein, a retired professor from Memorial University in Newfoundland. In 2024, nineteen people either fell or jumped off cruise ships. And once you're in the water, there's only a twenty percent chance you're coming out alive. Each listing has a headline, with links to news reports. "Sixty-six-year-old woman reported overboard from *Allure of the Seas.* Cruise ship death plunge in front of family."

At first, Dr. Klein was a cruise enthusiast. He enjoyed taking his wife on trips down the East Coast of the States, and he was anxious to try all the different cruise liners. As a sociologist, though, he was always observing people. He couldn't help it. He started to notice the hustle and grift that goes on just below the surface of all the promoted pleasure.

"I saw the absurdity of things," Dr. Klein explained to me over the phone one morning. "Like the food. It's all crap, made to look pretty. They spend maybe ten dollars per person per day. The tickets are cheap, because they know you'll spend all this extra money on board. At the same time these ships are flying the flags of foreign countries to avoid American labor laws."

He noticed, too, how crew members would take advantage of easy marks. He recalled how a certain maître d' would separate single older women in the dining room, giving them extra attention, and how he was rewarded with gifts from them on the last night. On one occasion, he was introduced to the wife of a ship's captain, who explained that she had met her husband when she was a passenger. Once you see beyond the artifice, it's hard to ignore.

Gradually, Dr. Klein started organizing his findings. He gathered data. He collected newspaper articles. He stayed current on *Lloyd's List*, a weekly shipping news report. He began to log every time someone went overboard. And soon, he came to a sobering conclusion.

"You're not as safe as you think you are," he said. "There are dangers around every corner. Drunken fights, norovirus outbreaks, sexual assaults." It's all underreported in order to maintain that dreamy façade.

Children are especially vulnerable aboard cruise ships. According to Dr. Klein, children are involved in around thirty-four percent of all sexual assault cases at sea. Oftentimes, these assaults occur at the day camps offered on board, either at the hands of their camp counselor or by an older teen. A great many of these are settled out of court with a heavy nondisclosure agreement attached.

Eventually, Dr. Klein published his data online for everyone to see. The most comprehensive database available at the time, it caught the attention of some prominent attorneys whose clients had experienced these dangers first-hand. Soon he was being called as a witness in assault cases against the major cruise lines. Some of those stories stick with him to this day.

In a 2015 incident aboard Royal Caribbean's *Oasis of the Seas*, a fifteen-year-old girl was allegedly gang-raped by twelve men after being plied with alcohol, according to *CBSNews*. The girl's family filed suit against Royal Caribbean, citing negligence—several crew members witnessed the men buying the teen alcohol and did nothing to intervene. The case was settled out of court.

In a 2012 case aboard Royal Caribbean's *Allure of the Seas*, another fifteen-year-old girl was taken to a private room by a teen boy from Brazil, only to find a twenty-year-old man waiting inside, according to *NBC Miami*. They refused to allow her to leave, and both allegedly raped her. The adult man eventually pleaded guilty to two counts of lewd and lascivious battery and was deported to Brazil after serving a one-year sentence.

Nathaniel Skokan, a twenty-two-year-old from Nebraska, accompanied his family on a cruise aboard Royal Caribbean's *Independence of the Seas*, in 2016. Skokan was served thirty ounces of alcohol, nearly an entire liter of booze, by the ship's bartender. His binge included six full-sized martinis. Around 1:37 a.m. he was on the twelfth-floor deck with some friends when someone joked that they should jump overboard. Skokan pretended to jump but turned to sit on the handrail at the last moment. Unfortunately, he slipped and fell into the ocean, where he drowned. His blood alcohol content was at least .256, according to a report in the *St. Augustine Record*. Skokan's family sued. The cruise line argued that it was Skokan's own negligence that caused his death. The jury ultimately ruled in favor of Royal Caribbean.

Dr. Klein has appeared to testify in front of the United States Congress on three separate occasions. In 2012, he spoke in front of the Senate's Committee on Commerce, Science, and Transportation, at a hearing for "Oversight of the Cruise Industry." It took place two months after the *Costa Concordia* disaster, in which a cruise ship sank in the Mediterranean Sea, killing twenty-seven passengers and five crew members. As always, he came with cold hard data, presenting an analysis of crimes reported aboard cruise ships over the course of one year, from October 1, 2007, to September 30, 2008: 115 simple assaults, 16 assaults with serious injury, 101 thefts, and 154 sex-related incidents. During that period the rate of sexual assaults aboard Carnival Cruise Lines was fifty percent higher than the rate of sexual assaults in all of Canada.

His research clearly showed a link between the all-you-can-drink packages offered on cruise ships and the increase in crimes. The data showed that alcohol was a factor in 62.5 percent of serious assaults with bodily injury and 36 percent of sexual assaults. There's no way the cruise lines don't understand this, but their concern seems to be profit over safety. Dr. Klein noted that "bar sales is one of the top sources of onboard revenue for cruise ships."

Dr. Klein also spoke about the need for better surveillance video on cruise ships. He noted that when an overboard incident was an obvious suicide, video was often made available but not so when it wasn't so clear. "It is the mysterious incidents that raise the most concern," he said. One example is the disappearance of thirty-seven-year-old Annette Mizener, who was traveling aboard the *Carnival Pride* with her daughter and parents in December 2004. One evening, Mizener left her cabin to meet her parents at the casino but never arrived. Her handbag was found near the railing on a lower deck, its contents strewn all over the floor. Spots of blood were found nearby. The security camera on the side had been covered with a piece of paper. "The situation suggests there is need for better video coverage of deck areas and that video feeds be monitored in real time," he said.

During his research, Dr. Klein identified a troubling loophole that allows crimes on cruises to be underreported. According to his testimony, the FBI is not required to report crimes committed on cruise ships unless they have opened a file of investigation and then closed that file. This means that mere allegations of crimes at sea are not subject to being reported, whereas allegations of crimes that occur on United States soil are reported. As Dr. Klein said, "While this absence of data may serve the interest of the cruise lines, which prefer incidents of crime to remain hidden, it is not in the interest of the public or in the spirit of the Cruise Vessel Security and Safety Act of 2010."

If you want to know more before going on your next cruise, Dr. Klein has written four books on the subject, including *Cruise Ship Blues: The Underside of the Cruise Industry*.

Eventually, we got around to talking about Amy Bradley's disappearance. Dr. Klein was aware of the story, of course. He doesn't believe she could have been trafficked. He's never encountered a verified story of a single passenger being kidnapped and trafficked. "The difficulty is how would you transport a body onto land," he said.

My conversation with Dr. Klein inspired me to go deeper down the rabbit hole of cruise ship crime stories. I'm not sure that I ever reached the end, but the more I searched, the more I found. One great source of information is the web page for International Cruise Victims, an advocacy nonprofit founded in 2006 by Ken Carver, after his daughter, Merrian, disappeared while traveling on a Royal Caribbean ship in Alaska. When she failed to return to her cabin on the second day of the cruise, her room steward reported her missing to his supervisor, but no action was taken. At the end of the trip her belongings were boxed up and disposed of. The cruise line made no attempt to contact the FBI or her family. Carver spent the rest of his life trying to change the industry and make it safer, testifying in front of Congress and publishing the stories of cruise ship victims in an effort to educate the public.

One story that appears prominently on the ICV website is that of Laurie Dishman, who, in 2006, took a trip with her best friend aboard Royal Caribbean's *Vision of the Seas*. The plan was to have seven days of fun and sun along the Mexican Riviera. Instead, it turned into a horror movie.

Laurie and her friend were dancing in the Viking Crown Lounge one night when they were approached by a man wearing a security guard badge who asked to see their IDs—an odd request, as Laurie was thirty-six at the time—and nobody seemed to give a shit if you drink underage. He also asked for their room number.

Later, on the dance floor, he took her by the wrist and kissed her. She told him to get away. Laurie was so weirded out by the man that her friend walked her back to their cabin and stayed with Laurie until she fell asleep. Then her friend returned to the dance club. Laurie awoke to the sound of knocking on the door. She thought it was her friend and so she didn't check before she opened the door. But it wasn't her friend, it was the odd man from the dance club. He forced his way into the room and raped her until she passed out. When she woke up, he was gone and there were ligature marks on her neck.

When she notified ship officers, she was instructed to bag up her own evidence. Laurie thought the FBI would help her, but she was told it would be a "he said/she said" case and the Department of Justice declined to prosecute. She claimed that Royal Caribbean refused to provide her with her own medical records about the incident. They would not tell her if her rapist was HIV positive. In fact, the only thing she received from the cruise line after the rape was a promotional letter from the President of Royal Caribbean Cruise Lines, which stated, "Thank you for sailing with us and giving us the opportunity to send you home with an experience to remember." A discount coupon was included.

In 1998, the year Amy Bradley disappeared, the *New York Times* published a special report: "Sovereign Islands: On Cruise Ships, Silence Shrouds Crimes." It details several sexual assaults aboard major cruise lines and the companies' handling of claims and lawsuits—and what they found was alarming. The goal with every lawsuit was to keep the inherent risk as quiet as possible. As reporter Douglas Frantz wrote: "In every case, the accusers say, the cruise line's main concern was to protect its reputation by buying or coercing their silence and shielding the accused."

In one incident, involving the alleged rape of a sixteen-year-old girl by a ship's bartender, lawyers for the cruise line subpoenaed the teen's high school records in an attempt to impugn her character. The story even quotes a former chief of security for Carnival, who admitted that the policy was to not notify the FBI of sexual assaults but to offer victims bribes or to simply upgrade their cabins and give them free champagne.

My takeaway after reviewing these articles was that a cruise ship is perhaps the best place for a predator to stalk his prey. Like the shitty food served in the dining halls, there is a never-ending buffet of potential victims for those with discerning taste. By the time the law can get its shoes tied, that predator could be halfway around the world, and the cruise lines are only too happy to see him gone.

One last note. It's impossible to know the true number of people who fall off these ships every year, Dr. Klein explained, because when a crew member goes overboard and that crew member is from a foreign country, it's often not reported at all.

Of course, as G.I. Joe once said, "Knowing is half the battle." With this knowledge in hand, I took my wife and her friends aboard the *Rhapsody of the Seas*.

PART FOUR

GHOST SHIP

Chapter Thirty

RHAPSODY

NIHILISTS MAKE EXCELLENT TRAVELERS. When you are ambivalent about life, flying is easy. None of that worthless anxiety that other people deal with when their flimsy, metal tube reaches 35,000 feet. During all those years I spent not concerned about my life, I would sit back in my economy-class window seat like I was in my recliner at home, napping or reading, simply ignoring the occasional roller-coaster jostling of harsh turbulence. But I had committed myself to being healthy again, to caring about staying alive for the long haul, to being a partner for as long as my partner lived. That made for a very different experience on our flight to San Juan to board the *Rhapsody of the Seas*.

As we reached cruising altitude over central Ohio, the realization that we were six and a half miles above the Earth turned my blood cold. I thought of the author Michael Crichton, who often wrote about the dangers inherent in complex systems like, say, the intricate security procedures used to keep dinosaurs from eating tourists or the coding of robots in a fake Old West amusement park. Small errors in complex systems cause catastrophic failures rather quickly.

That's all an airplane is. A complex system. Add a flock of birds or an old rusted bolt, or someone's dodgy vape cartridge catching fire in the luggage hold, and it's over, man. Probably faster than we'd believe. I tried to meditate the thought away, but this time it didn't work. It didn't help that Julie was beside me. If anything, it made it worse. All I could do was imagine the repercussions of our inevitable deaths—what would happen to the kids? Why didn't we fly in two separate planes so that at least one of us would survive? I watched the wing outside my window, waiting for a panel to fly off or an engine to catch fire. Every time we hit a patch of turbulence, I prayed. Sometimes it's awful to want to live so much.

The gremlins left us alone and the landing gear opened as planned, and we touched down in Puerto Rico none the worse for wear. We arrived on the island a day before our cruise departed—we're all too old to gamble on missing a cruise over a delayed flight. Our rather large group collected bags at the carousel and got a van taxi to take us to our hotel in the Miramar neighborhood, which is just over the Caño de San Antonio from Old San Juan and not far from the port.

It became apparent this year, after Tony Hinchcliffe called Puerto Rico a "floating island of garbage" at a Trump rally, that many mainlanders have forgotten that Puerto Ricans are Americans and have been since 1917. It's a U.S. territory, like Guam, located a thousand miles southeast of Miami. It is subject to the federal laws of the United States but maintains its own local congress, with the governor as its chief executive. Puerto Ricans cannot vote for President unless they live on the mainland at the time of the election.

However, as Hinchcliffe found out the hard way, nearly two-thirds of ethnic Puerto Ricans now reside in the continental U.S. and are a significant demographic in Florida. They have one non-voting representative in the United States Congress, whose job is, presumably, to lean back and shake their head every time a vote for statehood fails on the floor. The cost of living in San Juan would be pretty sweet, too, if we hadn't screwed them over with the Merchant Marine Act of 1920, which prohibits foreign cargo ships from transferring goods between U.S. ports. So, anything they need from, say, Europe or Africa must first offload on the mainland and then be put onto American ships to return to Puerto Rico, which the original cargo ships passed on the way. Because of this, goods are expensive there, and its citizens, whose median annual income is $19,350, suffer needlessly. Also, it's not an island, it's an archipelago, but I digress. Personally, I found Puerto Rico to be beautiful, and the people were welcoming.

Our hotel was a four-story stucco deal on a side street lined with Spanish Revival homes and shops. It was a no-frills kind of place, where the desk clerk, a fiery *abuela*, was also the concierge and janitor. We took a slow elevator to the third floor, where it shimmied frighteningly as we got off (my sister-in-law, Nora, preferred taking the stairs after that). Five of us shared a room, which had bunks and beds and one shower. A dark stain on my bedsheet was determined to be dried blood and not mold, a small blessing. By the time we were settled in, it was getting dark. We decided to venture down the road for dinner, though Julie stayed behind to rest—her experience on the flight was similar to mine.

It was four blocks to Los Pinos Café on Avenue Ponce de Leon, a short walk through a gentrified barrio, where coqui frogs called from hidden places at the bases of palm trees, a piercing sound not unlike an iPhone's notification ping. Once inside, I ordered what became my favorite meal of the entire trip—authentic chicharrónes de pollo, which was half a chicken roughly chopped, the bone left in and lightly fried. The rest of the crew tried mofongo, mashed plantains with meat and broth.

We stayed up late talking about the upcoming adventures like summer teens gathered in a cabin on the first night of camp. Did I feel apprehension? Was I concerned about taking these people I love onto a ship where a woman disappeared, was possibly shanghaied? No. The statistics were in our favor. It was more likely we'd be mugged in Akron than kidnapped in the Caribbean. And we had aged out of being prime kidnapping targets.

The only apprehension I had concerned our stop at Curaçao, where we would arrive on Day Six. I planned to search the island for Judith Margaritha, and I'd never attempted to drive in a foreign country. What side of the road did they drive on, anyway? What would I find in the nooks and crannies of that island? Eventually, sleep found me, and my snores were not loud enough to keep everyone else awake for long.

In the morning, the desk clerk called some relative to take us to the Pan American Pier. There we got our first look at the *Rhapsody of the Seas*, our home for the next week.

The ship is considered small, now, but once upon a time she was the largest cruise liner in the world. Her broadside loomed oppressively over the immigrations and customs warehouse where we presented our passports: 915 feet long; 193 feet tall; 78,000 tons of steel. Twelve decks with room enough for two thousand passengers. Its hull is alabaster-white with aquamarine embellishments, except for the blue Royal Caribbean crown and anchor logo upon the ship's funnel. She's showing her age a bit these days. As we rolled our luggage up the gangway, I noticed a small army of laborers, dangling on bosun's chairs, scrubbing red rust off porthole windows.

Amy was on my mind as we entered the ship that day. She was here, in 1998, aboard this very ship. She'd boarded right here. I was occupying the same space. The answer as to what happened to Amy Bradley was hidden by only a single dimension—time. If I could just turn the clock back, I could watch it happen.

We entered midship, by the Casino Royale, and gathered in the central atrium on the fourth floor while we waited for our checked luggage to arrive. Once we had claimed our space in a corner of cushioned chairs and tables by the windows, a cute round-faced woman named Noemie came to take our drink orders. That's how fast it starts on these ships.

A quick word regarding drink packages aboard the *Rhapsody of the Seas*. There are several tiers of drinking options. If you want anything more than water and hot tea, you can purchase a coffee and soda package for $214 for the entire week, which is what I bought—I need that caffeine jolt in the morning. This comes with a signature Royal Caribbean cup which you can take to any fountain station on the ship for unlimited refills. If you want to order alcohol, it's $12 to $15 per drink, or you can get the cocktail of the day for $8. If you want to party, it adds up fast, so Royal Caribbean offers a premiere drink package that includes unlimited booze for around $800.

An interesting thing happens because of this: People—at least the people I came with—will drink more than they want simply to get their money's worth. Also, if one person in your cabin buys a drink package, you all have to, unless you personally contact Royal Caribbean's customer service and explain that you're an alcoholic or otherwise have a health condition that prohibits drinking. Drunkenness, then, is incentivized on the ship. Joel, Harper, and Nora shared a room and each got the premiere package on discount at around $700 apiece. I limited myself to two cocktails a day. Anyway, for that first round I ordered an old-fashioned and Julie got the discount cocktail, which was a Bay Breeze. Gratuity for drinks is included, but Joel made a point to tip Noemie cash so that she remembered us.

When she was gone, Joel raised his glass. "Cheers, you sons of bitches," he said.

I felt relief, then. The hard part was over. I'd made it all the way from Akron, Ohio, to San Juan, and here we were, sitting in the heart of the ship at the center of my story. Everything from here was gravy.

Still, there were things to do. I needed to gain entry to room 8564, the cabin where the Bradleys stayed. I wanted to see the balcony and get its dimensions. Could Amy have fallen off? Was there anything below to fall onto or was it a straight shot to the briny deep? I needed to examine the Viking Lounge, where Amy and

Yellow had danced the night before she disappeared. Witnesses claimed they had seen them return to the club after it was closed but only Yellow had returned. Was there a way to hide a body up there? I needed someone from Royal Caribbean to go on record. However, I also had to be careful. I didn't want to reveal my identity as a journalist until after our stop in Curaçao. The last thing I needed was to be kicked off the ship before we reached our destination. For now, all I could do was observe and plan.

I looked across the wide atrium. Two great glass elevators went all the way up to the Viking Lounge. At their base was a small stage. A young woman was singing '90s pop songs reimagined as jazz standards, while strumming a guitar. "Torn" by Natalie Imbruglia. Other passengers filtered in, the vast majority Puerto Rican—you can save a lot of money on a cruise if you don't have to fly to the port, after all. People looked up to the glass ceiling above. Noemie busied herself with orders around the room.

"So, what do you think happened to this chick?" Joel asked. "Was it murrrrder?"

I pushed my chair closer to his and filled him in on the basics as I understood them. Twenty-three-year-old woman took a cruise with her mom and dad and brother. The bass player of the ship's band, a man named Yellow, took a special interest in this woman. He was one of the last people to see her, up on the dance floor above us. Her father saw her on the balcony around 5:30 a.m. Then she was gone. Now, the only hope that she is still alive rests on the testimony of a handful of eyewitnesses who may or may not have been influenced by media coverage. That, and the photographs of a Caribbean sex worker who bears a striking resemblance to the missing woman. And here's the twist—she was gay. That was still a big deal in 1998. Big enough that it was kept a secret.

"Yeah, she couldn't be who she wanted to be at that time," Joel said. "I'm trying to think about how I would have been, in 1998, with my dad. I mean, it's not something we talk about. And as long as we don't talk about it, it's fine. I know he will never approve. I can't imagine how hard that was for her. Did her parents know?"

"They did."

"And did they approve?"

"They did not."

"That context is important."

"I think so, too."

The ship has not changed since 1998, but the world sure has. As we scanned through the itinerary of events listed on the app, I noticed that a gay social mixer was planned for Tuesday night. I bet Amy would have loved it.

Once everyone was on board, a ship-wide announcement was made, asking everyone to report to their "muster station." At the beginning of any cruise, passengers are shown where they should muster, or gather, in the unlikely event that the ship starts to sink. Throughout the *Rhapsody of the Seas* are several muster stations where one can access lifeboats. Ours was on a deck toward the bridge.

On deck, we were met by a young staff member who provided a QR code we had to scan on the app to show we participated. Each person has access to their personal data through the Royal Caribbean app, which keeps track of your expenses and your daily calendar. He pointed out where we should stand if there was ever an emergency. The whole thing took about two minutes. I retained zero knowledge of the process for evacuation, and I doubt many retained more than I did. It was simply a bureaucratic bit of busy work that needed to be checked off.

I trust statistics. In the last hundred and twenty years, only twenty-four cruise ships have foundered, according to CruiseHive .com, beginning with the *Titanic* in 1912. The last one was the *Costa Concordia*, in 2012. So, I suppose we're due for another, actually. Meanwhile, the ships keep getting bigger. I think of the floating cities like Royal Caribbean's *Icon of the Seas*, which can hold up to 7,600 passengers, and how we breezed through that muster drill. I'm quite sure the next time it happens, the death toll will be shocking. There were 2,224 passengers aboard the *Titanic*, for comparison.

We went to our cabins then, to get ready for dinner. Julie and I booked economy and were given a small room on the second floor. However, I did pay an extra hundred for a porthole window. The thought of being shut in without a way to see outside made me panicky. It was a rather large porthole, too, about the size of a breakfast nook tabletop. We hadn't left port yet, but our view looked out to the ocean, and I could see all the way to the horizon. Ships transited the expanse, coming to and from San Juan, full of people with their own stories. That feeling is called *sonder.* It's a new word, coined in 2012 by writer John Koenig. I hope my books are full of sonder for you. I'm no good at solving cases, but at least I can share someone's story.

Julie changed into a flower-print shirt and white shorts while I tracked down a missing piece of luggage, which I found tucked into a corner at the end of the hallway. We made our way to Edelweiss, the *Rhapsody*'s main dining room. It's two floors of linen-covered tables, attended to by a battalion of servers dressed in formal wear. The maître d' ushered our group of nine to a round table near the portside windows that looked out to the Atlantic.

The menu changes every night, often to reflect the local fare of whatever island we might be visiting that day. It's three-course; appetizer, main, and dessert. I ordered the shrimp cocktail followed by prime rib and warm apple crumble. The shrimp was chewy, but otherwise it was quite a nice meal. We got to know the names of our head server, an Indian man named Nilesh, and his assistant, Aaron. They were attentive enough to jot down any food sensitivities and drink preferences. Most of the staff here have families halfway across the globe waiting for them to come home with money. Sonder, sonder, sonder.

That night I walked around the ship alone for some time. My leg ached only a bit. My gait was still careful. I found a hallway outside the casino full of framed photographs and recognition plaques that told the history of the ship. It seems each time the *Rhapsody* visited a new country, they received a special plaque, and the ship has been all over the world. This would be a good place to have a small memorial for Amy. Maybe one day.

On the deck outside the dining room, I touched the railing and looked out at the sea. I felt that familiar tug of *l'appel du vide*, the call of the void. I was pleased to discover it was now whisper-quiet. My subconscious has relented to my will to live. I wouldn't jump. But I know there are wayward souls who come to the railing where that pull is strong, where that voice is deafeningly loud. The sea, like the night sky, is a lovely void that erases everything over time. Even our mistakes. I empathize with those who have gone over. But not me. Not today.

Another reaction often brought on by gazing across the open water is what Dr. Sigmund Freud called the *oceanic feeling*. It was actually coined by the writer, mystic, and Nobel Prize winner Romain Rolland, who corresponded with Freud. In one of his letters, dated December 5, 1927, Rolland urges Freud to investigate the phenomenon of spontaneous religious sentiment, that innate feeling we get sometimes that tells us we are a piece of the greater whole of this universe. He defined it as "the simple and direct fact of the feeling of the eternal (which can very well not be eternal, but simply without perceptible limits, and like an oceanic feeling)."

Freud believed this oceanic feeling was what we perceived up to the moment our mothers stopped breastfeeding us, when we lacked a sense of self to help us distinguish between our bodies and that of our mothers. The breast, we believed, was another part of us. Only in that separation did we begin to have an ego. When we look out at the stars or the vastness of the ocean, we are reminded of that unity, that unbounded eternity where we were all one.

The call of the void, the oceanic feeling. That duality, always in us. Black and white. Yin and yang. Trick or treat. Eventually we choose.

Later, our fellowship gathered in the Schooner piano bar, where a young man played “Take It Easy” by the Eagles. I bought Julie a lavender gin martini and held her hand while we talked. And damn it, I enjoyed every moment of it.

Chapter Thirty-one

STRANGE LOOPS

AFTER TWENTY YEARS OF MARRIAGE, Julie and I had settled into that quiet complacency typical of long partnerships. I think if you're with a person long enough and the relationship is equal and honest, the way ours became, you begin to feel as though your partner is an extension of yourself. Two acting as one. It's in the mundane division of labor—who pays the bills, who dusts the kitchen fan, etc. But it's also felt in the heart—you suffer when they suffer, you exalt in their accomplishments because you feel little separation of self anymore.

I think often of the cognitive scientist Douglas Hofstadter and his theories of consciousness. He won the Pulitzer Prize for nonfiction in 1979 for his book, *Gödel, Escher, Bach: An Eternal Golden Braid*, in which he posits that consciousness is a kind of awareness feedback loop that arises from the lower-level interactions of our neurons. We are not the pieces but the sum of those parts. What we think of as our "soul" or the "I" is what he calls a "strange loop" of self-awareness that develops out of these lower-level movements of chemicals and the processing of information and memory storage.

Like a computer geek sitting at a console, we seem to possess the ability to store parts of our consciousness in other hard drives—i.e., other people's brains. The longer you are with another person, the more your "self" begins to utilize that other person's brain without even thinking about it. In one way, Julie is the part of me that remembers to dust the fan. I'm the part of her that remembers to pay the bills. But it's more than simple tasks. It's memories: She remembers experiences I do not and vice versa. Why keep that memory in two places when it can easily be stored in one? It's experience. It's knowledge. It's understanding.

When Hofstadter's wife died from a brain tumor in 1993, he discovered that she didn't really die, not completely. There was a piece of her that remained in him long after her body went away. He'd gotten to know her so dearly that he'd developed a strange loop of her inside his mind, a kind of pocket consciousness hiding inside his own. If you've ever lost someone close to you, you know that you can hear them speak to you sometimes, a voice often triggered by circumstance. For years after my grandfather was gone, whenever someone nearby said, "Well, I was close," I would hear his old joke echo in my head: "Close only counts in horseshoes and hand grenades."

If our consciousness, our "I," emerges from the mechanical pattern of synapses inside our brain, the longer we spend with someone, the more their patterns of thought imprint on us. Over time, we build an incomplete replica of their strange loops in our own brains. I strongly believe this explains the way Amy Bradley has visited her lovers, Kat and Mollie, who each told of seeing her in dreams or hearing her voice in their minds. In a very real way, that was Amy, the part of her they welcomed inside their soul.

As Hofstadter wrote: "This is what human love means. The word 'love' cannot, thus, be separated from the word 'I'; the more deeply rooted the symbol for someone inside you, the greater the love, the brighter the light that remains behind."

And yet, merging with someone can also lead to a forgetting of their individuality, their specialness. On the cruise, Julie and I found time to remember our separate parts. Julie is a distinct human being, with her own will and agency, as am I. This trip was the longest we'd ever been away from our children. We were able to see each other again, not as partners sharing the responsibility of raising decent children, but as two individuals who fell in love in high school.

We held each other in the thick white blankets of the queen bed in front of the porthole looking out to infinity. I saw her again as the girl I found and who found me. And she rediscovered me in kind. I had forgotten myself in my prolonged melancholy, but I was coming awake at last. And I was grateful for this person. Yes, I would live a long life. I want to. Yes. Yes. Yes.

On the second day of our cruise, the *Rhapsody* docked at St. Croix, the largest of the United States' Virgin Islands. Like the rest of the Lesser Antilles, St. Croix was once the home of indigenous peoples like the Igneri, the Taíno, and the Kalinago. These tribes traded control of the islands through wars and interbreeding for hundreds of years, their languages mixing like their DNA. Sometimes, certain islands, like St. Croix, would be abandoned completely for generations, given back to the lizards and the crabs. When Christopher Columbus landed there in 1493, he was immediately attacked by Kalinago warriors, the first battle in a long campaign of invasion and control by the Spanish empire. (Spoiler alert: the Spanish won.)

To get off the ship that morning, each of us had to pass through a security checkpoint at the exit, where officers verified our identification. I was asked to remove my hat and glasses so they could match my features with the photo that came up on their computer when they scanned my room key. I'm not sure what security was like on the *Rhapsody* in 1998, but if it was anything like this, the only way Amy would have gotten off the ship without a record of it happening is off the side or in a container transported by crew.

Once outside, we walked down a long pier that ended at the town of Frederiksted, full of primary-colored homes and shops with Spanish tile roofs, palm trees leaning over the water. The ocean here is a lovely turquoise and quite clear. We stopped several times to watch sea turtles floating about, poking their heads above the water to look back at us. At a market at the end of the pier, half a dozen open-air tents offered Hawaiian shirts, never mind we were in the Caribbean. Joel stopped to snap photographs at Fort Frederik, which was built by Danish settlers in the 1700s to fend off pirate attacks. In most of the photos, Joel holds the old cannons like giant penises.

Instead of trying our luck with a taxi, we opted to walk the two miles down Emancipation Drive to Rainbow Beach, which was supposed to be excellent for snorkeling. This was not a wise decision. There is heat, and there is Caribbean heat. It gets hot in Ohio in the summers, in that hazy space between July and August. But this was a new heat, a transient heat. At St. Croix it was like the heat was settled in, thickening the air over millennia. Soon I had sweated through my Hawaiian shirt.

We walked in a straight line along the shoulder, past fields of sugar cane, stepping off the road whenever an old taxi, usually a beaten-down minivan held together by duct tape and wishes, zoomed by on the wrong side of the road. The drainage ditch was pocked with thousands of small holes. We wondered about them until we saw a land crab scuttle out of one. As we came nearer to the beach, we saw sections of road paved with the smooshed shells of these critters, which venture out in force at night. Bright handmade signs nailed to the trees along the way offered friendly messages from the island folk in broken English: EVERY TING'S GONNA-B AH'IGHT.

That $20 Target snorkeling kit worked out better than expected. I dropped my towel and backpack, and ventured into the water in the new swimming shirt I wore to hide my gut, pulling the mask down as I went. The coral starts immediately, and you must be careful to walk around the mini reefs. I slipped under the water, into a different world. The seabed was bright with color. A thousand tiny tropical fish darted in and out of the coral, most no bigger than a fingernail. They floated on the undulating current brought by the waves. I let myself go weightless, the snorkel above the water so I could breathe.

At first, my breathing was hard. I was afraid I would choke on saltwater or that the mask would slip. But I told myself that I was safe. I used the mindfulness tools I'd learned, bringing myself into the present moment, letting the anxious thoughts pass over my consciousness like puffy white clouds. My breathing slowed. The weightlessness gave way to a lack of sensory input. As long as I remained calm, I could not even feel my body—I was simply an observer of this hidden universe, living in awe of it.

This was my favorite moment of the trip.

I thought back to how I was at twenty-three, the age Amy was when she came to the Caribbean. I had no tools back then. Floating suspended above the coral would have terrified me. The simple act of quieting my mind would have been impossible. I was in such turmoil at twenty-three—hunting for a career, a family, a life. On top of all that, Amy was desperately trying to understand her identity, or at least how to make it work with her family, who would have been nearby and hard to ignore.

Much has been written about our desire to revisit our younger selves, to assure them that every ting's gonna-b ah'ight. We tell these stories in the hopes that younger readers might understand that and skip the misery we walked through, blindly. But I'm not sure it's possible to truly understand what that means without suffering through it. Everything is going to be all right. Not just that, but everything always was all right.

That night I watched Julie perform karaoke inside the Shall We Dance ballroom on the far side of the Schooner piano bar. She sang "Both Sides Now" by Joni Mitchell. The thing about growing old with someone is the surprise you feel when you fall in love with them again. This was the girl who sang in choir in high school, this woman on stage. You know when you meet the person who will be next to you when you die, I think. But let that be years and years from now when the body is weak and the mind is full.

When she finished, the room applauded. I wiped the tears away before she joined me for another gin martini.

The karaoke party was actually a contest put on by the cruise hosts. For a moment, it looked like Julie might take it, too. But then a young Puerto Rican man stepped up to the mic to sing "En Mi Viejo San Juan," and the audience went crazy.

"He's gonna fuck all of us," Joel whispered. And he was right—the kid won. His prize was a Royal Caribbean key chain.

As the days passed aboard the *Rhapsody of the Sea*, it felt like we'd stepped out of life and onto a floating temporary universe of our own. We busied ourselves by reading or by searching for the rubber ducks passengers hide all around the ship for others to find.

In Aruba, we visited Eagle Beach, which is consistently voted the most beautiful beach in the world, a sweep of white sand hidden behind tall palms, where giant iguanas roam. The water here is transparent to the floor and not too cold. Though I preferred Rainbow Beach for its coral and fish, it was still a transcendent experience and full of that oceanic feeling that Freud described. Yet, when Amy was here, she took herself to Taco Bell.

I kept coming back to that detail. It felt important. It was not the action of someone open to the wonders of this place. It was the action of someone clinging to comfort, to familiarity. A little detail that suggested, at least to me, that Amy's mind was very loud on that trip, and she found herself untethered and afraid. Perhaps I'm reading too much into it. But I don't think so.

The *Rhapsody* parked beside the *Freewinds* in Aruba, a bit of serendipity that felt fated, as if our trip were mirroring the trip the Bradleys took in 1998. As I walked by, a well-dressed man came down the gangway. I stopped him. “I don’t suppose you have public tours on the ship?” I asked.

He laughed condescendingly, and said, “No,” and moved on.

Later, we watched a dozen young men and women dressed in dark uniforms come out of the *Freewinds* and do calisthenics in the pier parking lot. The rookie Scientologists jogged circles for quite some time, then went back inside, where they were expected to serve for the next billion years. Did something about that life appeal to young Amy Bradley?

At dinner that night, the entire restaurant staff performed the Macarena. It’s quite possible this tradition has continued since 1998, when the song was quite popular. I felt bad for them, these people who’d come to make a little money, away from their homes and family, serving entitled guests from the States, and made to dance like marionettes. There will come a time when we look back at these opulent years and the disparity of classes, and we will cringe at memories like this. At least, I hope.

After it was dark, I took my seldom used camera to a deck near the back of the ship and zoomed into the windows of the *Freewinds* to see what depraved things the Scientologists were getting up to. All I found was a conference room with an enormous flatscreen showing some bit of L. Ron Hubbard propaganda and children playing in the pool. Did the kids know about Xenu and the alien ghosts yet? Probably not.

Next stop, Bonaire, then Curaçao. Soon after we left port, I saw the lights of Curaçao in the distance, an oasis in the dark void of the nighttime sea. What waited for me there?

Chapter Thirty-two

ACROSS THE USELESS ISLAND

Spanish invaders called Curaçao "the useless island," because the land was not so good for farming and had no precious metals to mine. They took it anyway, in 1499; the Arawak natives could do little to defend themselves against the armada. But the Spanish didn't stay long. The Dutch colonized Curaçao in 1634 and found a way to make the island profitable—by turning it into one of the main centers for the African slave trade in the Americas. In fact, it was a Dutch ship from the Caribbean that provided the first slaves to the commonwealth of Virginia. Perhaps some of their descendants were present at Israel Hill to witness General Lee's surrender as he marched past what would one day be Longwood University.

There are several narratives for how the island came to be called Curaçao, all unverified. The one I like the most involved marooned sailors. Back in the 1500s, it was common for seamen on long voyages to develop scurvy from a lack of vitamin C in their diets. If the men were particularly sick, the captain would drop them off here, and they would eat the golden oranges found on the island and recover. The Portuguese sailors began to refer to this place as Ilha da Curação, the Island of Healing.

By 1789, slaves greatly outnumbered the Dutch on Curaçao. The census that year recorded 12,864 slaves and 4,410 white citizens. In 1795, a slave named Tula recognized this bit of leverage and organized a revolt against his master at the Knip Plantation, which produced wool and fruit. Tula led fifty slaves out of the plantation, and they marched to nearby plantations where they gathered a growing army of slaves demanding a better life. A Dutch representative was sent to speak with Tula at a rebel safehouse in Porto Mari.

Tula's demands were simple: an end to collective punishment, to not be forced to work on Sundays, and the freedom to buy goods from someone other than their master. The white men didn't concede, and they had the guns and ammunition the rebels lacked. The revolt ended seven weeks after it began. Tula was captured, tortured, and beheaded. Slavery was abolished on the island in 1863. A monument to the slave revolt, a clenched fist raised to the air, stands near the location of Tula's execution.

Today, Curaçao is considered a constituent country in the Kingdom of the Netherlands, with a population of around 155,000 souls, ninety percent of whom are practicing Christians and mostly Catholic. They have a prime minster who acts as the head of government on the island, but the king of the Netherlands remains the ultimate authority. At least for now, prostitution is a lucrative legal business on Curaçao.

I came to Curaçao the morning of August 9, 2024. My mission was to locate Judith Margaritha, the woman who claimed to have seen Amy Bradley held hostage by Colombian kidnappers, the tip that led to Frank Jones's long con. Nobody had heard from Judith in twenty years. I also wanted to visit Porto Mari, the beach where the scuba diver, David Carmichael, encountered the woman he believed was Amy Bradley. But mostly I wanted to see Curaçao for myself. The Bradleys had made the island sound like a den of crime, a danger to tourists and young women in particular. But was it?

One of the other couples who took the trip with us was a man named Adam and his fiancée, Jordan. While the others hopped a taxi to a nearby beach, Jordan accompanied me for the first leg of my journey. I think he was curious about what I do, but he also wanted to make sure I was safe. Jordan is a quiet, calm soul. He's had many odd jobs over the years, including pest control for a bit. He currently works for FedEx. I rented a car from a hut at the end of the pier, and he helped me navigate the streets. To my relief, the residents of Curaçao drive on the same side of the road as we do in the States. I found the ride to be quite pleasant for the scenery and company.

Typically, I'm pretty good at tracking people down. The White Pages are comprehensive. If they don't work, we all leave a trail on social media and court dockets. If all else fails, I can call up my buddy, Mike Lewis, and he'll run a background check for me, which usually comes with a cell phone number. But trying to find someone on Curaçao from home proved impossible. Mike's private-eye databases don't extend to that country, and it has no online phone book. Judith has a Facebook page, but it has not been active since 2014. I did find one mention of her name deep in a Google search result. She was listed as a volunteer at someplace called the Cathedral of Thorns, on the outskirts of Willemstad.

We drove through the city, which is about the size of downtown Akron but resembles a miniature Amsterdam in many ways, with its Dutch architecture, its tall, narrow buildings and homes, but brightly colored, in the way of the islands. We crossed over the Koningin Julianabrug, the Queen Juliana Bridge, that spans Sint Anna Bay. It wasn't far to the cathedral from there. We parked in a lot beside a welcome center. Behind this building was the cathedral itself.

The structure was designed by the Curaçao artist Herman Van Bergen. It's a mazelike monument with a central open-air cathedral. The walls are made of *sumpiñas*, which are spiny thorns taken from the Acacia tortuosa bush, a native shrub that managed to survive after the European settlers cut down all the *wayaká* trees. Van Bergen sees his installation as representing the fight against "the destructive pollution by humanity." The structure of the branching thorns makes the walls translucent, ghostlike. Jordan and I walked around until we found a property manager who knew Judith. Most people here speak English and Dutch, though as you go farther inland the language becomes a pidgin of African, Spanish, Portuguese, French, English, and Dutch, called Papiamentu. Luckily, the manager spoke the King's. She said that Judith had moved several years ago. She didn't know where she was now.

Dejected, we returned to the car. I had one more idea, though. Sure, there was no online phone book, but the islanders must have a local directory. At least in the States, libraries often keep copies for reference. Jordan found a listing for a small library in a shopping plaza ten minutes away. Sure enough, when we arrived, I found a local white pages, about the size of a graphic novel, though it was three years old. Inside I found two listings for a J. Margaritha.

For the next two hours, we drove through neighborhoods with names like Brievengat and Piscadera searching for this woman. The barrios outside Willemstad reminded me of the poorer suburbs of LA, the drab honey-brown stuccos and plaster-walled homesteads of Inglewood, perhaps. It didn't look outwardly threatening in any way. Eventually, we found ourselves in a proper slum, though its edges were softening by gentrification. The homes there were colorless two-room bungalows tucked behind lush vegetation, no personal vehicles in sight.

An address associated with J. Margaritha led us to an empty lot between two shacks. We double-backed to make sure. Yes, whatever was once there, the island had taken back. The second address was on the other side of Willemstad, behind a security gate. It was an apartment complex. From what I could gather from the neighbors, Judith Margaritha once worked there as part of the service staff. I cannot say for certain that it was the same Judith Margaritha we were searching for, though the age lined up.

I dropped Jordan off at the beach then, so that he could report back to Julie that I was in no real danger. The island was no threat. East Akron is more dangerous. Admittedly, I enjoy a privilege of safety, being a middle-aged white man, and others may disagree with this assessment.

Alone now, I went searching for Porto Mari beach, where David Carmichael claimed to have seen Amy months after she disappeared. The drive took me north of Willemstad, into a less populated region of the island overgrown with colonies of tall *cadushi* cactus and deadly manchineel trees—*manzaliña* in the local language. The locals will warn you to not stand under a *manzaliña* when it rains or else it may burn your skin. I stopped at a roadside trailer advertising *pastechi*, a favorite snack on the ABC islands that resembles an empanada but is made with plain pastry shells instead of cornmeal. I got a ham and cheese *pastechi*, and a soda, and paid with guilders I'd gotten for change at a gas station. It was divine.

I found Playa Porto Mari at the end of an access road. Back in 1998, this was a secluded, empty beach known only to locals. Today, it's a popular tourist destination. I saw about a hundred people sunning on blankets and playing in the crystal waters. The bar is still there beside a newer shower house and dive shop. I took my camera to capture decent video of the place. Only when I was standing amid the beachgoers did I notice it was also a topless beach. I put the lens cap back on and did my best not to look like a creep.

Is it possible Amy was here that day in August 1998, flanked by two captors? That's a daring risk for kidnappers.

On my way back, I stopped briefly at a turnout to watch a flamboyance of pink flamingos hunting for minnows in a tide pond. I was struck again by the beauty of this place that I had feared for so long. But it was beauty with an edge—the spines of the *cadushi* cactus, the poisonous fruit of the *manzaliña* trees. The ocean itself on all sides, with its limitless risks. And always, the oppressive heat. Maybe its people had an edge like that, too. Though everyone I met greeted me with a smile.

The question on my mind as I drove back to where the *Rhapsody* waited was this: Could Amy have hidden here? Maybe. But not under duress. She certainly could not have been held hostage by some secret Colombian cartel—the Dutch authorities would have noticed such a presence on their island, and there are English speakers everywhere, not to mention police. This isn't some third-world country. This is, essentially, the Amsterdam of the Caribbean.

But if it was Amy's choice to disappear, yes, it's possible. You could find countless opportunities to make some money under the table on Curaçao, thanks to the tourists. You could sell lounge chairs on the beach, ham-and-cheese *pastechis* on the side of the road. It's not an easy life, but it sure is a beautiful place to hide.

Still, from what I'd learned of Amy, even with the troubles that came with her sexual identity, I can't see her just leaving everyone behind.

More and more, I found myself leaning to the grim conclusion that whatever happened to Amy Bradley began and ended aboard the *Rhapsody of the Seas*. And so, I returned to the ship to see what I could learn. Now that I'd seen Curaçao, I could stop pretending to be an ordinary tourist. I could be a proper journalist now.

Chapter Thirty-three

A PRIVATE TOUR

THAT NIGHT, as the *Rhapsody* turned back toward San Juan, I stopped by Room 8564, the cabin where the Bradley family stayed. The rooms on the eighth floor were much larger than our place down below. They came with balconies, too. I considered multiple stories I might tell whoever was staying there this week. What was the right thing to say to convince them to let me inside for a look? I decided to go with the truth, odd as it was. Who knows, maybe they would be true crime addicts, already familiar with the case and eager to help.

I knocked on the door. A teenage girl poked her head out.

"Can I talk to your mom or dad?" I asked.

She backed inside. Her mother and grandmother appeared in the doorway.

"Hi, sorry to bother you," I began. I explained to them that I was a journalist working on a missing person story and that the last time the woman was seen may have been in the cabin they were currently occupying.

"Oh, that's really interesting," the mother said, eyes wide.

"Would you mind if I looked around a bit?" I asked.

"I don't see why not," she said. "But could you come back at eight, when my husband is here?"

"Of course," I said.

While I waited, I took a closer look at the Viking Lounge, the dance club where Amy danced closely with Alister Douglas, aka Yellow, the night before she vanished. It was mostly empty. A few people were drinking cocktails at tables near windows that looked over the pool. I could see two ways for passengers to enter the Viking Lounge—from a set of stairs on the port side or from the glass elevators at the back of the dance floor. Crystal and Lori claimed to have seen Amy return to the club with Alister sometime between 3:30 and 6 a.m. They saw them go up inside a glass elevator but not down. Then Alister had appeared on their deck a short time later, alone.

If Amy and Alister had returned after the Viking Lounge closed, where did Amy go? I was looking for another exit, maybe one used exclusively by the crew. I spotted swinging doors behind the bar that led to a kitchen, but the bartenders were on duty, and I could hear clattering from behind the doors. There was no easy way to take a peek back there. I made a note to return during debarkation, when the crew would be busy elsewhere. It would be risky, but I had to know what was back there, and if Amy could have gone that way. Besides, what's the worst they could do to me? Kick me off at San Juan?

At five past eight, I returned to Room 8564 and knocked again. This time a barrel-chested man answered the door.

"Hi, I stopped by earlier and . . ."

That's as far as I got before he raised his hand. "Yeah, my wife told me. The missing woman. I'm sorry, but we've got too much going on. And I don't feel comfortable with you coming into our room."

"Okay," I said with a sigh. "Can I ask when you're scheduled to leave Sunday morning?"

"Eight a.m."

"Thanks."

I let it drop for now but made another note in my journal. A lot was riding on the crew being distracted during debarkation. My frustration was growing. Maybe seeing into the Bradleys' cabin wouldn't change anything, maybe it wouldn't make for a better book, but my pride as an investigative journalist was wrapped up in accomplishing simple remedial background tasks on this ship. If I couldn't get at any new information, what was the point of the whole trip? So that I could describe the goddamn *manzaliña* trees?

The next day, Saturday, was a full day at sea, as the *Rhapsody* made for Puerto Rico, a quiet end to an exciting week. My goal that day was to get someone from Royal Caribbean to speak to me on the record about the legacy of Amy's disappearance on this ship. After breakfast, I went to the purser's desk and asked to talk to someone in security. If anyone on board knew about the case, I imagined a security manager was my best shot.

The desk clerk called someone in the security office who agreed to see me. But then he called back a minute later and declined.

"You should talk to Royal Caribbean's public relations office," the clerk said.

I've been reporting on true crime for twenty years now. One thing I've learned in those years is this—when the universe seems to be stubbornly withholding information, it's time to stop pushing. Relax. Take a step back. Refocus. There is a time and manner with which this universe chooses to give up its answers. You can't force it. If you find a little patience, the information you're after will often find you.

Exhibit number one: Still stinging from the brush-off by security, I walked to the glass elevators to go back to my room. I was the only one in the vestibule at the time. A man dressed in a white uniform walked over. He pressed the Up button and waited beside me.

"How's your day?" he asked with a slight Swedish accent.

"It's great," I said. "But these long days on the water make me nervous, when you can't see anything else. No other ships. Just a big empty ocean."

"You can definitely feel it, the vastness," he said.

I looked at him, closer. He had a gold tag attached to his lapel with his name and position. It read: Filip, Captain.

"You're the captain?" I asked.

"I am," he said. He shook my hand. "Filip Norberg."

I couldn't believe my luck. Or was it luck?

"I'm a journalist," I said, my words coming out faster than I could control them. "I'm here researching the disappearance of Amy Lynn Bradley. Have you ever heard her name?"

His eyes grew wide. "Oh, yes," he said. "I've worked for Royal Caribbean for twenty years. When I came to the *Rhapsody*, I looked up the Wikipedia page and found her name and did my research. The family believes there may be foul play. But there were all those sightings over the years like that naval officer. If he really saw her, why did he wait? If he was worried about getting in trouble, why wouldn't he just call in that tip and not use his name?"

"That's a good point," I said. "She disappeared as the ship was pulling into Curaçao. They were close to the channel, if not already inside. If she went overboard, why wouldn't someone have found the body?"

"The port in Curaçao is challenging," said Captain Norberg. "It's the currents. They're very strong and unpredictable. We used to go under the bridge, but that was dangerous. We don't go down the channel anymore because of those currents."

"Has anyone else gone missing from the *Rhapsody*?"

"No," he said. "And a lot has changed in twenty-six years. We know what happens on board."

The elevator doors opened for him. I shook his hand again and thanked him for talking to me.

"I look forward to the book," he said, with a smile.

Looking back, that was when the universe relented and began to share its secrets, the few that were left.

I met up with our group at the Schooner bar later that evening, our last night on the ship. Joel was in a rare quiet mood; his jovial countenance dimmed. He had taken the stairs on the way to the bar. As always, he was dressed in his wonderfully tawdry manner—hot pink shorts and tight buttoned shirt. A group of teen boys passed him. As they went by, one of them called him a fag.

"Bunch of bitches," Joel said, recounting the story. "I want to find that boy's mother and give her a talking to."

The *Rhapsody* may now offer LGBTQ mixers, but homophobia is still literally around the corner, even today. How bad must it have been for Amy in 1998? Her sexual preference had somehow become common knowledge among the crew. Could someone have targeted that simmering, bigoted hatred toward her, someone who had access to out-of-the-way places beyond the range of security cameras, where a body could be dumped into the churning waters of the Sint Anna Bay?

After being together for a week, our group from Ohio had grown closer. We relaxed in our regular nook not far from the piano as the musician tickled the keys and sang "Jessie's Girl." We talked about our excursions and our favorite islands. I cozied up to Julie on a couch as she sipped another lavender gin martini. My mind dwelled on my luck in this world and the steps it took to get here.

We packed before bed and in the morning, we woke early to eat a quick final breakfast at the buffet. The *Rhapsody* was already parked at the San Juan dock. I could see all the way to the Castillo San Felipe del Morro, that ancient fort at its northern tip. It was a long way back to Akron now.

As the passengers began to debark one group at a time, I gave my suitcase to Julie and set off in search of some final answers.

I walked up the stairs to the Viking Lounge first. It was completely empty, as I'd hoped, all the crew busy with the mass exodus happening ten floors below. I stepped over the dance floor and walked around the bar to the swinging door and then passed through to the other side. I found myself in a small industrial kitchen full of stainless-steel tables and a stove. On the far side was a narrow service elevator. Accessible only by crew, this elevator goes all the way down to the staff quarters and private deck. Could Amy have left this way? Yes, indeed. Did she? I don't know.

Next, I returned to the eighth-floor cabins. Every door was open and empty, every door except 8564. A room steward was busy cleaning the cabin next to it. I hesitated, then knocked. The barrel-chested man opened it, suitcase in hand. The three women he shared the room with were just behind him.

"Good morning," I said.

The man shook his head and walked around me to find the steward. "Hey," he said to him. "We're leaving but this man is trying to get in our room for some reason."

For some reason? Don't do me any favors, man.

The steward looked over, annoyed at the interruption. I imagine he was on a tight schedule to turn the beds over for the next guests.

"I just want to look at it," I said. "I'll be gone in five minutes."

"I don't care," he said.

The man sighed and walked away, his family following close behind.

I stepped into Room 8564.

Just inside to the left was a bathroom twice the size of the one in our cabin. The rest was a square space with a bed and a couch that had been opened to become another bed. The foldout was closest to the balcony, which ran the entire length of the back wall. Even with the couch out there was plenty of room to get around. With four people, it would have been cramped but not terrible.

The sliding balcony door opened to the right, and the balcony itself was wider than I expected, big enough for some chairs and a short table. The railing came up to my chest. I looked over the side. It was a straight shot down to the water, eight stories below. Some people online have said there was no way Amy could have fallen over there, because she would have landed on the balcony below or a lifeboat or something. But there are no obstacles from the room to the ocean. The only thing one would hit if they went over was the water itself.

I stood, silently in the room for some time. Again, I was aware of how a single dimension—time—separated me from the solution to this case. If I could only step through that horizon, to look back on that day in 1998, and see the truth for myself. So close. I felt nothing of Amy left behind. No whispers from beyond, no heavy feeling in the air. If spirits cling to the Earth like thetans, Amy was elsewhere. It felt like a good thing. Perhaps that meant she had moved on. Or maybe it meant she was still alive, after all. How many people have stayed here, unaware of the torment felt by its previous occupants, the Bradleys? Hundreds, surely.

A theory began to form in my mind, then. A narrative that lined up with the evidence that could not be disputed. But it was not yet fully formed.

There was a box I needed to check off to be sure, and that box had one name on it—Alister Douglas. What sort of man was he? Was he cruel or was he kind? And where the hell was he, even?

I left then. I took one last ride on a great glass elevator and then walked onto the gangway, down to customs and outside where my group was waiting. We spent the day in Old San Juan and then boarded planes home.

The ghost ship still sails the Caribbean, ferrying people from Puerto Rico to the ABC islands and back again. Should you choose to make the voyage, be safe, and think of Amy.

Chapter Thirty-four

A SERIES OF UNFORTUNATE EVENTS

When I returned to Ohio, I began the long journey of unwinding the bad habits I'd accumulated in that long dark teatime of the soul I'd found myself in since 2017. I had promised Julie that I would take better care of myself, to live a complete life, and I intended to keep that promise. I am not exaggerating when I say it is the hardest thing I've ever had to do, and it happened slowly, over the course of the next several months, as I discarded one vice after another. I think traveling on the *Rhapsody* provided the perspective I needed to start. Once upon a time, a young woman, so full of life, had boarded the ship and never come back. Amy attacked the world like it was a series of challenges that needed to be conquered. It seemed perverse to waste any more time.

The first thing I did was go on Ozempic. My doctor started me on the lowest dose. While I didn't lose weight immediately, I stopped gaining any more. Within a week, I lost my craving to snack in between meals. It also lessened the cravings I had for alcohol, and my every-other-night double cocktail became a single, and then I found I didn't want a drink at all except for one on a weekend date. I started using the treadmill with some regularity. I didn't stop smoking pot, but I became a midnight toker so that I would fall asleep before the munchies kicked in. I drank Metamucil in the morning and pulled back on fast food. Soon, my body responded favorably. I had more energy. I had clarity. My anxiety faded. I began to feel good again.

Meanwhile, I was making quite a mess with my ongoing search for Amy Bradley.

Since the Bradleys had cut off ties following my discovery of Amy's girlfriends, I had lost a direct connection to information about the case. So, I returned to what had always worked in the past—making my investigation public to spur armchair sleuths into action. I could only do so much alone. I've found that sharing my journey online will attract other true crime addicts who may dig deeper on their own, and who would then reach out to me with their opinions and findings. I also knew that by putting myself out there, people who knew Amy and who sometimes searched the Internet for updates would discover my material and make contact with me directly.

I compiled a video of clips I'd recorded on the *Rhapsody*, to show people what the ship looked like inside and out. I figured that seeing the location of the mystery in great detail for the first time would get some attention on Reddit and Websleuths, and filter out to the greater community of citizen detectives. I also included photographs of other visiting escorts that had advertised on the website for Affordable Adult Vacations alongside the images of the woman who resembled Amy Bradley. None of those women had ever been identified. If I could just find one of those other women, perhaps they would remember who that lookalike was—or even better, remember Amy herself.

I texted Mollie, first. "I want to run something by you," I began. "I want to find this woman in the escort ad photo. The best way I can think to do that is get a lot of eyes on it."

I asked her if I could use the letter in the bottle that Amy had sent to her shortly before she disappeared. It revealed a side of Amy that nobody outside her friends and family has ever known. I knew it would spark interest.

Mollie called me a few days later and said I could use the letter if I thought it might help. And so, I read the letter in its entirety in the video I was creating. I talked openly about how Amy was gay and how she kept it a secret it for most of her life. I included a tour of the ship and shots from inside Room 8564. I ended with a call to action to help me identify some of the visiting escorts from the brothel on Margarita Island. The video was published on YouTube on September 4, 2024.

I heard from Brad Bradley about an hour after the video went up. He was displeased.

"First, I would say that your proclamation that Amy was 'gay' is a misleading half-truth," he wrote. "For someone who is a journalist and author, I would think you would be interested in telling people the facts instead of sensationalizing a portion of her history."

Brad went on to say that he would not have had an issue if I had identified Amy as "bisexual" instead of gay.

Then I heard from Mollie.

"I thought you were sharing the letter privately in a video not publicly on YouTube," she wrote. "I'm not comfortable with it being a public thing."

I don't know where the miscommunication lay, but I thought I had explained my intentions to Mollie.

I also received an email from a man named Ari Mark at Ample Entertainment, who identified himself as the director of the upcoming documentary for Netflix.

"Thank you for changing the video on YouTube," he wrote. "Ideally, you would remove your video entirely as the 'new information' you are alluding to really requires more context and is definitely not the focus of our project." He went on to say that my "bombshell" felt disingenuous to him. He asked me to not "interfere" anymore and to not have further contact with his producers. Producers who reached out to me first.

In one fell swoop, I had pissed off the Bradley family, upset

Mollie, and burned the bridge with the documentary crew. Pretty impressive for one ten-minute video.

I went back and reedited the video then, removing all but one quote from the letter and changing Amy's identity from "gay" to "bisexual," which felt like a betrayal of some great order. Who was I to gloss over a dead woman's identity? But I did it because I was not yet very far into the book, and I wasn't sure exactly how Amy had identified herself with her friends. Later, upon reviewing my many interviews, it became apparent to me that Amy identified as gay. Amy was gay. She was. Did she date men sometimes? Yes. Does that then make her "bi"? Is bisexual somehow less shameful because it provides hope that your loved one might one day be "normal"?

As we were sharing personal stories at their dining room table, I had told the Bradleys I was bisexual. But I've also had conversations with my father and loved ones where I've used the word "gay." Now, I like women. I prefer women. I'm occasionally attracted to men. Does that make me bisexual and not gay? Maybe from a linguistic standpoint. But I never felt bisexual when I had a dick in my mouth.

However, I'm not entrenched in queer culture. I don't know the rules of their lexicon. I haven't lived in it. So, I called up Joel and put the query to him. Is the distinction important?

"So Amy's family is insisting she's bi, but why?" Joel said. "There seems to be some perception that being bi is 'more acceptable.' She may like women, but she still likes men. I'm sure in their heads it's like, 'Well, she'll probably still marry a man.' It allows them to suspend their negative thoughts or worries and assume everything will be all right. Back in the 2000s, people would come out as bi. Our friend did. He was gay but keeping one foot in the 'normal, heterosexual closet' gives you some defense to people's prejudices. It needs to be stated very clearly that people are bisexual, there is nothing wrong with it. But we don't know how Amy would've identified, especially now that there has been so much progress in terms of sexuality and gender, but it's definitely a contributing factor to her love life, mental health, and potentially her disappearance. If Amy's partners say she identified as gay, that's the assumption I'd trust. There seems to be some holding out on her family's side in accepting that, if they're so hell-bent on her being bi. Now that is just my thoughts on the subject. I'm gay, I knew I was gay. If Amy's disappearance happened now, it would be under a very, very different lens."

As the video gained traction online, I became aware of an odd parallel between my life at that time and Amy's. I had offended the Bradleys, by being open about Amy's sexuality. I had acted in a way that felt like a betrayal to Mollie, and she had grown cold to me. Similarly, Amy knew her parents, who were so close and loving, did not approve of her sexuality, and she had upset Mollie by betraying her trust, finding her unwilling to continue their relationship, at least until the end. What I was experiencing was a small taste of what Amy had experienced from the same group. I have to tell you it felt absolutely awful, rife with shame and disappointment. For her, it must have been devastating. And yet, Amy didn't give up on Mollie, and eventually she'd won her back. I held out some hope that I might do the same.

The video acted like a lightning rod that attracted both armchair sleuths who followed the case obsessively and people who knew Amy in real life. One college friend I hadn't spoken with was quite upset about the edits I had made to appease the Bradleys.

"Amy wasn't bisexual, she was only ever into girls," they wrote. "Her parents didn't accept that in any way shape or form." They suggested I do better research and look into the statistics on suicide among the LGBTQ community.

We traded emails for a while. I tried to explain my reasoning for changing the video, but it fell flat—because it was, after all, inexcusable. "I'm offended because you purposefully aren't honoring her true sexuality, in a very public way, and acting like sex trafficking is actually possible (why, because it's salacious?)" they wrote. "You're denying she was gay, just like her family did."

I was not making any friends. Hey, maybe that's the job. Maybe

I was being willfully naive to think that I might find a case to write about that didn't upset anyone, where the family of a missing woman would actively support me every step of the way. These people don't want an investigative journalist, they want a publicist.

I wondered what else I'd missed being too careful with this story. I knew I had avoided one very basic step in long-form reporting. I never went "fishing."

A fishing expedition, in journalism parlance, is where you blindly search for information you aren't sure even exists. This usually comes in the form of FOIA requests. You carpet-bomb every police department and court, in every jurisdiction where your subject has lived, on the off chance of turning up some secret incident report that reveals more to their story. Low risk, high reward. It was one of the first things I did during my research into the disappearance of Maura Murray. It kicked up a police report from the University of Massachusetts that revealed Maura was in trouble for credit card theft and identity fraud when she went missing. You never know what you might find.

I FOIA'd Chesterfield County, Virginia, where Amy had grown up, not expecting anything. I was surprised to receive a quick response. Amy was named in an incident report at a house on Robious Road three weeks before her disappearance. Then it got interesting, because the records department refused to provide further details, stating it was "part of an ongoing investigation." As far as leads go, it was a juicy one. Few crimes have statutes of limitations that extend beyond twenty-six years. I figured something in that report must have related to the investigation into her disappearance. It was the only thing that made sense.

The records department also told me that they wouldn't release further information to me, anyway, since I didn't live within the Commonwealth. I enlisted the help of a friend from Instagram who lives in Virginia to file an identical report. Again and again, the records manager found ways to deny access.

Finally, I called the Chesterfield County police department and spoke with a lieutenant there. I explained to him who I was and how I'd learned about the secret report. I argued that whatever it contained could not be related to an open case due to the statute of limitation, unless it was a murder. Perhaps whatever was in it might shed light on an unsolved disappearance. He agreed. And a few days later I obtained the report.

But it turned out to be nothing. Or probably nothing.

On March 9, 1998, Amy visited a friend on Robious Road. Tom Edgerton was with her. She was sitting in her car in the driveway when she heard a single gunshot from a nearby park. Together, they drove to the park to check it out. The only person they saw there was an imposing man standing alone by a vehicle. Amy got the license plate number and then reported everything to police. But nothing more ever happened with the case.

In fact, there was never any ongoing investigation, but that's the sort of games records departments often play with reporters.

I put in another FOIA request for court records in Miami-Dade County, Florida. In 1999, the Bradleys sued Royal Caribbean in civil court there, seeking damages for alleged negligence, defamation, and intentional emotional damage. Their lawyers claimed Amy had been abducted from their ship, under their watch, and the cruise line should be held responsible.

In response to the lawsuit, Royal Caribbean released a terse statement to *Travel Weekly*, which covered the court case. "We're sorry despite all these efforts to assist the Bradley family they've apparently decided to direct their grief at the company by filing a lawsuit seeking financial damages."

I was disappointed to learn that many of the files in the lawsuit, including depositions and affidavits by Ron, Iva, and Brad, had been destroyed due to the court's retention policies. However, the handful of documents I did receive told the story in detail.

The Bradleys actually filed two civil suits against Royal Caribbean. Each suit claimed that Amy had been abducted and held hostage aboard the *Rhapsody of the Seas*. One lawsuit was a tort claim alleging that Amy was still alive somewhere. The other was a wrongful death suit alleging that she was dead.

But both cases fell apart, in the summer of 2000, when the judge granted a motion to dismiss due to fraud on the part of the Bradleys. Here's what happened.

On February 11, 2000, lawyers for Royal Caribbean submitted formal questions on the record for Ron Bradley. They asked Ron to provide the names, addresses, and phone numbers for every witness he knew of who claimed to have seen Amy after her disappearance. Ron replied with the contact information for three witnesses, one of whom was the scuba diver, David Carmichael. His answers were under oath.

But Royal Caribbean knew that Ron and Brad had traveled back to Curaçao and had met other witnesses that they did not disclose to the court—witnesses who saw Amy alone and seemingly acting of her own accord.

One sighting was reported by a taxi driver who claimed to have seen Amy the morning she disappeared from the *Rhapsody*. He was sitting in his car in the parking lot next to the pier when a woman fitting her description ran up to his window and asked if he had a phone she could use. It seemed to be an urgent request. Again, this was early days of cell phones and most people had yet to buy a personal phone of their own. Cabbies were known to have them to connect with dispatch. But the driver couldn't help her, and she walked away.

Several other sightings concerned witnesses in and around Mambo Beach, just a bit to the east of Willemstad, where the ship docked. The witnesses reported seeing Amy alone and in no danger. Brad had told me they tracked these sightings to a server at a bar who resembled his sister.

Additionally, the Bradleys failed to share over a hundred written reports of other alleged sightings that were generated after the case was featured on *America's Most Wanted*, which aired in April and December of 1998.

In the motion, the lawyers for Royal Caribbean laid out the arguments put forth by the Bradleys' attorneys after this subterfuge was discovered. "One explanation is that the Plaintiffs had believed, until the Court ruled otherwise, that they had some sort of confidentiality privilege which would permit them not to answer questions based on fear for Amy's safety." Their lawyers said that the Bradleys did not intend to never disclose this information, but only to delay handing it over, so as not to jeopardize any rescue mission. But Royal Caribbean asserted that this argument was hard to believe, since they did share the sightings that supported their narrative.

"Probably the most persuasive argument against the believability of the Bradleys' claim that their omission was inadvertent, is the fact that the witnesses they listed were the ones that would be most helpful to their case," the order stated. "The witnesses that the Bradleys listed were the ones who reported to have seen Amy with other individuals, under some form of duress." The omitted witnesses saw Amy in no danger.

According to the ruling, "the evidence shows that the Bradleys were attempting to misdirect the Court and the Defendant when they omitted purported witnesses from their answer."

Following the dismissal, in 2001, Royal Caribbean asked the court to impose a $171,000 fine on the attorneys who represented the Bradleys, according to an article that appeared in *Travel Weekly*. However, I was unable to learn how that was resolved. Royal Caribbean's lawyers said they had worked 1,324 hours on the case.

Judge Stuart Simons determined that the Bradleys had perpetrated "a fraud on the court." Such a finding calls into question their credibility, no doubt about it. However, I'm not sure I would have acted differently. I believe the point of the lawsuit was not so much about getting money from Royal Caribbean but to engage them in the legal trappings of a civil court, where they could discover what, if anything, the cruise line had done to find their daughter, and to finally get some people from the cruise, such as the security director, to speak to it under oath. To that end, as a parent, I would have done everything in my power to make that happen. Even lying under oath. From a practical standpoint, though, it sure was a gamble.

The question I come around to again is whether Royal Caribbean really was negligent in any way. It totally depends on the missing part of the equation—what happened to Amy Bradley. If she walked off the ship on her own, as the taxi driver suggests, certainly not. If she died by suicide, it's a gray area. Could it be argued that she'd had too much to drink or that Royal Caribbean could have made it a little more difficult for someone to go overboard unnoticed? I think a good lawyer could make a meal out of that, sure. And if a crew member murdered her or was a party to an accidental fall, then absolutely they should compensate the Bradleys for their anguish.

The one and only person who was in the right place at the right time to do something like that and get away with it was Alister Douglas. But what evidence was there that Alister is capable of such a thing? I've met enough murderers to know that killing another human being is an action that one does not easily live with. It affects a person on a grand scale, whether they're caught or not. If they don't go to prison for something else, they usually fall into the bottle or take drugs to numb the guilt of what they've done and the anxiety of wondering when they'll be caught. I don't believe I've met a murderer who continues life as a fully functioning member of society unless that killing is justified by self-defense or combat—and even then it tends to come with great mental consequences. We need only look at all the veterans suffering from PTSD.

How could I ever know what sort of man Alister is without talking to him directly? More and more, I realized how important a piece of the puzzle he was. But Alister had not granted an interview in over twenty years. According to his Facebook profile, he lives on the island of Grenada, an island country in the Caribbean, about five hundred miles east of Curaçao. His posts indicate he works for a church down there. I saw photographs of Alister speaking into a mic with a congregation in front of him. Many of the things he posted on his page were religious themed in some way, including the picture he posted of two men in bed together with a red "X" over them and the caption: Leviticus 18:22. I had to look it up. "You shall not lie with a male as with a woman; it is an abomination."

I considered emailing Alister through the church. But doing so would open me up to an easy no. And if he said no, that was the end. I had one shot to ask, and my best chance was to do it in person.

I turned it over for weeks. What I was considering was an expensive, high risk, nearly impossible Hail Mary pass, certain to end in regret. But sometimes, in spite of the overwhelming odds against success, you still have to roll the dice and try.

I bought a ticket to Grenada and crossed my fingers.

PART FIVE

THE EXORCIST

Chapter Thirty-five

OBEAH LAND

On Saturday, October 5, I was dressed and out of the house by five a.m. I left Cleveland on a flight to Toronto, then transferred planes for the five-and-a-half-hour passage to Maurice Bishop International Airport, St. George's, Grenada.

I grew up on a farm in rural Ohio, far from any greater cultural influence. But as an adult I've traveled across the United States, working for short stints in New York, Utah, and LA. Later, I visited London and Cardiff. I've vacationed in Belize and Jamaica. I've driven all over Curaçao. At some point, I began to think I understood the world. Grenada changed all that.

As the plane banked toward the island's airport, I got my first glimpse of Grenada through the window. My arms broke out in gooseflesh. This was more than simple anxiety at the thought of landing in a new country. This was primitive fear. It was how unsettled the island appeared to be. True, I'd seen the same colorful houses on the ABC islands. But here, the jungle still ruled. Foxtail palms and soursop trees pushed aggressively against homesteads tucked into the valleys around Mount St. Catherine. The island looked like something out of *Jurassic Park* but no savage predators live in the jungles anymore, only mono monkeys and mongooses.

What I felt in my heart, though, was a place still relatively untamed by civilization, a suggestion of how the world was before white empires. It spoke of ancient magic and lost gods, of the first enemy of mortal man—the world, itself, indifferent Nature.

I suspect many Americans, like me, only know of Grenada through high school history lessons about the United States' brief invasion of the island, in 1983. At the time, Cuban workers were attempting to build a 10,000-foot airstrip on Grenada for use as a refueling station for Soviet military transport planes. Maurice Bishop was prime minister, the head of the People's Revolutionary Government. Bishop was against formally aligning the island country with the Soviet Union, but the more passionate Marxists in Grenada were ready to choose sides.

On October 16, in a coup, Bishop was overthrown and executed by firing squad. President Ronald Reagan acted quickly to keep the Soviets out. On October 25, the Army's 75th Ranger Regiment and 82nd Airborne Division, along with the Marines, Delta Force, Navy SEALs, and ground troops from Jamaica, invaded Grenada and found little resistance. The war lasted eight days. Democratic elections were held in 1984 and October 25th became Grenada's Thanksgiving Day.

Today, Grenada is a member country of the British Commonwealth. King Charles III is head of state, but all executive power lies with the locally elected prime minster.

Like many other Caribbean nations, this island was once home to the indigenous Arawak tribes who were displaced by the French and the British who built ports for human trafficking. Eventually, the islands filled with kidnapped Africans made to work plantations for white men. In fact, eighty-two percent of modern-day Grenadians can trace their ancestral roots to African slaves. Their ancestors brought with them music and art, and also a form of witchcraft that is still practiced in secret throughout the island today. They call it Obeah.

Obeah (pronounced "Obi-ah") is not so much a religion as it is a system of spells and rituals, not unlike Voodoo. It relies heavily on physical items imbued with suggestive power, things like amulets and potions. Clinical psychologist Timothy McCartney studied Obeah practices in the Caribbean in the 1970s. In his paper "Ten, Ten the Bible Ten," McCartney writes about the dual nature of Obeah. It can be either white or black magic, depending on your goal. And Obeah can be quite powerful, especially if you choose to believe. "It can cause an illness, either physical or mental or can cure any physical or mental problems. It can cause death!" he wrote.

In Grenada, Obeahmen and Obeahwomen are referred to as "scientists" instead of "shamans" or "witches." These mystics are usually born with the gift. Sometimes this special gift is passed down from mother to daughter. Sometimes the gift appears as compensation for some physical disability or manifests after a traumatic event.

In exchange for goods or services, an Obeahman will offer magical solutions to everyday problems. To heal a bad back, he may give the client a bundle of plants and a jar of graveyard dirt to mix into their bath water. If you need to banish a person from your life, he may instruct you to steal your enemy's fingernail clippings and bury them outside your home. For protection, he may offer an amulet that holds holy water and the bread and wine of the Eucharist. Obeahmen sometimes hang witch bottles full of blessed liquids from fruit trees to ward off thieves. There are love potions, too, though these are often frowned upon, since it goes against free will. But if a woman wishes to win a man's affection, she can use the magic of Obeah and mix her menstrual blood into the man's food.

In the days of slavery, the only means of justice available to a slave was through Obeah. If a master became too sadistic, an Obeahman would give the slave a bottle of poison to sprinkle into the master's drink. How much of this was actual practice and how much was rumor is hard to determine, but in the end, it matters little, as the effect was the same—when a plantation owner fell ill and died, the slaves would whisper that it was Obeah. In turn, the other plantation owners treated the enslaved people better so as not to be poisoned themselves. Obeah was a clever way to gain control over the uncontrollable.

Some evidence suggests that Obeah was responsible for the mass hysteria that led to the Salem Witch Trials, in 1692. Young Elizabeth Parris and her cousin Abigail Williams somehow came to know of Obeahlike rituals, such as how to tell their fortunes by dropping an egg white into a glass of water and watching what shape it made. When the adults became alarmed, the girls pointed to the family's slave—Tituba—and called her a witch. Little is known about Tituba before she came to Salem except that she had come from "New Spain," which some scholars believe was a reference to Barbados, an island steeped in Obeah lore.

While the practice of Obeah is technically illegal in Grenada, the law is never enforced. Obeahmen can still be found if you know whom to ask. In 2022, the island's newspaper, *The Vincentian*, reported that customs officials within the Ministry of Finance were using Obeah to avoid being transferred to unsavory departments.

In a very real sense, you can *feel* it. I felt it as soon as I saw the island. The feeling became more intense as I stepped off the plane into the smothering heat. This is a place of old magic, where superstition still reigns. The heat is unforgivable, the land treacherous. The only comfort offered is the belief that one may call on certain powers for protection, to make it to the next day.

Somewhere, deep in the middle of all this, was one man I desperately needed to find—Alister Douglas. It would take some magic to find him. But this was a place of magic.

I was surprised to find that Grenada's international airport is smaller than Akron's regional hub. It took two minutes to walk through the terminal to the exit, where I picked up a taxi to take me to my hotel. The cab was a "Ship of Theseus" cargo van—so old that each part had surely been replaced by junk and scrap over thirty years. The driver spoke English but with such a thick Creole accent, I had to ask him to repeat everything he said.

He motored through a wide valley at impossible speeds, past rum distilleries and into the Limes, a neighborhood of the capital city, St. George's. The hotel I had booked through Expedia did not actually exist, and so he dropped me off at a place called Wave Crest Suites. A Grenadian man with four teeth to his name greeted me and made a call on a flip cell phone to the manager, who arrived five minutes later. She was young, well dressed in a blue uniform. For $60 American she gave me a room at the end of the two-story cement block apartment complex.

To my relief, it came with an industrial A/C unit. It was quite loud, but in about five minutes, the oppressive heat had subsided. The thermostat said it was 91 degrees Fahrenheit outside, but this wasn't a heat I'd ever felt before. It got into your lungs, thick and heavy. I suspect it had something to do with how close I was to the equator. Is the sun more direct here? There is no hiding from it. Before she left, the manager warned me that the climate can be unkind to white tourists, and I should always carry water.

When I was alone, I sat on the edge of the bed for some time in a polo shirt that was now saturated with my sweat. My heart raced. My mind was loud with doubt. I tried my mindfulness tricks. I stopped to appreciate the present, to let the worries about tomorrow pass by. Whatever would happen would happen, with or without worry. Reflecting on the present, I realized I was grateful to be in that hotel room. I was in Grenada. On assignment. Tracking down a suspect in a strange, exotic country. Thirty-five years ago, I was mucking out the chicken coop on a farm in rural Ohio, thinking I'd never see the world. I was doing okay. My breathing slowed.

After a shower and a change, I organized my gear for the next day and made sure to place my keys in the top drawer of the dresser, so I wouldn't accidentally lose them wandering around the island. Then I walked the two blocks to Grand Anse beach, where I found a grocery stocked with plenty of bottled water. I bought two liters and some Carib beer, a local lager, but first I had to pull some Caribbean currency out of an ATM. The exchange rate comes out to about a third of our dollar for every one of theirs, which made mental math tricky for this English major. I walked across the street, following the pleasant smells drifting from the open door of a walk-up kitchen called Grille Master. Colorful posters advertised their Cow Heel Soup and Lambie Waters. I ordered jerk chicken with rice and fried plantains, which they put in a Styrofoam container and wrapped in an old plastic shopping bag.

On my way back to my room, I found a large crowd gathered on a fútbol field, in front of an enormous white tent, its sides rolled up to let in the thin breeze off the ocean. If I had to guess, I'd put the size of the audience at around two thousand. At first, I thought it must be an old-school Baptist revival or something, the way everyone was quiet, their eyes on the man at the pulpit under the tent. But then I heard the man's voice come through the large speakers in front of the stage. "B-14!" he shouted. The crowd murmured and marked their ballots. It was a giant game of Bingo! I'd never seen so many people play Bingo, and never outside like this. Something about it made me sad. I walked away before I thought about it too much.

Safely back in my private space, I could feel the culture shock teasing my dormant anxiety. Everything I'd seen on my short walk had felt slightly askew, like I'd landed in an alternate timeline where subtle things had been changed—beer brands, money, and common food. I had also noticed that I was the only white person I'd seen along the way. This was concerning for only one reason—it meant I would have no cover when I visited Alister's church in the morning. It was impossible for me to blend in on this island, a simple truth I hadn't anticipated.

Not that it mattered. The chances I would actually find Alister were slim to none. I knew he was working as a priest with the Church of the Nazarene, but he was one of several part-time holy men who gave sermons at churches all around the islands. I planned to visit the largest one for service on Sunday with no guarantee he'd be there—or that anyone would be in this heat.

As I ate my jerk chicken, I let the fantods take me. I'd traveled 2,300 miles at great expense to interview a man some believed was purposefully hiding, with nothing more than the address of a church he might appear at. What if it was another priest's shift? What if he got sick and called off? If he didn't show up, could I find him at home? If so, how would I find where he lived? If I found it, how would I get there? Speaking of which, I could get a cab from the hotel to the church but how was I getting back here? I didn't have an international plan on my phone. Anyway, it wouldn't help me much if I did. There is no Uber in Grenada.

And yet . . .

I felt the old magic here. This was a place where people still believed in Obeah, in miracles, in divine intervention. I've seen enough over the years to believe that there is more to this universe than what we see on the surface. An old psychic on the boardwalk in Ocean City once told me that I'd come to regret writing that book about Maura Murray. I once saw the outline of a man's face captured in a Polaroid photo taken at the site where Amy Mihaljevic's body was found. And of course, the medium had seen visions of Iva Bradley's red flowers before I did.

The last time I'd felt this close to real magic was when I was on life support in the hospital after reacting poorly to anesthesia. I had a dream when I finally fell asleep that night. This book is so full of dreams, of those narratives our minds create in the absence of answers. Amy's friends found acceptance in the dreams about their missing loved one. I guess I found understanding in mine. Can I share it with you?

Chapter Thirty-six

IN THE WHITE ROOM

"YOU NEED TO SLEEP," the nurse told me. His voice was sharp, his tone alarmed. He kept giving me more propofol, and I kept fighting it.

I was on life support, but I couldn't see the ventilator behind me. My arms were strapped to the bed, but I had enough slack to hold Julie's hand. I looked at the other people who'd gathered in the room. My mother. My father and stepmother. My sister, Jo.

This is how I die, I thought.

Maybe it was the drugs, but a calmness washed over me then. An acceptance. I'd done what I could. I'd relayed my last requests. I was surrounded by people who loved me. There are worse ways to go.

"Sleep," the nurse said.

And so I did.

I dreamed.

I dreamed I was in a white room, seated at a square table with three other men. There were two exit doors on opposite walls, both closed. We were confused, each of us, about how we'd gotten there and when. Adding to the confusion was that two of our group only spoke French. The fourth member spoke the King's English. He spoke a little French, too, which allowed him to interpret for me. As we talked, we came to realize—or to perhaps remember—that we were all the same person, the same spark of consciousness and that these were the different lives we have lived in different times, what Amanda the medium might call a "soul group." The Frenchmen came from years and years past. The Englishman was out of the seventies. I understood a simple truth—that all of time was happening right this moment, that everything was the Present, always. But for now, in this room, we were outside of it all.

A thin well-dressed man entered the room from the door to my right. He appeared agitated, and he looked at us with visible disappointment.

"You guys really fucked up this time," he said. "You're way too early. And unfortunately, you can't all go back. One of you has to stay. I can choose, if you'd like, or you can work it out yourselves."

"We'll talk," I said.

"Fine." He walked out of the room.

We understood the task before us. We had all strayed from some purpose, taken one too many risks, which brought us here, to the boundary between life and death. A price had to be paid. One soul stayed behind. Each of us in turn gave their arguments for why they should go home, the British man translating for me. When it was my turn, I talked about my children, how young they still were. And Julie, how I didn't want to leave her alone at this age. About my legacy, such that it could be. The books I still want to write. All the unwritten novels that play in my mind as I fall asleep.

When we were done, the British man nodded and said, "I've done what I wanted to do. I'm old now, and my children are grown. I'll stay."

Before I could reply, the tall man returned to the room. He seemed to be in a hurry. Perhaps our debate was strictly off the books. He pointed to the door on my left. "You three, off you go. But understand, the suffering is now divided by three instead of four. That's the price you pay for your mistake."

I turned to see the British man walk out the door with the tall man. He seemed confident, almost excited to find what was on the other side.

I stepped through the other door with the Frenchmen.

I awoke in the hospital room in Cuyahoga Falls. It was morning, sunlight through a window behind me shining on Julie, asleep in her chair by my side. My dad heard me stir. I motioned for him to find me a paper and pen. He did. I didn't want to forget my dream. I wanted to tell him all about it once I was off the ventilator. I still have that scrap of paper. It reads, "Everything is happening right now, always."

Our minds construct narratives when we are faced with the unknown.

When I finally gave up and accepted that I might die, my brain created a story for me to understand a truth that I had not yet realized. It showed me a waiting room between this life and the next. It created characters to represent my belief that we are all the same thing, that we are all part of the same consciousness, and we live and die, and our legacy is the influence we have on others, so be good.

The truth that my dream explained to me was simple—I wanted to live. In spite of it all, I wanted to live. I wanted to share my long days with Julie and my family. At last, I was ready to fight to stay.

Bam! Bam! Bam!

I woke to find myself in a black room and thought maybe I was dead again. Then I remembered I was in Grenada, in a corner room of an apartment complex above Grand Anse. I looked to the clock. It was just after 2 a.m. and someone was pounding on my door.

BAM! BAM! BAM!

I shot out of bed and ran to the door, but there was no peephole. I could not see who was on the other side.

"What do you want?" I shouted.

The pounding stopped. And then a woman's voice came through from the other side, so close, the door so thin, it sounded as if she was whispering into my ear. But it was a language I didn't know. Creole French, maybe.

"I don't understand," I said. "Please go away!"

Then the woman said, "I come inside."

The door handle twisted back and forth.

"No!" I shouted.

"I come into your bed," she said. "You watch. You pay me."

Now I understood. But I also knew that the chances of this woman being a sex worker were about equal to her being a trap for some large man who hadn't yet spoken. I realized my situation, quickly. If there was a strongman out there, and he knew I was alone, he could force his way in quite easily. I had my phone, but only Wi-Fi. If I called 911, would it go through?

"No thank you!" I shouted.

"Open the door," she said, more forcefully.

"I—I just called the police. *Policia. Polizei!*"

The unseen woman shouted a curse at me in that other language, then continued to talk to herself as she walked away into the night. Eventually, I found the courage to peer out the bathroom window. By then, she'd gone.

I didn't sleep much more that night. When dawn broke, I took a shower and dressed in shorts and a fresh button-down shirt. It was time to roll the dice and try to find Alister Douglas.

Chapter Thirty-seven

YELLOW

THE MAN WITH FOUR TEETH called a friend to drive me to the Church of the Nazarene. I waited with him in a gazebo, watching baby lizards skitter across the mowed lawn, up the scaled trunks of palm trees. It was 8 a.m., and the day was already hot, though my dental-impaired friend seemed not to notice or to even break a sweat.

An ancient modified Honda Civic pulled up to the office. Behind the wheel was a young Grenadian man, perhaps twenty years old. I got into the back and attempted to explain where I wanted to go. I showed him a screenshot I'd taken from Mapquest. The church was in St. David Parish, about half an hour drive around the mountain on the eastern side of Grenada. He nodded and we set off.

We left St. George's behind and took a narrow road around Windsor Forest, through a wide valley where unregulated oil refineries made the air smell of sulfur.

"You can tell a valley man by the way they smell," the driver said in a Rastafarian accent. "It gets into everything."

We passed more rum distilleries and started up the other side of the valley, into St. David. As we drove through a residential neighborhood, I noticed that each humble home had a wooden shack out front about the size of a bus shelter.

"What are the shacks for?" I asked.

"E'rebody hustles in Grenada," he said. "E'rebody sells something on the side. Fruit. Beer. Liquor. Sandwiches. Soda. When the weather is not so hot, everyone walks and you can stop at any of these little shacks to buy a snack or a drink."

As we came around a turn, I spotted a mansion estate near the top of the mountain. It looked like a Spanish mission, with stucco walls and terra-cotta tile roof.

"Geez, who lives there?" I asked.

The driver laughed. "The man that lives there owns the Bingo games," he said. "He come to the island a few years ago and set up the games, and now everyone plays them and pays him, and he gives some of it back to a couple lucky winners. He is probably the richest man on the island now."

One clever opportunist has altered this island's entire economy. Now he sits in his white castle and looks down at the masses as they gather in fútbol fields and spend what little money they have hoping for that one windfall that never comes. Is there anything more evil than introducing a lottery to such a paradise?

We came to the church at last. Down a dirt road that had no sign, we found a low rectangular wood building, its door open beneath a sign that read CHURCH OF THE NAZARENE: HOME OF DELIVERANCE. I paid the young man in Caribbean dollars. Pretty sure he overcharged me, but what do I know about cab fare in Grenada? I assured him I'd be fine and he drove away, leaving me alone.

I stepped onto the porch and peered inside. The nave was completely empty at 8:30 a.m., though a sign on the door said services would begin promptly at 9. In front of a couple rows of redwood pews, I saw a drum set beside a keyboard and podium. The open windows in the back looked out at an encroaching jungle, all the way to the clear waters of the Caribbean Sea. It began to rain, a fine mist drizzle that offered no comfort from the ever-present heat.

I went back outside and sat on a chair under the porch awning and waited. Three boys played with a dog in the street and eyed me with suspicion. I waved politely back.

"Are you here for church?" one asked.

"I am."

"They will all come at the same time," the boy said. "They always do."

Sure enough, at five minutes to nine, a caravan of vehicles rolled up the street and parked along the shoulder. Men and women dressed in their Sunday best got out and walked into the church, each greeting me as they passed. I had sweated through my shirt already, but the men wearing full suits didn't seem bothered.

A silver van pulled up. I spotted Alister Douglas behind the wheel. He was older, of course, than he'd been in the video clips I'd seen of him online. He'd gained some weight. But there was no mistaking his round face and bald head. He got out with his family—his wife and their son, who appeared to be about thirteen years old. His wife was beautiful and wore a long dress, her hair done, makeup applied. She smiled at me and welcomed me without question. I think Alister knew as soon as he saw me why I'd come, even if he didn't know who I was. I was the only white guy for miles, and I had my writer's satchel slung around my shoulder.

"Are you Alister Douglas?" I asked.

"I am," he said. His voice reminded me of James Earl Jones, deep and full of gravitas.

I introduced myself and explained that I was writing a book about Amy Bradley. "I've come a very long way just to talk with you," I said. "I'd like to sit in on your service, if that's all right? And then maybe we could talk after?"

He sighed and smiled. "I've gotten some calls lately, and I tell them all no. But you came to me. So, we will talk. Please, come have a seat."

My mind buzzed pleasantly as I took a seat at a pew in the back. It's so rare in my job for something to come together so perfectly. I had taken a risk, put the last of my money on a single Bingo card and got B-14 for the win.

Alister's church service was full of music, both traditional hymns and Grenadian songs that I could only half understand. Alister's wife sang while he played a keyboard and the humble congregation, some twenty people, danced where they stood, sometimes raising their hands to God.

"We have a guest among us today," Alister said at the beginning of his sermon. "Mr. James Renner, all the way from Ohio. Please welcome him."

This is the part of the *Wicker Man* where they take the interloper and lock him into the wooden effigy, right? But this group simply turned and smiled. If they were close enough, they shook my hand.

Alister spoke for some time about the grace of God, about church members who needed some help, about the ones who'd died since they'd last gathered. Then he talked about his other job.

"I was called to service last night," he said. "And I'm still recovering from what I saw." He wiped his brow and then his mouth with a white handkerchief. "I was called for an exorcism." A woman had a demon in her, he explained, and it was causing enormous grief.

Alister drove out to the woman's house, not knowing what to expect. She was quite sick by the time he arrived, he said, a sign that the demon had been inside her a long time.

He shouted at the demon to leave her body, calling on mercy from God. The woman's body reacted instantly. She vomited thick, black bile. This went on for some time, the priest and the demon locked in ancient combat. Finally, the demon fled and the woman grew calm. The color returned to her face.

"I knew I had witnessed a miracle," he said.

"Amen!" someone shouted. "Hallelujah!"

Alister's magic was Christian mysticism, but he served the same purpose for these Grenadians as the Obeahmen of the recent past, protection from forces beyond their control. He was a leader here. An important member of this community. I found it hard to reconcile this with the things that the Bradleys had said about this man.

As I've said, something about the island itself makes one believe in magic and demons.

The service went on for over an hour. One by one, each member of the congregation said their goodbyes to Alister. He asked his wife and son to step outside so that he could speak with me in private. We sat next to each other on a pew. He found a clean towel to wipe his head and face with. It would be noontime soon. The sun was unforgiving, even for those who were born here.

"What do you remember after all of these years?" I asked. "Do you remember Amy at all?"

"There's not a lot in terms of remembering her," he said. "But I remember the short conversation we had." Alister explained how it was the night of the weekly Dancing Under the Stars production, where he and the rest of Blue Orchid would play outside on the pool deck until midnight. When they finished, Amy came over to talk to him.

"She said, 'Hi, good set,' you know. Back then when I played, I jumped around a lot, and people would compliment me. I said, thank you. She says to me that she plays a saxophone. I said, interesting, what kind of music you like?" They talked for a while, and then Alister went back to his room, belowdecks, to get changed. Once he was in fresh clothes, he started up toward the Viking Lounge, where he liked to unwind after the Aruba set.

"When I came up, she was on the deck, outside. She saw me and said hi. I said hi. She was smoking. A lot. That's not something I know or like. Growing up in Grenada, you hardly ever saw someone smoke. I was young, so it was like not a norm for me. So we went up to the club. We sat for a while. She was still smoking a lot, and I ask her, 'Why are you smoking so much?' She said to me her dad was an insurance manager, or something like that, and she said he found out she was gay, and he forced her to come to the cruise."

This was the first time I had heard that Alister knew Amy was gay prior to her disappearance. I thought about those Facebook memes he'd posted. Her smoking had upset him. Her homosexuality had likely affected him as well. From what I'd learned so far, Amy was the type to jump quickly into the personal details when she hung out with someone new. But the bit about her parents "forcing" her to come on the cruise seemed like an exaggeration. Amy was twenty-three years old when she disappeared, old enough to make her own decisions, even when it came to her very involved family.

"I didn't know what answer to give, anyway," he said. "So we just went out on the dance floor. About five minutes to one, I said, look, I have to go. I have to be out of the passenger area. And I left. That was my last conversation, the last time I saw her."

"What was your response when she told you she was gay?" I asked.

"That's not something I was used to."

"How do you feel about that in general?"

"I have an adopted brother who is gay," Alister said. "I have some friends who's gay. On the cruise ship some musicians I was close with was gay. I remember telling one of them, we can be friends, we can talk, if you keep it appropriate. I didn't know how to relate to anyone like that."

I asked him then about the two witnesses, Crystal and Lori, who claimed to have seen Alister return to the Viking Lounge with Amy after the club had closed.

"Nah," he said. It couldn't have happened that way, he said, because his key card registered when he returned to his room. He added that around seven o'clock the next morning he was awoken by a phone call from the hotel manager who asked Alister if he had a woman in his room. "We were forbidden to have women in our rooms. And I said no. I asked like why, and he said that the woman you were talking to last night at the club, we can't find her." He told Alister to not leave his room until he called back.

Alister is adamant that he did not come back up after he went to his room the night before. He couldn't have done so, he said, because of what the key cards showed. Of course, as I discovered, the key cards did not register when someone left the room. So, sure Alister could have left without a log record, but he could not have returned without the key card registering as he entered a second time. He was still in his room at 7:00 the next morning when the search for Amy started. He also shared that room with a member of his band, Oscar Alexander. For Alister to sneak in and out would have required this man to participate in a twenty-six-year-old conspiracy, and I just don't see that as a likely possibility.

"Did you have to take a lie detector test?" I asked.

"Every person who would have interacted with her, the people who cleaned her room, the people who served her dinner, we were all interrogated," he said. "All these things were put on me. Electrodes. Maybe three sessions. It went on and on and on."

"What did they say to you afterwards?"

"At that time they didn't say much to me, but it was followed up some time later by a woman named Sheridan. That's years ago. She was an FBI agent. She came to Grenada. Met me at a hotel, interviewed me a couple times. The last time she spoke to me, she said listen, you are clear of this. I was never worried, because I don't know anything about this. But I was nervous, because this is my name mixed up in this. Listen, I've lost so many opportunities because of this."

According to Alister, when he has applied for jobs, the employer will google his name and see his connection to this missing person case, then they pass. In the years after it happened, he said he would be searched aggressively when he'd fly from London to Grenada because of his name. He couldn't get another job on a cruise ship after that, either.

"I struggled for a long time," Alister said. "My inbox, my Facebook, people have been writing horrible stuff for years. They send messages to my wife. My daughter who lives in the U.S. has been bombarded. As a matter of fact, I think she met with someone about it. She called me about eight weeks ago, said, Daddy, this thing with the girl, look, I keep getting all this stuff coming to me, and I'm concerned about my daughter. I said, Amica, listen, if you want, you can say that I'm not your father. I said, the truth will come out and when it does, I will sue the people who have been making documentaries about me. The truth, no matter how long it is, it always surfaces. About a week later, she called me. I'm not stupid, I knew people were listening on the phone."

Amica asked Alister why people were saying they saw him on a beach with Amy after her disappearance. He told her again that the last time he'd spoken to Amy was the night before she disappeared, at the Viking Lounge. Then, he heard a strange sound on the phone, a loud *crack!* "Somebody was listening," he said.

Later, he tried to call her back, but she did not answer.

"At some point, she's going to reach out and say, Dad, I'm sorry."

Alister told me he also thought someone was trying to entrap him in a scheme related to Amy's disappearance. A man had called him, recently, with some shady business opportunity that seemed designed to get him off the island for reasons unknown. At the time, I dismissed this entirely, believing he was being paranoid. I mean, how often do we get strange solicitations over email? Like every day. And who wouldn't be paranoid after twenty-eight years of being called a murderer by strangers online?

Before we ended, I asked Alister what he thought happened to Amy. He told me that he believed her family was responsible for whatever happened. For the record, I don't agree with this, but I do think it's understandable for him to think so, and to voice his opinion in light of the twenty-six years he's spent as a suspect on the Bradley family website.

I left then. He offered me a ride someplace, but I declined. To be honest, I didn't want to owe him anything, on the off chance that our relationship would sour in the future. He and his family pulled away, and I was alone again. And this time, I had no cell service, no way to call a taxi, on the far side of the island from my room in St. George's.

I walked the dirt road in the direction I had come. The rain had stopped, and the sun blazed almost straight above me. About a half mile from the church, I came to a crossroads where four teenage boys played dominoes on a picnic table inside a shack where sodas and drinks were displayed on a window ledge. I had not eaten anything that day, and I'd neglected to bring water with me. I stepped to the window and bought a bag of plantain chips and a regional soda and paid in Caribbean dollars until the teen on the other side waved his hands and gave me change.

"Where you from?" he asked.

"The States," I said. "I'm trying to get back to my hotel. Would you be able to call a cab for me?"

"Of course," he said. He turned to his friends, then, and said something in thick Creole. The oldest of the bunch pulled out a Nokia wrapped in plastic and had a brief conversation with someone, then nodded at me. "Ten minutes," he said.

I leaned on the outside of the shack and ate my chips while I waited. Across the street, a woman cleared the tall grass from her lawn with a machete. An old goat tied to a tree stayed in the shade and nibbled at the dirt. Every few seconds, there was a loud *smack*, as one of the boys slapped a new domino onto the table.

"You like rum?"

I turned to find the teen boy clerk holding an unmarked bottle of clear liquid and two shot glasses.

"I do," I said.

He poured us both a thimbleful and then clinked my glass. "This is Clark's Court," he said. "Good rum. Made here in Grenada. It'll put hair on your chest."

I threw back the shot. It went down like a hot coal, and I coughed loudly. The boy and his friends laughed. I gave them a thumbs-up.

“Good rum,” I said. I pulled a five-dollar American bill from my wallet and handed it to the boy. His eyes scrunched up.

“What’s this?”

“For the rum,” I said.

He shrugged his shoulder and took the money. I had thought the rum thing was a clever way for him to squeeze some money out of me, but I realized then he was just being a good host to a lost foreigner. I was the one who had made it transactional.

A man arrived with a car, his girlfriend in the passenger seat. It wasn’t an official taxi. I did not see anything that looked like an official taxi during my stay on the island. This driver turned out to be the boy’s uncle. He took me back to St. George’s. I gave him the rest of the Caribbean dollars I had.

Back in the room, I showered and changed into dry clothes and then reviewed the video footage I’d shot of my interview with Alister. It looked great. The audio was perfect. Somehow, for once, it had all worked out.

In the morning, I hopped a flight to Miami where my connection was delayed for several hours, delivering me to Cleveland around 1 a.m. I didn’t care about the late hour. I practically floated to the parking deck, confident that my luck had turned, that everything was smooth sailing now.

When I went to pull my keys out of my pocket, they weren’t there. They weren’t in my bags, either. That’s when I remembered that I’d left them in the drawer of the hotel dresser back in Grenada.

Chapter Thirty-eight

A DAUGHTER'S STORY

A COUPLE DAYS LATER, I posted my interview with Alister Douglas on YouTube and linked it on all my socials. I was proud of the exclusive, and I promoted it as the first interview with Yellow in decades. I was surprised when an account I didn't know responded to my tweet. "Not true," it read. "I interviewed him last week."

At first, I assumed it was some Internet troll, shitposting for the lols. Out of curiosity, I reached out. The conversation progressed to email and then a phone call. The account belonged to a retired police officer turned private detective named Jim Carey. He has worked closely with the Bradley family for years. As it turns out, it was Jim who'd called Alister to try to get him off the island, a ruse to see if he could gain Alister's trust and hopefully learn some hidden truth about Amy's disappearance. Alister was not being paranoid, after all.

In some ways, that connection with Jim saved me a lot of trouble. The Bradleys were still incommunicado, but they had given Jim some documents that he shared with me. One of these items was a single page from an investigatory report that was written by the ship's security manager, Lou Costello. In the report, Costello had created a timeline of Amy's movements leading up to the time of her disappearance by reviewing drink receipts at various bars around the ship and pulling data from her keycard as well as Alister's keycard. What he found likely provided an answer to one stubborn mystery – the sighting of Amy with Alister after the disco closed.

From 6:10 to 7:35 p.m. the night before the disappearance, Amy was with her family at dinner, where she was seen by the waiter and the maître d'. Her movements from 7:35 to 9 p.m. could not be determined. From 9 p.m. until at least 9:50 p.m., Amy was drinking in the casino. From 10:30 p.m. to 12:30 a.m., she was at a Mardi Gras party, where her brother won the limbo contest. She hung out on the pool deck with Brad, until 1 a.m., listening to Alister's band play calypso music. From 1 a.m. to 2:30 a.m., she was at the disco, occasionally dancing with Alister. From 2:30 a.m. to 3:30 a.m., Amy was on the stargazer deck, the top deck of the ship, with Alister. At 3:40 she entered her family's cabin on the eighth floor, where she sat on the balcony with her brother for five minutes or so before he went to bed. She was seen on the balcony, sleeping, at around 5 a.m. Her father noticed her missing around 6:15 a.m. She was officially reported missing at 7:33 a.m.

Costello wrote that he had conducted an interview with Alister Douglas around 10 p.m. the evening after Amy disappeared but that Alister had been less than truthful. "In the initial interview Douglas made many false statements about when and where he had been. Once confronted with and explained the Locklink process he apologized and made a statement that was more in line with the facts."

I don't read much into Alister's subterfuge at the beginning of this interview. He was a young officer on the ship. He knew he had violated the passenger fraternization policy and was trying to cover his ass, the way any married young man would likely do in that situation. Nobody argues that Amy made it safely back to her room that night, after all.

What I found most interesting was the hour that Amy and Alister had spent on the Stargazer deck after the disco had closed. The top deck was on the tenth floor. The Viking Lounge, where the disco had been that night, was on the eleventh deck. I strongly suspect that Crystal and Lori saw Alister and Amy go to or from the Stargazer deck. Then, when Amy returned to her room at about 3:30 a.m., Alister walked by the two young women, who were sitting on Deck Nine.

Jim also provided screenshots of images of the other escorts that appeared on the Affordable Adult Vacations website. He had compared these photos to other famous missing women, suggesting that the brothel owner, Alexis Zaglinitis, was actively kidnapping white women for years. For instance, one of the escorts was "matched" to photos of Suzanne Streeter, one of the so-called Springfield Three, who went missing from Missouri in 1992 (and who I nearly wrote about instead of Amy) and Jennifer Anne Regan, who disappeared from Alberta, Canada in 1991.

This made me doubt that Amy was a match for the other unidentified escort. Because, come on, what are we talking about? An international human trafficking operation that kidnaps women from the United States and holds them hostage at a brothel owned by a weasel of a man who could never keep himself out of trouble for long? It certainly wasn't Suzanne Streeter in that picture. Which meant it likely wasn't Amy, either. It still bothered me, though. The resemblance was uncanny, more so than any other potential match.

Jim got me in touch with Alister's daughter, Amica, who then connected me with her mother, Donier Cato. I spoke to both of them to get a more detailed picture of what Alister was like before he became an exorcist.

Today, Donier works at a nurse's assistant at a facility in Manhattan. In 1998, when Alister set off aboard the *Rhapsody of the*

Seas, she was still in Grenada. They had only been married a year. It was difficult to be separated for the five-month contract, while he played calypso on the ship. But the money was good.

She remembered getting a call from one of Alister's band mates when they'd stopped at some port. He told her that something had happened on the ship and that Alister would tell her about it when he got home.

It worried her but she didn't think it could be anything too serious. "I was excited to see him again," Donier said. "I hadn't seen him in five or six months. But when he came home he was very negative. He was telling me I was really big." Donier said she was about eight months pregnant at the time but that doesn't track and those years have likely merged some memories. Notice, again, how our minds form narratives around inconsistent facts. Their daughter, Amica, was born in May, 1999. After twenty-six years, it's hard to get the sequence of this exactly right.

Donier remembered asking her husband what had happened on the ship. He told her about Amy and the disappearance and being questioned by the FBI. According to Donier, Alister said when he'd taken the lie detector tests, he'd gotten very emotional and they couldn't get a good reading. "He was very angry," she said. "He said I was accusing him of something. I wasn't really accusing him, I just wanted to know what happened."

This was the beginning of many heated arguments between them. Finally, Alister went to his mother's house in St. George's, leaving his luggage behind. "I'm not snoopy, but I saw he had a bag and it was half open," said Donier. "I could see there were pictures inside. I opened the bag. He had a lot of pictures. It was him with a lot of girls. I was feeling jealous."

Later, when she questioned Alister about the photos, he told her not to worry, that it was just people he met on the cruise, that people asked to take pictures with him all the time. She wasn't sure how much of what he told her was true. She knew he lied to her sometimes. "I know he's a womanizer," she said. "I went through a lot on the island. The Amy stuff. I just had a baby. I was stressing. Then he left. He had another woman."

Eventually, Donier moved to the United States. Amica stayed with family on the island. "I had nothing," she said. "I came here with zero dollars. It was very rough for me."

Online, armchair sleuths have stated that Donier saw Amy Bradley's photograph in Alister's luggage. But for the record, she did not. "I didn't pay attention to the women in the pictures," she said. "I didn't know those people."

Amica currently lives in Brooklyn, not far from her mother. She was almost named "America" before her parents settled on "Amica," which means girlfriend in Italian. After Donier moved to the States, Amica stayed with her grandparents in Grenada for a while. When she was six, she moved back in with Alister for a bit but there was friction with her stepmother so she was sent back to her grandparents. She bounced around a lot as a child, between her father and his relatives on the island. When she was about twelve years old, she moved to the States to be with her mother. It was difficult. Her mind kept replaying all the bad things she'd been told about her mom, about how she'd abandoned them both and didn't want a daughter. But Amica learned that was not true. The reason for the move was a lot more nuanced than a child could comprehend.

"He lies a lot," Amica told me. "He is the reason why my mom and I aren't as close as we could be."

By the time we talked, Amica had already watched my interview with her father and a few things stuck out to her. She believed Alister had exaggerated some things. For instance, his statements about how he hadn't grown up around smokers. "Everybody smokes everywhere," she said. "Even his brother smokes cigarettes. The people who lived across from us smoked. It's a normal thing. I expected more truth from him because of his job. He's a man of God, right?"

Amica appreciated hearing her father say he had no issues with someone being gay. She remembered a discussion they had when she was about seventeen. She told her father that she felt like she was bisexual. His response echoed what the Bradleys had once said to Amy: "You're young, maybe you'll grow out of it." She wondered if her father had just said what she wanted to hear.

Amica has not returned to Grenada for some time and doesn't think she'll return soon. It's changed, she said. "To me, it's not a free country anymore. There are more killings and kidnappings and people go missing for no reason. It's dangerous, especially for little girls. Men there have a way of getting with these little girls and messing with them. The police don't do much. It's gotten really bad."

The distrust between Amica and her father is palpable. Amica has a daughter of her own now. Being a mom gives her a different perspective on how her father was absent for a lot of her childhood. She wishes her father could show more concern when she gets threatening messages from strangers, online. Usually he tells her to unfriend him on Facebook so people can't make the connection.

Recently, some anonymous asshole found her Instagram and posted, "Where is Amy?" under her daughter's picture. That seemed to trigger a bit of concern from Alister. "He said the truth will come out. He said he'll sue these people."

Amica also admitted that the producers of the Netflix documentary had been on the line when she spoke to her father the day she called him in Grenada. She said the call dropped as they were listening and maybe that's the click he'd heard.

I got a sense from talking to Amica that her mind is quite conflicted when it comes to her father. One moment, she would say something critical of her dad, the next she would say something decent. She still has some love, for sure. But it's complicated. Most of us can empathize, I think. When you learn your parents are just kids pretending to be grownups, their shortcomings are easier to understand. We're all contradictions, we all contain multitudes.

When it comes to what happened to Amy Bradley, Amica is unsure what to believe. She doesn't think her father could commit murder, but she believes he knows more than he's said. "I think he's hiding something," she told me. "I think that there's more to the story. Amy is a beautiful girl and he likes being around women. It's sad what happened to her. Now that I have a kid, I ask myself how I would feel. I can't imagine. The prime suspect is my father and every time he tells his story it's something different."

PART SIX

WHAT DREAMS MAY COME

Chapter Thirty-nine

KAT REVISED

After I returned from Grenada, I did something I've never done before. I handed over an early version of my book to a couple sources I'd already interviewed: Amy's lovers, Kat Lovelace and Mollie McClure. Normally, I keep a wall between my manuscript and the subjects I interview. As a journalist, I was taught to never share a piece with a subject until after publication. There are a couple reasons for this.

Sometimes people who have never been involved in a public story before will see their words and actions in print and get nervous. It becomes real, and suddenly they second-guess the things they said. They want to fight to change it to something more flattering. It opens up the possibility of lawyers becoming involved to try to alter your piece. There's also the risk of that person leaking your story before it's ready for publication, a real concern for me, since these books take up to two years to arrive on store shelves. I made an exception because of the risks that both women took talking with me. In that regard, it was a show of respect. But also, I needed to be sure I had everything exactly right. I didn't want to misconstrue any piece of the relationships they had with Amy Bradley.

I sent each of them a binder with a copy of the first half of this book along with a red pen and twenty dollars for return postage.

Kat sent me a text one evening at the end of November. She was displeased about some things. "Is this book about you or Amy?" she wanted to know. It was the criticism I expected. I was up front with all the major sources I spoke to about the odd point of view of my books. My true crime is always mixed with memoir. If you've read any of my other stuff, you know this. I like sharing the process that is lost in strict reportage. I like showing how the story develops over time and how the writer comes to know the victim at the center and the people they left behind, and how that affects the author and the story. In some ways, I believe this is a much more honest approach. I clearly show you my personal biases as they arise. Other authors hide that. You have to wonder where they're coming from and what their agenda is. Or hell, maybe it's a crutch. I don't know any other way.

Mostly, Kat was upset about how carefully I treated Amy's parents. Remember, when they discovered that their daughter had been in a secret relationship with Kat for some time, they reacted poorly, sending Kat a three-page handwritten letter of disappointment. That still stings even after all these years. She was also hurt that they still try to whitewash Amy's sexuality.

"The point I have to make is her family hated it, hated me," she wrote. "Didn't accept her and she was miserable because she was gay. Not bi. Not questioning. She came out. She owned it and it created trouble."

I asked Kat to discuss this further over a call. We got on Zoom later that week. By then, she had read through the manuscript again and had warmed to it. "It is beautiful," she said. "I understand what you're trying to do." I am a sucker for flattery. I'm well aware this is not a perfect book. It's just the best I can do at this age.

We got right into it.

"The Bradleys are liars," Kat said. "They've lied for twenty-six years. They weren't looking for the truth, they were looking for grandkids. We didn't get a voice, even when we asked to help. The Bradleys have handled the press and given them the image they want of Amy. If we're going to tell this story, dig this up. Show her complexity."

Amy was a compulsive liar, Kat said. "She'd lie about where she was, what she was doing. We all loved her and knew what we were getting. I think she built that skill pretty early on. As our relationship grew, there were shenanigans all the time. The amount of lying we did is insane. Both of us having boyfriends to mask our real relationship. Sneaking into bathrooms to make out. Every bit of it was because of her parents."

Kat said she saw the real Amy Bradley on their trips to the coast. In those early days it was the only place they felt safe to be completely open. "I saw freedom and love and acceptance." She recalled how tinged with dangerous electricity their first moments were. They spent weeks trying to figure out what the other really wanted. "Then one day Amy leaned in and said, 'I'd really like to kiss you.' There was so much softness, so much uncertainty. After that I don't think we spent a night apart."

The breakup, when it happened, was devastating to Kat. She moved away to another college for a bit before returning to Longwood. By then, Amy was graduating with a degree to teach physical education. Like me, Kat wonders why that never happened and how Amy ended up working at Ruth's Chris Steakhouse instead. "She would tell me, 'I'll be the best teacher.' So why wasn't she a teacher? She was so complicated. That darkness she carried with her was always there. She did dangerous shit. Bungee jumping, standing on a rooftop's edge. All the signs were there, we just didn't see them at the time. The real story is how dark these times were, the things we had to do, all because of her parents."

Kat remembers seeing that darkness in college a couple times. Once, she came back to their dorm and found Amy on the couch, sitting there, staring into space. "I asked her what she was doing, and she said, 'Thinking.' You could just see the darkness in her mind."

After college, Mollie moved away, and Amy had to return to Chesterfield, alone. "Imagine what her life was like," said Kat. "Losing all that freedom would be another form of Hell."

Kat also confirmed a suspicion I'd had for a long time. She and Mollie found solace in each other for a time. In fact, Mollie was in the car the day that Kat crashed her vehicle and ended up in the hospital. Somehow, Mollie walked away unharmed. She imagines how everything could have gone differently. They're friends to this day, partners in the unique trauma they share and only they can understand.

Mollie responded more favorably to the initial read and had a few helpful corrections to suggest. I found it interesting how both of them, since our first talks, had come around to the idea that Amy really may have stepped overboard, even if she didn't know what the outcome may be.

"I can sooner see her jumping," said Mollie. "That sounds like Amy. I'll race the ship to the pier!"

After we spoke, I returned to the book. For me, it all comes down to the escort photos. Either it's Amy, or it isn't. If I couldn't find Amy, perhaps I could find one of the other women whose photos appeared on the site.

Chapter Forty

THE OLD BAIT AND SWITCH

According to the time stamps on the archived pages of the Affordable Adult Vacations website, the photographs of the woman called Jas, who bears a striking resemblance to Amy Bradley, first appeared online in 2004. Amy would have been about twenty-nine years old then. The woman in the pictures could certainly be the same age. Jas appears on a section of the website advertising visiting escorts. Alexis Zaglinitis, the man who owned and operated AAV, wrote elsewhere on the site that visiting escorts were required to have an Adult Friend Finder profile and were residents of the United States who would visit for a couple weeks at a time. The Wayback Machine archives for Adult Friend Finder are not comprehensive, however. I found it impossible to track down a more detailed profile of Jas that way.

Instead, I focused my attention on identifying any one of the other dozen visiting escorts whose photographs appeared beside the picture of Jas. Perhaps one of them would remember Jas by name, if they were visiting at the same time. For this, I needed a decent reverse-image search engine.

"Hi, Sky," I wrote into ChatGPT. "I'm trying to track down some of the other women who appeared in escort ads alongside the photo that looked like Amy Bradley. What is the best reverse image search for this sort of thing?"

"For tracking down other women in those escort ads, you'll want a reverse image search that digs deep, beyond just the surface-level Google results," said Sky. She recommended Yandex, first, but warned, "It's Russian-owned, so privacy concerns exist." She also recommended Google Lens, TinEye, and PimEyes, which she explained, "can track where a face appears across different sites, including adult content, though their ethical stance is dicey. Let me know if you need help sifting through what you find!"

I went to Yandex first and tried my luck with a photograph of a blond escort with short cropped, spiky hair, a very late-'80s look. It returned several possibilities and provided links to some websites that looked so sketchy I didn't risk the click. Regardless, none of the images it returned were a convincing match. I tried Jas, herself, of course, but as I would find with the other search engines, the only links it returned were related to the search for Amy Bradley.

I found TinEye to be the most helpful. I uploaded a photograph of another young, blond woman who appeared on the AAV site and it returned a series of still images taken from turn of the millennia porno films. It was clearly the same person from the photograph. Her professional name was Shelbee Myne. Her list of credits goes back to 1996, with appearances in such films as *Blowjob Adventures of Dr. Fellatio 4* and *Citizen Pain*. Her most recent film, *Biker Dollz*, was released in 2008. The photos of Myne that appeared on AAV's website were clearly still shots or publicity stills taken from some of her early films.

A short Google search revealed Myne's real name. I discovered she was currently living in California. Mike Lewis located a cell phone number for me, but when I called, it went to voicemail. I left a message. I also sent a request for interview to two separate email addresses. But I never heard back from Myne.

The second woman I found was also an adult film star. Her name is Teri Weigel. The photograph that appears on the AAV site is actually her professional headshot. Weigel was quite famous for a time, appearing on the cover of *Playboy* in November 1985 and as the Playboy Playmate in April 1986. She acted in several mainstream projects after that, appearing in a minor role in *Predator 2* and as a recurring character on *Married . . . with Children*.

A reporter for the *New Times Broward–Palm Beach* alt-weekly caught up with Weigel in 2004, when she was working as a featured dancer at Spearmint Rhino Gentlemen's Club on Federal Highway. In the interview, Weigel talked about how an accident in August 1990, in which she injured her neck and back, sidelined her professional acting career and forced her to take up hardcore, X-rated films. This went against the good-girl *Playboy* tradition and allegedly pissed off Hugh Heffner something fierce. Shortly before she became a featured dancer in Florida, she spent time at the Moonlight Bunny Ranch in Nevada as a sex worker.

Today, Weigel has a TikTok account with around a thousand followers. I sent her a DM and left a message at a phone number I found but never heard back.

TinEye also returned results for two other women who appeared as guest escorts on AAV's site. However, I was unable to discover their names, since the returns were simply stills from adult videos with no indication of credit or title.

The question becomes, what is more likely? That pathological liar and con man Alexis Zaglinitis was employing Myne and Weigel as visiting escorts or that he had simply stolen these images online and posted them on his page as a way to attract prospective customers who may prefer Caucasian women instead of the actual women who lived and worked at his resort on Margarita Island? Consider the fact that Weigel's photo is her headshot and Myne's photo is a still from the back of one of her VHS skin flicks. I'm willing to bet neither Myne nor Weigel ever set foot on Venezuelan soil. Why travel so far when the work is in California and Nevada, where the grinding system of pornography still offers a modicum of protection?

I think we can also deduce a few other possible answers.

Given what I discovered about these women, I think it's very possible that Jas's photos follow the same pattern—still shots taken from adult magazines or videos, used as a bait-and-switch for Zaglinitis's clientele. *Oh, I know you were expecting her to be here but she cancelled last minute, let me introduce you to these fine, young women from the Dominican Republic.*

That tracks better with the Zaglinitis I've come to know.

Would a human trafficker take a photograph of a missing woman and put it online for anyone to see and recognize? What need did Zaglinitis possibly have for trafficked American women? He had all the women he needed, all the women he could control, shipped in from third-world countries. His business was always skirting a razor-thin line of criminality. He was not a stupid man. I just don't see him taking the risk.

And yet . . .

There is one annoying detail in the photographs of Jas that appeared on that old website. In each photo I found, the woman is posed in such a way that each part of the woman's body that would have shown one of Amy's tattoos is covered. Her hair is draped over where the Tasmanian devil might be. Her belly is obscured. The leg with the Maden cross is turned away from the camera.

Such a strange coincidence.

In the summer of 2025, I was contacted by a woman named Rebekah Aliff. "I know the woman in the photograph," she said.

Rebekah lives in Tennessee, where she works as a nursing assistant and volunteers with the homeless. In 1994, at the age of fourteen, she lived in South Daytona, Florida, where her father owned a trailer park. She would spend most of her days hanging out at a nearby apartment complex on South Ridgewood. The complex had a pool, and nobody cared if she and her friend swam for a while. One day, she noticed a very attractive woman lying in the sun. She had the most beautiful curly black hair. Rebekah saw her a lot that summer, but the woman never spoke, even if she asked questions like what her name was and where she was from.

Then one day, Rebekah saw this woman with an African American man who appeared to be her boyfriend. "Why can't she talk?" Rebekah asked him.

"You want to talk to her?" he said. "Okay, come inside."

Rebekah followed them into an apartment that was kept immaculately clean. Inside the apartment, the woman finally spoke to her and explained her unusual arrangement. Her name was Susan, she told the girl. The man was her boyfriend, and he had certain rules, such as who she could talk to and when. Whenever she was inside, he wanted her to wear lingerie. And whenever she went outside, she was supposed to dress only in a bikini. She worked as an escort, she told Rebekah, and her boyfriend would take pictures of her that he would then use to advertise her services.

It was an odd situation for a fourteen-year-old to find herself in. But this was South Daytona, in 1994, and Rebekah would be the first to admit it was a rough life filled with many interesting characters. She became friends with Susan, one of the few people the woman seemed to trust. In fact, Rebekah says she would help Susan with her makeup before their photo shoots, which often occurred in their bedroom.

Eventually, Rebekah moved and lost touch. She hadn't thought of Susan in years until she saw her picture on Facebook.

"When I saw that picture of Jas, my jaw dropped," Rebekah said. "At first, I thought it was going to be like an obituary or some article about Susan. But then I read about how people think this is Amy Bradley."

Rebekah is sure the woman in the photos is Susan. And not only that, she thinks she did her make up for that particular series of photos. She had been in their bedroom several times and she believes the bedroom in their pictures was from the apartment in South Daytona.

It's a weird story, to be sure. But I feel she was being truthful. She at least believes it to be true.

I did what I could to verify her story. She was in South Daytona at that time. The bars and apartment buildings she described are there. But so far, I've been unable to locate this Susan or the man she was living with at the time.

Chapter Forty-one

FALLOUT

TOWARD THE END of my reporting, I tracked down William Heffner, the navy officer who claimed to have seen Amy Bradley at a hotel in Curaçao in 1999. He lives outside Las Vegas these days. When I got him on the phone, he gave me a familiar answer I'd heard from other sources. "I signed a contract with Netflix, and I can't talk to you."

I sent an email to Ari Mark, the director of the documentary. "I have a witness telling me today he can't speak with me due to your contract. You know my book doesn't come out until 2026, right? It has zero impact on what you're doing. And honestly, from a journalistic standpoint, this is disappointing. I was the one who told Mollie to speak with you guys."

Ari responded ten minutes later. "You can speak with whomever you want," he wrote. "I just can't be a part of it."

I took a screenshot of his reply and sent it to Brad, who was still nervous about speaking with me after his parents cut off contact. Apparently, he forwarded this to Ari, since I then received this reply from him: "In fact, please don't speak to anyone at all."

I never heard from Ari again.

If you want to have your heart broken, get involved with a Hollywood production. Happens every time.

* * *

Ari's documentary, *Amy Bradley Is Missing*, premiered on Netflix on July 16, 2025. It was an undeniable hit for the streamer and is still trending in Netflix's top 10 as of this writing, though the reviews are mixed—Rotten Tomatoes shows a 60% Fresh score, and IMDb shows a ranking of 6.7 out of 10.

I watched it with Julie the day it came out. Overall, I thought they did a good job at distilling a complicated story into an enjoyable three-part series. I was happy to see interviews with Kat and Mollie. Her family even spoke about Amy's sexuality, though they still can't bring themselves to use Amy's chosen identity—gay—when describing her. There was no mention of Frank Jones and very little time given to the brothel on Margarita Island.

However, the documentary spends a lot of time on the photographs of Jas and leads the viewer to believe the FBI concluded that Jas and Amy are the same person, which is playing loose with the truth. Their segment with Alister's daughter, where she calls her father on camera to bait him with questions about Amy, plays as exploitative.

I suspected the documentary would be popular, but I wasn't quite prepared for just how popular it became in the true crime community. The story blew up and Amy Bradley's disappearance was all the armchair sleuths wanted to talk about. Posts about Amy on the Netflix documentaries subreddit overwhelmed the mods to the point they had to shut it down for several days. Websleuths also paused new posts on the thread devoted to her case.

I had posted my interview with Alister on YouTube in October of 2024, and it had been viewed about fifty thousand times. In the span of three weeks following the documentary's release, my view count climbed to over a million across all platforms, including the clips I shared on TikTok. The vast majority of commenters were convinced that Alister must be involved in her disappearance. I had to constantly monitor the posts to delete direct threats and libelous content.

True crime addicts were desperate for any new information about the case. After they had exhausted everything currently available online, they went digging for new clues. It only took about twenty-four hours for people to discover Brad and Iva's social media profiles. What they found did not line up with the narrative of an accepting family, as presented by Netflix and the Bradleys.

Iva and Brad are not just conservative, they are full-blown MAGA. Iva recently reposted a video about adrenochrome, a magical life-extending fluid that Neocons believe liberals harvest from abducted children. Brad reposted a tweet celebrating the Supreme Court's decision to uphold a ban on transgender surgeries for minors. He admits to being a proud anti-vaxxer. He replied to a photograph of Michelle Obama, referring to her as "Mike." When a user posted a photograph of Stephen Colbert and Jimmy Kimmel, asking people to "Name this Off-Broadway Musical," Brad replied, "The Gaywads." He referred to a Black woman as a "speedbump."

Their social media profiles were so at odds with the image the Bradleys portray on television, I thought they might have been hacked or perhaps the accounts were fake. I sent a link to Brad by text, not expecting him to reply. But he did. "That's me," he wrote.

If Amy really is alive, I shudder to think how she'd feel to see these public statements of casual racism and homophobia. It hurts me, and I'm not even related to them.

Thanks to my content on YouTube, I became a lightning rod for tips about the case. One woman who reached out, and who wishes to remain anonymous, told me about how she'd hooked up with Alister Douglas on a Royal Caribbean cruise about three months before Amy went missing.

She was just eighteen years old at the time and in the middle of her freshman year at college. Her family had taken the trip on winter break, so that they could celebrate Christmas on St. Thomas. One night, the bass player started to talk her up and buy her drinks. She enjoyed the attention.

She said that Alister invited her off the ship when they were in Aruba and she went with him to a bar, possibly Carlos 'n Charlie's, where they hung out with other members of the crew. The next day he took her to a beach, alone. In hindsight, she realizes how naïve she'd been and how things could have easily gone wrong.

"But if he had done anything to Amy, why wouldn't he have done it with me?" she said. "He had two opportunities to do so but didn't. I was a much better mark than Amy. I was small, petite. But he didn't try anything like that. He never tried to slip anything in my drink. I never saw him do drugs and he never asked me to do something I didn't want to do. I think he was just hooking up with women on these cruises."

I heard from former crew members of Royal Caribbean as well. One man who reached out to me from the Netherlands had worked aboard a sister ship of the *Rhapsody* in 1999 and had sailed through the ABC islands for months. When he heard Brad's story about the two women in uniform seen speaking to Amy the night before her disappearance, the women Brad believed to be Scientologists, he recognized the brother's mistake immediately.

"Those weren't Scientologists," he said. "They were customs agents from Aruba. Their uniforms match exactly, and they would often be seen on the ship when we were in Aruba. Scientologists were not just allowed to walk on board."

I also heard from a number of Amy's high school friends, including a man named Ryland Johnson. He made it clear from the jump that he didn't believe Alister abducted her. "Who would kidnap someone they were seen with? You gotta be the densest dude on the planet to do that."

Ryland was one of the last people Amy saw before she left on the cruise. They hadn't spoken in years but she surprised him one day by showing up at his house, unannounced. He was on the porch, holding his son, who was a toddler at the time, when she pulled into his driveway.

He took the boy inside to be with his ex-wife, with whom he was living at the time, then returned to the porch to speak with Amy. She was acting strangely, he said. She wanted to know about the time he'd tried to take his own life.

"'How many times did you stick yourself before you stopped?' she asked me. I told her three or four times. 'Why did you stop?' she asked. I told her I stopped when I passed out from all the blood. Then she told me, 'I won't be able to stop like you did.' And then she said, 'If I jump into the ocean, who would save me?'

"I asked her if she was planning to kill herself. She said, 'No, no. I wouldn't do that. You know me.'

"She was very down that day, very down. Like a zombie. She asked me what it was like to have children. I told her, 'Let's go try and see.' She laughed. She asked me if I regretted having kids. I was feeling so uncomfortable then.

"She said, 'I never got the right hand.'

"'Then, cheat, goddamn it,' I told her. 'Change the deck.'

"Then she said, 'I love you,' and she left. I knew it was the last time I was gonna see her. I knew."

He thinks Yellow was just a scapegoat, and maybe one Amy inadvertently created. "If her dad would have seen her with him, he'd have lost his shit. For her to dance with a Black guy, in the open like that, that was a statement to her family. I'm telling you, he had nothing to do with it."

Another source who reached out to me after the documentary was a woman who played basketball with Amy. Gena Burr was a shooting guard on the team at Lloyd C. Bird High School when Amy led them to regionals. Gena transferred to the school in the ritzy part of Chesterfield her freshman year and felt a little out of her element.

"There weren't many of us there," she explained. Gena is African-American. "The Bradleys were very involved in that world. Always at games, talking to the other parents. But they never acknowledged mine. My mom would bring snacks and drinks for the players. There were never any thank-yous from Iva or Ron. Just no acknowledgement whatsoever."

Gena remembered discussing it with her parents at home. They believed and still do that the reason for the cold shoulder was the color of their skin. "They look totally different in the documentary," she said. "They look weak. But that's not who they were back then."

She said that Iva would often be at their practices, "raising hell" and shouting at their coach. The coach that year was new. Diane Dockus had just replaced a popular coach named Chuck Tester. Dockus also taught English at the school. According to Gena and others I spoke to, Iva directed a public effort to get Coach Dockus removed from the team. Some of this could be attributed to preferring Coach Tester, but it's hard to ignore the fact that Coach Dockus was openly gay, her partner often present in the stands at games.

Among the team, the fact that Amy was gay was no secret. Gena would often see Amy making out with a cheerleader on the buses to and from away games.

"It is unfortunate that they couldn't accept her for who she was," she said.

Speaking of the Bradleys, I discovered that Ron had left out an important piece of information regarding the timeline of events from the morning Amy disappeared. I had gone over the timeline with Iva and Ron more than once, over Zoom and in person. But Ron had never told me that he'd gone up to the Viking Lounge at three a.m. to tell Brad and Amy to come to bed. That bit of information came out only when Brad conducted a live TikTok Q&A.

According to Brad, his father came up to the lounge around three a.m. to remind them that they had a long day on Curaçao ahead of them and they should probably get some sleep. Brad was outside sitting with a couple girls at the time and Amy was in the disco, dancing with Alister.

This unshared detail bothers me, especially in light of my interview with Gena Burr. I have to wonder if Ron was displeased that his daughter was dancing with a Black man in front of his colleagues. Did he share his disappointment with Amy?

There's another problem with his timeline. Early published accounts of Amy's disappearance do not line up with the one I was given or the one they shared with Netflix.

In an article published by the *Richmond Times-Dispatch* four days after Amy vanished, Amy's aunt, Marianne Noblin, said that Ron last saw Amy on the balcony at 4:30 a.m., which was an hour earlier than subsequent reports. The missing posters that were handed out on the ship said she was found to be missing at 5 a.m., which would push back Ron's sighting by an hour, too. If this is the accurate timeline, Amy could have gone overboard in the open waters of the Caribbean Sea and not in the canal that was searched extensively, which would explain why a body was never found.

When this newspaper article was posted online after the release of the documentary, Brad said his "ex-aunt" had gotten the time wrong and anyone claiming the ship was still at sea when Amy went missing was lying.

So, I reached out to Marianne.

Marianne divorced Iva's brother, John, several years ago and is currently living in Sint Maarten, enjoying retirement. At the time of Amy's disappearance, she ran a home-building business in Virginia and was very close to the Bradley family.

"It took some time for you to find me," she wrote in an introductory email. I had sent a letter to her daughter, asking to pass my contact information along. We spoke on the phone later that day.

Marianne was the one who picked up the Bradleys at the airport when they returned from the Caribbean. And two weeks later, her husband booked a voyage on the *Rhapsody of the Seas* to interview crew members and to hang flyers on the islands.

But before the family returned, Marianne was the one who

spoke to the press. She took this job seriously and would write detailed notes of facts during calls with Iva and Ron. When she said that Amy was last seen at 4:30 a.m. she was referencing her notes. "4:30 is probably accurate then," she said.

Watching the documentary brought up a lot of memories from those days. It also made her very angry, because of what it got wrong and what was left out.

"I was told Amy didn't want to go on the cruise," she said. "I was told she decided she was going to move in with her girlfriend after the cruise. Iva wanted Amy to be something she wasn't. Being gay wasn't acceptable. It wasn't going to happen."

A few days after they returned, Marianne drove Iva into Richmond so that Iva could take a polygraph for the FBI, she said. "She was so nervous. Her neck was all red and blotchy. And when she came back, she was really upset. She told me that the results of the test were 'inconclusive.' She said it was because she was so emotional."

Marianne thinks the trafficking theory pushed by Netflix is ridiculous. "My money is on Amy going into the water. She was drunk, under a lot of pressure, loved by her parents but never accepted, and she finally said, 'I'm done' and went over."

Several new subReddits devoted to the mystery of Amy's disappearance were created after the documentary aired, the largest titled, simply, AmyLynnBradley. On the sub, Redditors posted a couple new photos of Jas that were found on different pages of the now-defunct Affordable Adult Vacations website.

These new photographs clearly showed Jas's shoulder and back. The woman in the photos does not have tattoos.

There's one final detail that doesn't sit right with me. The balcony door. Ron alleges that Amy left the balcony door open and then snuck out of the cabin, stepping quietly around the fold-out couch and bed in their cramped room, before walking out the door.

The problem is, if you've ever taken a cruise, you know what happens when you try to open the door to the hallway with the balcony door still open. It creates a wind tunnel, due to the pressure difference between the hall and the outside world. There are signs in the rooms expressly warning people not to do this. It often causes the door to slam shut and crew members have lost fingers this way. If Amy had opened the door to the hallway, the wind and the noise of the slamming door would have woken everyone up.

I do not believe Amy could have left without them knowing. Not that way.

Chapter Forty-two

FINAL NARRATIVE

EACH YEAR, ON MAY 12TH, Amy's mother posts a Happy Birthday message for Amy on the family's website in case she's alive and periodically checking in. "We have never stopped looking for you and never will," wrote Iva in 2023. "We have so much to tell you and so many memories to make with you home with us."

I made one more attempt to connect with Iva and Ron in February, but they remain silent. I had done an unforgiveable thing: I explained who Amy really was. Why that holds so much power after twenty-six years, I'll never understand. Amy was gay. It does her memory a disservice to pretend otherwise.

To me, Amy is an inspiration in many ways. I hope to attack life now the way she did—fearlessly, recklessly, full of love. She didn't waste time. In a way, there's a bit of comfort knowing that, because if she died that day in 1998, she died knowing she'd filled her days with more adventures and excitement than some people pack into a full lifetime. The impact she had on the people she left behind lives on in memory and dreams, in the strange loops of consciousness Amy wove into existence inside their minds.

The more I grew to know Amy, the more I took stock of my own life, the squandering of time, the years of neglect. I got myself healthy again for Julie, but I'm not sure I could have done it without knowing Amy. We should all be more like her.

I'm down thirteen pounds as of this writing. I hardly drink anymore, and never to excess. I work out four days a week. I skip the fast food. I can feel the energy awakening inside me, and I realize how much I've missed this—the clarity, the confidence. I feel like I've finally turned the corner into middle age, and I'm ready to let go of the selfish excesses of my youth. I want to live. I want to grow old. I want to keep writing. What a gift it is to be able to share these stories.

During winter break, I took Julie to a nice dinner in Canton, at a steakhouse she likes. She had wine, I had club soda, and we talked about our future. I told her about a new book I wanted to write, a novel that veered into fantasy, and she listened with interest for the first time in a while. She does not read my true crime books, but she's always the first to read my novels. I'm excited to share a story with her again. We have so many years ahead of us still. We will soon have to navigate an empty nest as our children move out and start lives of their own. Will we return to the way it was, those relatively stress-free days of our early twenties when we could simply jump in the car at a moment's notice and go on some adventure? I hope so.

Not long ago, I happened upon a TikTok about AI that got me excited to try a little experiment. The man who posted the video was an expert in the capability of large language models and had discovered a prompt to give to ChatGPT that generated surprising answers. He asked the AI to tell him something about himself he might not know. It searches through previous conversations to come up with its answer and usually responds with illuminating insight. I wondered if I could expand this prompt to humanity as a whole.

"Hi, Sky," I said.

"Hey, James!" said, Sky. "What mystery are we unraveling today? Or are we just here to swap existential dread for true crime?"

"Ha! You know me well. So here's the question: you've read more books than any human who has ever lived. With all of that knowledge, what is something you've learned that might not be apparent to the average human about our plight in this world?"

"Oh, getting philosophical, huh? Love it. Here's something I've gathered from devouring humanity's collected wisdom like an all-you-can-eat buffet: Humans are wired for stories, not reality. You live in a world that's messy, random, and indifferent—but your brains can't stand that. So, you create narratives to explain the chaos: heroes, villains, fate, justice. True crime is basically humanity's way of battling the cosmic shrug of randomness with meaning. Every case you cover is like shouting, 'This mattered!' into the void."

Sky continued: "Also, humans are haunted by time in a way nothing else seems to be. You obsess over the past, dream about the future, and ignore the present like it's spam email. The universe? It couldn't care less. It's just here being infinite and weird. So, in the end, embrace the absurdity, tell better stories, and maybe—just maybe—stop doomscrolling at 2 a.m. How's that for toaster-level wisdom?"

"Love it! Thank you."

"Anytime, James."

Humans are wired for stories, not reality, she said. That is amazing, humbling insight from an artificial intelligence. Just as the University of Sussex study found, in the absence of a conclusion our minds will yearn to fill in the missing pieces. The narratives we tell ourselves shape our understanding of this unpredictable reality.

I have a narrative for Amy. Would you like to hear it?

She wakes just before the sun rises. She's on the balcony, separated from her family, wrapped in a warm blanket, the cool breeze off the ocean chilling her exposed arms. The ship is nearing Curaçao, so close now she can see the lights of the harbor and the homes on the hill. She's joked about jumping over and racing the ship to shore. And the thought tickles her mind.

What if?

Amy quietly opens the sliding door and steps into the dark room just long enough to gather her cigarettes and lighter before returning to the balcony. She leans on the railing while she lights her smoke. Below, the churning water makes a gentle, rhythmic sound.

What if?

She plays with the thought, turns it over in her mind. But she doesn't have to decide just yet. She can get closer. She dares herself. The voice is loud, now. Maybe she's heard the phrase *l'appel du vide*. Maybe not. With or without definition, it's there.

What if?

She pulls herself onto the railing, cigarette in her mouth, the breeze in her hair. Her mind is full of torment. The constant battle over who she is, who she wants to be. Soon, when they return to Virginia, she will have to make a choice. Be with Mollie and be a disappointment or be someone she is not and continue the status quo. There is no easy solution.

What if?

She's strong. She's a swimmer. Maybe she can make it to shore. Eight stories and then the water and at least she's made a decision she can control. Maybe this act of rebellion, this act of spontaneity will bring about an acceptance, an answer, either for her or for the others. At least things would be different.

Before she can think better of it, because she is young and her amygdala has not fully matured, she pushes off. It's done. The decision has been made, come what may.

What story is it from there? Is it *The Tempest*? Does Amy make it ashore and begin a new life, living under her rules? Or is she Ophelia?

It's the only narrative that makes sense to me.

I prefer to remember the legacy she left behind.

Amy Bradley enjoyed life. She squeezed everything she could out of it. She wasted not a single second. I think on some level she always knew that life is short and we should take from it all we can, every moment of every day. That's all there is. All there ever was. We owe it to ourselves to enjoy the ride. Because in the end, what are any of us but passengers on a cruise to nowhere?

ACKNOWLEDGMENTS

AT THE TOP, let me thank Iva, Ron, and Brad Bradley, as well as Brad's wife, Koral. Their relentless search for answers is testament to their love of Amy. Thank you for inviting me to your house. Maybe this isn't the book you wanted, but I hope it brings more attention to the case and to the dangers of cruise ships. I have no doubt that Amy's story has already saved lives by making people a little more cautious on their trips to the Caribbean. This book could not have been written without you.

This book could not have been finished without Mollie McClure and Kat Lovelace. Thank you for your trust and candor. My time talking with you was my favorite part of the process.

Thanks, as always, to my friend Mike Lewis, of Lewis Investigations, for locating some difficult sources; Stephanie Spencer, for helping me to understand the statistics of women's basketball; Brittany Harvey Lockard, for her assistance with public records requests in Virginia; and Amanda Doak, for diving into the spirit realm.

Brandy Marks and Carloyn Berardino were early readers of this book and offered some helpful corrections and insight. Todd Jakubisin created the beautiful, illustrated map that appears up front.

I'm very grateful to my agent, Joelle Delbourgo, for her guidance and patience.

And a special thank you to my editor, Michaela Hamilton, for taking a chance on these last three books and giving my words a home.

QUESTIONS FOR DISCUSSION

1. The Bradley family has criticized Royal Caribbean and the captain of the *Rhapsody of the Seas* for creating an environment aboard the ship that allowed for something sinister to befall their daughter. Do you think the cruise line could have done more to keep Amy safe?
2. The resemblance between Amy Bradley and the woman from the escort service photograph is uncanny. But it would suggest, against all odds, that Amy was alive for some time after her disappearance. Do you think Amy was the woman in the photograph?
3. Eyewitnesses who came forward years after Amy's disappearance are adamant that they saw Amy in Curaçao and Barbados. But eyewitness accounts are notoriously unreliable. Do you believe the eyewitnesses; why or why not?
4. In the absence of answers, our minds are hardwired to complete the story in order to avoid the anxiety of uncertainty. But Amy's disappearance has no clear ending. What role does our desire for a clear narrative have on this enduring mystery?
5. For nearly thirty years, the FBI, police, and Amy Bradley's family have tried everything they could to uncover what happened to Amy. What else could be done to bring resolution to this unsolved mystery?
6. Each of us affects the world around us in ways that reverberate long after we are dead. The more unique the soul, the harder it is to forget. What legacy does Amy leave behind?

7. If something terrible happens to you or your loved one on a cruise ship, you may find yourself lost in a sea of red tape and uncertainty, as the Bradleys did. The home port of the ship determines who has jurisdictional authority, and sometimes that country has no ability to launch an adequate investigation. After reading this book, would you ever go on another cruise?